Get Started in Latin

GDA Sharpley

First published in Great Britain in 1997 by Hodder Education. An Hachette UK company.

First published in US in 1997 by The McGraw-Hill Companies, Inc.

This edition published in 2014 by John Murray Learning

Copyright © GDA Sharpley 1997, 2003, 2010, 2014

The right of GDA Sharpley to be identified as the Author of the Work has been asserted by him in accordance with the Copyright, Designs and Patents Act 1988.

Database right Hodder & Stoughton (makers)

The *Teach Yourself* name is a registered trademark of Hachette UK.

British Library Cataloguing in Publication Data: a catalogue record for this title is available from the British Library.

Library of Congress Catalog Card Number: on file.

Paperback ISBN: 978 1 444 17478 6

eBook ISBN: 978 1 473 60438 4

1

The publisher has used its best endeavours to ensure that any website addresses referred to in this book are correct and active at the time of going to press. However, the publisher and the author have no responsibility for the websites and can make no guarantee that a site will remain live or that the content will remain relevant, decent or appropriate.

The publisher has made every effort to mark as such all words which it believes to be trademarks. The publisher should also like to make it clear that the presence of a word in the book, whether marked or unmarked, in no way affects its legal status as a trademark.

Every reasonable effort has been made by the publisher to trace the copyright holders of material in this book. Any errors or omissions should be notified in writing to the publisher, who will endeavour to rectify the situation for any reprints and future editions.

Cover image © [cover image credit line to be inserted here]

Typeset by Cenveo Publisher Services.

Printed and bound in Great Britain by CPI Group (UK) Ltd., Croydon, CR0 4YY.

John Murray Learning policy is to use papers that are natural, renewable and recyclable products and made from wood grown in sustainable forests. The logging and manufacturing processes are expected to conform to the environmental regulations of the country of origin.

Hodder & Stoughton Ltd

338 Euston Road

London NW1 3BH

www.hodder.co.uk

Contents

Introduction

The aim of this course is to give a grounding in the language, whether you are learning classical or medieval Latin. It is broadly the same as the three previous editions (*Teach Yourself Beginner's Latin* in 1997 and 2003, and *Get Started in Latin* in 2010), but this edition is the most radically revised and cannot be used alongside a previous one in a class.

Latin grammar is essentially the rules of classical Latin (broadly, the 1st centuries BC and AD). Most Latin since has been modelled on classical Latin, and that includes the medieval story here, the story of Augustinus, which is set at a monastery in northern Europe around the ninth century AD and serves as a foil for the grammar and exercises. A translation of the story is available online: www.lingua.co.uk/latin/get-started.

Each chapter introduces a classical Latin author with a few quotations, and there are brief digressions on how Latin evolved and Latin's influence on English. The quotations are intended to give you a taste of ancient texts: you will not at this stage understand these in every detail, but see how many words you can match to the accompanying translations. There are also plenty of exercises in each unit, along with learning vocabularies.

In my experience the Latin-English connection is a major source of curiosity and interest. There will be Latin words which are new to you but you'll recognize them all the same because of their rebirth in English. This is not altogether secure, of course, as in time words gather different meanings, but it's still a great prop for unravelling Latin's meaning.

Answers to the exercises are included towards the end of the book, along with Grammar tables listing the different word-endings, and Latin-to-English and English-to-Latin vocabularies. There is a Grammar index to help you find explanations for grammatical words which appear in the course, and the Sound of Latin provides a letter-by-letter guide to pronunciation. A translation of the story is available online, as listed above.

The audio

In the audio that accompanies this book you can hear readings of the story of Augustinus and of the quotations from classical authors.

Some language courses attach more importance to the audio than to the text, for the reason that speaking aloud and listening are at least as important as reading and writing. One might argue that the audio with this course is not so necessary. It does not drill grammar or teach conversation skills as it might for a modern language. Indeed students of Latin inscriptions and other 'silent' texts may feel that the sound of Latin is something they can live without. For it is true that the Latin we find in books or inscribed in stone has fossilized into something rather silent. And yet two thousand years ago classical Latin was written to be *heard*. 'Reading' for a classical Roman usually meant listening to someone reading aloud. The speeches, poems and histories of classical literature were recorded in writing and so survive on the page. In their time they were essentially transcripts of live performances.

Thus the audio is for listening, to help with comprehension, to provide a pronunciation model, to enhance enjoyment of the texts, and to recreate a vocal dimension which was once at the heart of the ancient language.

See also a guide to the sound of Latin at the back of the book.

The Latin alphabet

The English alphabet is based upon the Latin alphabet with one or two additions. The Romans had no **j** but used **i** for the consonant ('j') or vowel ('i'). Likewise there was no **u** in Latin, in which **v** served as either consonant ('v') or vowel ('u'). Romans wrote everything in upper case.

Some of these conventions have changed. Now we always write **u** for 'u' and in some texts – not this one – **u** represents a 'v' as well (e.g. **seruus** for **servus**). Names keep their initial capital letters, as in English, but otherwise the lower case is used, even for the first letter of a sentence. In medieval Latin, **j** was introduced in place of **i** for the consonantal 'i', e.g. **hic jacet** (*here lies*); in most modern texts this has now reverted to **i** (hic iacet).

Y appears in a few names and imported Greek words, almost always as a vowel; **k** and **z** are occasional, in words borrowed from other languages.

The Pronunciation guide has an explanation of long and short vowels (**ā**, **a**, etc).

Online support

More information on the language can be found online at the same page where you access the English translation of the story of Augustinus: www. lingua.co.uk/latin/get-started.

Acknowledgements

I am grateful to my students at the University of Bristol for their input to earlier editions, and for this edition to my beginner students at Gloucester Cathedral; to Cecilia Giussani for reading through the revised story and to the Latin Qvarter for permission to use it in this course; to Robert Williams, my editor at Hodder, for his care and guidance, to Keely Mitchell, many of whose cartoons in the earlier editions have reappeared here, and to a number of users of the previous editions for their comments and suggestions; to my daughters, Becca, Meg and Flora, for putting up with a Latin story at bedtime; and to Sarah, my wife, for far more forbearance, support and love than I'll ever deserve.

In this unit you will learn about:
▶ *classical Latin*
▶ *nouns and verbs, subjects and objects*
▶ *the cases*
▶ *The story of Augustinus: meet the mule*
▶ *the poet Catullus*

This course assumes you are a beginner. Let's see. These Latin phrases appear from time to time in English. What do they mean?

1 bona fide
   a of good character
   b in good faith
   c good dog!

2 vice versa
   a the other way around
   b a promise to behave well
   c adult poetry

3 tempus fugit
   a the mist is only temporary
   b time is escaping
   c tempers cloud the issue

You can find the answers in the Answer key at the back of the book.

Introduction to classical Latin

Latin was the language spoken in Rome and the surrounding region as early as the sixth century BC and possibly earlier. The number of Latin speakers grew as the Roman empire expanded around the Mediterranean, and the vocabulary swelled and forms modified under the influence of languages in the new subject territories (especially Greek).

The classical Latin authors lived within a few decades either side of the life of Christ. In the first century BC Cicero, a brilliant public speaker, had his performances recorded in writing, and so his speeches survive along with his letters and more reflective philosophical works. His Latin became the model for almost all later writers of Latin prose. He was followed by, among others, the historian Tacitus, whose sharp comments on the theme of moral collapse enliven his account of Rome under the early emperors. Among the classical poets there is Virgil, whose story of Aeneas founding Rome was quickly recognized as a masterpiece, and Horace, a friend of Virgil, who is remembered for his Odes, short poems on themes of love, friendship and mortality; and Ovid, a decade or two later, a poet whose wit and fresh invention remained hugely popular in the centuries that followed.

Like any living language, Latin of the classical period would not stay the same forever – despite the efforts of later writers to reproduce literary models like Cicero. The spoken language gradually evolved into French, Italian, Spanish and other 'Romance' languages, while the much-prized literary language, by its nature preservable, was embalmed for future generations to study and imitate.

Thus the rules of Latin, the grammar and syntax, have been the same for two thousand years. Later writers of Latin were not always accurate in their reproduction of the classical language, but they knew that was how they would be judged. Of course it was almost impossible to recreate it without sticking closely to the content of classical texts. Things were emerging all the time which needed words to describe them. So new words appeared, or existing ones picked up new meanings – but the rules and grammar remained rooted in the past.

So it is in this course with the story of Augustinus, set in a medieval monastery. One or two medieval words appear (e.g. **ecclēsia** *church* and **presbyter** *priest*), but throughout the course you are in fact learning the rules of classical Latin. Indeed Augustinus loved classical Latin so much his recording of the story follows the rules of classical pronunciation!

Latin nouns

> **LANGUAGE TIP**
>
> Nouns are 'things', the essential building blocks. When we speak or think or write, we have to have something in mind. Take the noun *food*, for instance. It might be *fast food*, *hot food* or *delicious food*, but the thing is the food.

Mūlus (*a mule*) and **silva** (*a wood*) are both Latin nouns. An English noun is a word which may have 'the' or 'a' in front of it. In Latin there is no word for 'the' or 'a', so when you translate **mūlus**, for instance, you decide whether it is *a mule* or *the mule* or just *mule*. Names of people and places are also nouns, called 'proper' nouns, and have capital letters in both Latin and English (**Paulus** *Paul*).

Latin verbs

Latin verbs usually come at the *end* of their sentence or word-group, as **spectat** (*watches, is watching*) below.

PRACTICE 1A

1 **Some English words can act as a noun or a verb. We talk of a good** *walk* **(noun), but** <u>*walk*</u> **is also a verb** (*John and Clare walk to the town*)**. Are the underlined words nouns or verbs?**
   i She went for a long <u>run</u> before breakfast.
   ii I <u>run</u> to work every day.
   iii Why do you <u>ask</u>?
   iv Shall I <u>bin</u> these old clothes?

2 **With the help of the picture translate:**
   mūlus silvam spectat.

Subjects and objects

There are two nouns in the above sentence, **mūlus** (*the mule*) and **silvam** (*the wood*). One is doing the watching, the other is being watched. The doer is the <u>subject</u> noun, and the done-to is the <u>object</u> noun.

In English we usually make this clear by the word order, with who is doing it first (subject), then the verb, and finally the one being done to (object):

the mule is watching the wood

In the next sentence the same words appear, in the same order. But changes to the word-endings tell us that the subject and object have been switched:

mūlum silva spectat   *the wood watches the mule*

In Latin it is the word-endings rather than the word order which tell us who is doing it and to whom.

With both **mūlum** and **silvam**, the final **-m** flags up the object:

as subject:	**mūl<u>us</u>**	**silv<u>a</u>**
as object:	**mūl<u>um</u>**	**silv<u>am</u>**

> **LANGUAGE TIP**
>
> Note that nouns may have functions other than subject or object. For instance, *the mule watches the wood in <u>alarm</u>; the wood was dark with <u>trees</u>*.

PRACTICE 1B

1 **There are a handful of English words which change according to whether they are subject or object. These are pronouns, words we use in place of nouns (Latin** prō = *on behalf of***). Complete the table with the missing English pronouns:**

as subject:	I	she	_____	we	_____
as object:	_____	_____	him	_____	them

2 **A noun may have a function other than subject or object. In each sentence below there are three nouns. Identify the subject noun, the object noun and a noun which is neither:**
   i The mule watches the wood in silence.
   ii The huntsman chases the animal out of the wood.
   iii The woman eats supper with her friends.

Word order: verbs

A Latin verb usually (although not always) comes at the end of its sentence or word-group. In the sentences above, the verb (**spectat**) comes at the end, where in English it would be sandwiched between the subject and object. Thus, in a simple English sentence it is the object which we predict:

This morning the milkman delivered ...

What did he deliver? Presumably *the milk*. Possibly *the mail* or maybe even *twins*?

In Latin the final piece of meaning is the action, i.e. the verb:

Today the milkman ... three bottles of milk.

Did what? *Delivered*? *Stole*? *Threw at the vicar*?

The story of Augustinus (1)

Now start to read the story, with help from the words given below. You can also hear it read on the audio. A macron over a vowel (e.g. **ā**) shows that the vowel is 'long' as opposed to 'short' (see the section on long and short vowels which appears with the pronunciation guide). Macrons are a recent addition to help pronunciation and only appear in coursebooks. Their use follows the classical pronunciation, as per the strict instructions of Augustinus. An English translation of the story of Augustinus is available online at www.lingua.co.uk/latin/get-started

 01.01

> Paulus in silvā ambulat. mūlus cum Paulō ambulat. mūlus nōn Paulum portat sed sarcinam. fessus est Paulus et mūlus est lentus. mūlus silvam spectat. silva mūlum spectat. mūlus silvam nōn amat sed timet.

Paulus, Paulum *Paulus (subject and object endings)*
in silvā *in the wood*
ambulat *walks, is walking*
mūlus, mūlum *mule*
cum Paulō *with Paulus*
nōn *not*
portat *carries, is carrying*
sed *but*

sarcina, sarcinam *bag, sack*
fessus *tired*
est *is*
et *and*
lentus *slow*
silva, silvam *wood*
spectat *watches, is watching*
amat *likes, loves*
timet *fears, is afraid of*

PRACTICE 1C

1 **What is the mule carrying in the story above?**

2 **From the story identify three subject nouns and three object nouns.**

3 **Identify two other nouns which are neither subject nor object.**

4 **In the last sentence there are two verbs with the same object. What is that object?**

5 **Complete the table:**

as subject:	**sarcina**	_____	_____	**mūlus**
as object:	_____	**silvam**	**Paulum**	_____

Cases

Each ending of a noun represents a 'case'. So far we have seen the subject and object endings of nouns like **mūlus** or **Paulus** and **silva** or **puella** *(a girl)*. The subject ending is called the nominative case and the object ending is called the accusative case.

We have also seen one or two uses of another case, the ablative case:

mūlus est in <u>silvā</u>
the mule is in the wood

puella cum <u>Paulō</u> ambulat
a girl walks with Paulus

The ablative case usually describes how or where or when something happens. Typically we translate it with one of the English prepositions *in, on, by, with* or *from*.

Latin nouns in the ablative case may appear with or without a Latin preposition. The prepositions **in** (*in, on*) and **cum** (*with, together with*) are used with nouns in the ablative.

PRACTICE 1D

Complete the endings of the nouns in these tables:

i

Nominative (subject):	puella	mūl____
Accusative (object):	puell____	mūl____
Ablative (*in, on, by, with* or *from*):	puellā	mūlō

ii

Nominative (subject):	silv____	Paulus
Accusative (object):	silvam	Paul____
Ablative (*in, on, by, with* or *from*):	silv____	Paul____

Est and sunt

Est (*is*) and **sunt** (*are*) do not take objects like other verbs do. The 'object' of the verb *to be* is not on the receiving end of anything, but describes the subject. So any 'object' as such of the verb *to be* (we call it a 'complement') will be in the same case as the subject:

Paulus monachus est   *Paulus is a monk*

The story of Augustinus (2)

01.02 Paulus and the mule are bringing food to the monastery.

> Paulus est monachus. Benedictus etiam est monachus.
> Benedictus cēnam dēsīderat. nunc Paulus cum mūlō ad
> monasterium venit et in silvā ambulat. cēna est in sarcinā.
> mūlus sarcinam portat. mūlus lentē ambulat et silvam spectat.
> aquam dēsīderat mūlus.

monachus	*monk*		ad	*to, towards*
etiam	*also*		monasterium	*monastery*
cēna, cēnam	*dinner*		venit	*comes*
dēsīderat	*desires, longs for*		lentē	*slowly*
nunc	*now*		aqua, aquam	*water*

PRACTICE 1E

1 **Complete each sentence with the correct Latin noun (and its correct ending), and then translate the sentence into English:**

   i mūlus _____ (*dinner*) dēsīderat.

   ii Benedictus nōn in _____ (*the wood*) est.

   iii puella _____ (*the mule*) amat.

   iv Benedictus cum _____ (*Paul*) nōn ambulat.

   v Paulus nōn _____ (*a girl*) est.

2 **Read the following sentence. Who is carrying what?**

   nōn Benedictum sed sarcinam portat Paulus.

Catullus

 01.03 Gaius Valerius Catullus is one of the first of the classical poets, born around 84 BC. He came from Verona in northern Italy, which at the time was a part of Gaul. His father was a friend of Julius Caesar.

Over a hundred poems survive, most quite short, a few much longer. Several are addressed to a girlfriend called 'Lesbia', which is probably a pseudonym for Clodia, a consul's wife, whose beach parties and sexual antics were rarely out of the news. Catullus died young, close to his 30th year.

In this poem Catullus invites his friend Fabullus to dinner, but says he has nothing to offer him.

Many of the words and endings in the Latin quoted from ancient authors will be new, but see how many Latin words you can match to the English.

cēnābis bene, mī Fabulle, apud mē

paucīs – sī tibi dī favent – diēbus,

sī tēcum attuleris bonam atque magnam

cēnam, nōn sine candidā puellā

et vīnō et sale et omnibus cachinnīs.

You will dine well, my Fabullus, at my place
within a few – if the gods favour you – days,
if, with you, you bring a good and large
dinner, not without a radiant girl
and with wine and wit and all the jokes.

Poems 13.1–5

The next poem shows how distressed he was by his on-off affair:

ōdī et amō. quārē id faciam, fortasse requīris.
nescio sed fierī sentiō et excrucior.
I hate and I love. Why I do that, perhaps you ask.
I do not know, but I feel it happening and I am in torment.

Poems 85

Word discovery 1

1 What meaning do *spectator, spectacles* **and** *spectacular* **have in common? And what about** *porter, transport* **and** *support*?

2 From this unit can you find Latin ancestors of *favour, sentiment* **and** *vine*?

3 Identify English words with origins in
   i aqua
   ii musca
   iii equus

Like **puella** and **silva**		Like **Paulus** and **mūlus**	
aqua	*water*	Benedictus	*Benedictus*
cēna	*dinner*	Catullus	*Catullus*
musca	*fly*	equus	*horse*
sarcina	*bag, sack*	Fabullus	*Fabullus*
		monachus	*monk*

Words with fixed endings			
ad	*to, towards*	nōn	*not*
et	*and*	nunc	*now*
in	*in, on, into, on to*	sed	*but*

Test yourself 1

1 The names **Benedictus, Paulus, Catullus** and **Fabullus** are all nouns. How do they appear in the accusative case (i.e. as object)?

2 Complete each sentence with the right Latin word with its correct ending, and then translate the sentence into English:

   i Fabullus cēnam in _____ (*the bag*) portat.
   ii Catullus _____ (*the girl*) amat.
   iii nunc _____ (*the mule*) aquam in sarcinā portat.
   iv in aquā est _____ (*a fly*).
   v musca _____ (*the dinner*) spectat.
   vi Catullus cum _____ (*Fabullus*) ambulat.
   vii Benedictus _____ (*the horse*) spectat.
   viii mūlus _____ (*Benedictus*) nōn amat.
   ix in silvā nōn est _____ (*Benedictus*).
   x _____ (*the girl*) nōn Catullum amat sed Fabullum.

3 Who is said to have announced **vēnī, vīdī, vīcī?**
   a Cleopatra
   b Julius Caesar
   c Nero

In this unit you will learn about:
▶ *Latin and English: early days*
▶ *singular and plural of nouns and verbs*
▶ *The story of Augustinus: the mule wants to go home*
▶ *Cicero: orator and writer*

Latin and English: early days

Some Latin-derived words are obvious, especially phrases such as *et cetera* and *status quo*. But the majority of ex-Latin words are less noticeable, e.g. *ambulance, exit, mister, ridiculous*.

Welsh has many more traces than English of the Roman occupation of Britain, e.g. **ffenestr** *window*, **pont** *bridge* and **port** *harbour*, for English only arrived in Britain with the Anglo-Saxons as the Roman era was coming to an end. However, Latin words soon started to appear in English, like **cūpa** *cup*, **haereticus** *heretic*, **uncia** *inch*, *ounce* (lit. *a twelfth*), **magister** *master*, **mīlle** *mile*, **monachus** *monk*, **papyrus** *paper*, **bursa** *purse*, **schola** *school* and **vīnum** *wine*.

The word *street* was probably first used by Anglo-Saxons while they were still on the continent. It survives from a pair of Latin words meaning 'straight road': **via strāta**. From the same root comes German *Strasse*.

It was not until the second millennium that the trickle of Latin words into English became a flood. **Mīlle** (*thousand*) gave us *mile*, 'a thousand (paces)'. Centuries later comes the creation *millennium* to mean a thousand years.

The story of Augustinus (3)

 06.02 The mule does not like horses who live at the monastery because he does most of the work.

> Benedictus et Stephanus monachī sunt. monachī in monasteriō habitant. Paulus discipulus in scholā est. discipulī cum monachīs in monasteriō habitant. mūlus cum equīs habitat. mūlus semper labōrat, sed equī cum mūlō nōn labōrant. equōs mūlus nōn amat.

monachī (nominative)   *monks*
sunt   *are*
habitat, habitant   *lives, live*
discipulus/discipulī   *student/ students* (both nominative)

schola   *school*
equī/equōs/equīs   *horses* (nominative/accusative/ablative)
semper   *always*
labōrat, labōrant   *works, work*

PRACTICE 2A

1 **Where do the students live?**
2 **Which word is the object in the last sentence (**equōs mūlus nōn amat**)?**
3 **Some verbs above end -nt, others just -t. Can you see why?**

Singular and plural of **puella** and **mūlus**

Latin nouns have plural forms, in fact more than one, for there is an ending for each case in the plural as there is in the singular.

> **INSIGHT**
> One of the few surviving word-endings in English is the plural. We usually add an 's' to a noun to indicate more than one. Some nouns take '-es' (*branch – branches*); others take '-ies' in place of '-y' (*baby – babies*). A few change more internally (*man – men; mouse – mice; tooth – teeth*).

The plural of **mūlus** is **mūlī** if nominative (subject), **mūlōs** if accusative (object) or **mūlīs** if ablative (*in, with*, etc):

monachī mūlōs spectant

the monks watch (are watching) the mules

monachī cum mūlīs ambulant

the monks walk (are walking) with the mules

The plural of **puella** is **puellae** if nominative (subject), **puellās** if accusative (object) or **puellīs** if ablative (*in, with,* etc):

puellae equōs spectant

the girls watch the horses

mūlus puellās spectat

the mule watches the girls

discipulus nōn cum puellīs labōrat

the student does not work with the girls

Singular		
Nominative	mūl**us**	puell**a**
Accusative	mūl**um**	puell**am**
Ablative	mūl**ō**	puell**ā**
Plural		
Nominative	mūl**ī**	puell**ae**
Accusative	mūl**ōs**	puell**ās**
Ablative	mūl**īs**	puell**īs**

The ablative plural is the same for both types of noun (**-īs**).

PRACTICE 2B

1 Complete each sentence with the correct Latin word, and then translate the sentence into English:

  i muscae _____ (*the mules*) amant.

  ii Stephanus in scholā cum _____ (*with the students*) labōrat.

  iii mūlī _____ (*the flies*) nōn amant.

  iv Catullus nōn est _____ (*a monk*).

  v discipulus cum _____ (*with the girls*) nōn labōrat.

Like **puella**	Like **mūlus**
schola *school*	amīcus *friend*
	coquus *cook*
	discipulus *student*
	populus *people*
	Stephanus *Stephen*

Verbs: singular and plural

All the verbs you have seen so far end **-t**. That is the 3rd person ending of a verb. The 1st person is *I* …, the 2nd person is *you* … and the 3rd person is *he/she* …, or a noun in the nominative.

These three persons have plural forms (*we*, *you* and *they* respectively). You have already seen the 3rd person plural, which ends **-nt**:

monachī mūlōs specta<u>nt</u>
the monks <u>watch</u> (are watching) the mules

A verb is plural (in both Latin and English) if and only if the subject is plural:

<u>equī</u> muscās nōn <u>amant</u>
the <u>horses</u> do not <u>like</u> flies

So if you see a verb ending **-nt** look for a plural subject, and if it just ends **-t**, look for a singular one. An object, singular or plural, makes no difference to the verb.

A verb in the third person usually has as a <u>subject</u> a noun in the nominative:

<u>Paulus</u> in silvā ambulat
<u>Paulus</u> walks in the wood

If no subject noun appears, then we add *he*, *she*, *it* or *they* to the translation:

mūlus in silvā ambulat, sed silvam nōn amat
the mule walks in the wood, but <u>he</u> does not like the wood

> **LANGUAGE TIP**
>
> Remember that **ambulat** can mean either *walks* or *is walking*, and **ambulant** either *walk* or *are walking*. In vocabularies and translations the longer version will not always be shown.

Singular verbs (*he/she* …)

amat	*likes, loves*
ambulat	*walks*
dēsīderat	*longs for*
est	*is*
fugit	*flees, escapes*
habitat	*lives*
iacet	*lies*
labōrat	*works*
portat	*carries*
spectat	*watches*
timet	*fears*
venit	*comes*
videt	*sees*

Plural verbs (*they*…)

amant	*like, love*
ambulant	*walk*
dēsīderant	*long for*
sunt	*are*
fugiunt	*flee, escape*
habitant	*live*
iacent	*lie*
labōrant	*work*
portant	*carry*
spectant	*watch*
timent	*fear*
veniunt	*come*
vident	*see*

1 **If you know Caesar's famous phrase** vēnī, vīdī, vīcī, **can you say whether these verbs are 1st, 2nd or 3rd person?**

2 **Complete each sentence with the correct Latin word, and then translate the sentence into English:**

   i mūlus in silvam _____ (*comes*).

   ii Paulus cum monachīs _____ (*works*).

   iii Fabullus puellam _____ (*loves*).

   iv monachus in terrā _____ (*lies*).

   v mūlus aquam _____ (*longs for*).

   vi Paulus cēnam in sarcinā _____ (*carries*).

3 **Choose the correct verb in each case, and then translate the sentence into English:**

   i mūlus sarcinam <u>portat/portant</u>.

   ii equī cum mūlīs nōn <u>labōrat/labōrant.</u>

   iii puellae in terrā <u>iacet/iacent</u>.

   iv equī aquam <u>dēsīderat/dēsīderant</u>.

   v discipulus <u>fugit/fugiunt</u>.

   vi in aquā <u>est/sunt</u> muscae.

4 **Where would you expect to find the Latin words** hic iacet?

The story of Augustinus (4)

02.02 **The mule is scared by the shadows in the wood.**

> Benedictus vīnum dēsīderat. Paulus igitur vīnum in oppidō petit et ad monasterium cum mūlō ambulat. mūlus vīnum portat. nunc sunt in silvā. mūlus saepe in silvīs ambulat, sed nōn silvās amat quod in silvīs sunt umbrae. mūlus umbrās videt. mūlus neque umbrās neque sarcinās amat. mūlus amīcōs dēsīderat.

vīnum *wine*	quod *because*
igitur *therefore*	umbra (like puella) *shadow*
oppidō (ablative) *town*	videt *(he/she) sees*
petit *(he/she) seeks*	neque … neque *neither … nor*
saepe *often*	amīcōs *his friends*¹

¹*his friends* is a more natural translation than *the friends* (Latin does have words for *his*, *her*, etc, but they are only used to avoid confusion or for emphasis).

PRACTICE 2D

1 Name one thing that Benedictus likes and three things which the mule does not.

2 With help from the pictures, complete each sentence with one word, and then translate the sentence into English:

   i mūlus silvam nōn amat quod in silvā sunt _____

   ii mūlus equōs nōn amat quod equī cum mūlō nōn _____

3 Change the underlined word to the plural (remember that if you change the subject, you will need to change the verb too):

   i Paulus cum <u>monachō</u> saepe labōrat.

   ii <u>sarcina</u> in mūlō est.

   iii <u>discipulus</u> in monasteriō habitat.

   iv mūlus <u>amīcum</u> dēsīderat.

4 Complete each sentence with the correct word, and then translate the sentence into English:

   i mūlī _____ (*the shadows*) spectant.

   ii discipulī cum _____ (*the monks*) labōrant.

   iii in sarcinīs sunt _____ (*flies*).

   iv _____ (*the mules*) cum _____ (*the horses*) nōn habitant.

Cicero

02.03 Marcus Tullius Cicero (106–43 BC) was not born in Rome, but in Arpinum, a town 70 miles to the south-east. In his teens many of the towns in Italy together rebelled against Rome because they felt that their contribution to Rome's growing power went unrewarded. Arpinum was one that stayed loyal: Gaius Marius, born half a century earlier, was also from this town, and he had risen to the top of Roman politics – probably a good thing for his townspeople and for the young Cicero.

Once in Rome he soon impressed his peers with his ability as a public speaker. In a world with no TV, internet or other media, these skills were much in demand. Cicero's talent brought him to the attention of the rich and powerful, including Caesar and Pompey.

Speakers would plead cases in the lawcourts and participate in political debate, which in Cicero's time would shape major policies (under the later rule of emperors more decisions were made behind closed doors). Cicero was an ardent supporter of the Republic, which shared the responsibility for government between two annually elected consuls and a senate of elite citizens. He himself was consul in 63 BC. He was no soldier, but throughout his career used his skills as a speaker to stand up to various intimidating characters – Catiline, Clodius (brother of Catullus' 'Lesbia'), Julius Caesar and Mark Antony.

Catiline tried to seize power when Cicero was consul. Catiline even had the nerve to attend the senate, where Cicero stood up and denounced him.

> **ō tempora ō mōrēs! senātus haec intellegit, cōnsul videt.**
> *What times, what moral standards! The senate understands this,*
> *the consul sees it.*

> *Against Catiline* 1.2

Cicero's speeches were carefully rehearsed in advance and written copies made. He was considered brilliantly effective in his time, and has been much studied and imitated since. But things did not always go to plan. The historian Cassius Dio tells us that after Clodius was killed by Milo in a street fight, Cicero tried and failed to defend Milo in court, and Milo was banished to Massilia (Marseille). The trial was a particularly nervous occasion. Gangs loyal to the hostile parties were milling about in the forum and soldiers lined up to keep order. Milo later reflected that if Cicero had said on the day what he had written afterwards he would not be an exile in Gaul eating fish.

In his defence of Milo, Cicero claimed that Clodius had been the aggressor and Milo had to defend himself.

silent enim lēgēs inter arma.
Indeed laws are silent in time of conflict.

In Defence of Milo 11

Cicero's efforts on behalf of the Republic managed only to delay the inevitable. Caesar became dictator in Cicero's lifetime, and after Caesar's murder in 44 BC Mark Antony stepped forward as his lieutenant. Antony had little love for Cicero. He was the stepson of one of Catiline's supporters who had been executed on Cicero's instructions in 63 BC. To make matters worse, Antony had recently married Clodius' widow, Fulvia. Relations between the two men openly deteriorated. Cicero accused Antony of trying to take over:

Antōnius contrā populum Rōmānum exercitum addūcēbat.
Antony led an army against the Roman people.

Philippics 3.11

Cicero backed Caesar's heir, Octavian, who was still in his teens, but Octavian soon fell out with the old senators, especially those who had been less than wholehearted in their support of his adoptive father. Octavian threw in his lot with Antony, another partnership which wouldn't last (Octavian would later become Augustus, the first of the emperors), and he agreed that Antony could have Cicero executed.

Word discovery 2

1 **Can you see which of Cicero's words represent the following?**
   i are silent
   ii laws
   iii people

2 **The word** castra **originally meant a military camp or settlement. Can you think of any place-names which contain a form of this word?**

3 **Find Latin ancestors in this unit of** *inhabitant,* *intelligent,* *labour,* *temporary* **and** *video.*

More words with fixed endings

igitur *therefore*

neque … neque *neither … nor*

quod *because* (this word can also mean *which* or *any*)

saepe *often*

semper *always*

Test yourself 2

1 Which of Cicero's verbs above does *not* come at the end of its sentence or word-group?

2 Change the underlined words to the plural (remember that if the subject is plural, the verb will have to be plural too):

   i <u>puella</u> semper in silvā est.

   ii nunc mūlus <u>puellam</u> portat.

   iii <u>musca</u> mūlum amat, sed mūlus <u>muscam</u> nōn amat.

3 Complete each sentence with the correct noun, and then translate the sentence into English:

   i discipulus in silvā cum _____ (*the mules*) saepe ambulat.

   ii equī _____ (*the monks*) nōn portant.

   iii mūlī neque _____ (*the flies*) neque umbrās amant.

   iv muscae saepe in _____ (*the water*) sunt.

4 Which of the following is the correct definition for **vespa**?

   a an ancient two-wheeled transport for one person

   b a short monastic song sung in the evening

   c a wasp

In this unit you will learn about:
▶ *Latin and English: English words from Latin via French*
▶ *gender*
▶ **puella**, **mūlus** *and* **vīnum**
▶ *prepositions*
▶ *The story of Augustinus: the mule struggles on through the wood*
▶ *Caesar: politician, soldier and writer*

Latin and English: English words from Latin via French

In the centuries after the Norman conquest of 1066 a great number of French words drifted into English. As Latin is the parent language of French many of these French arrivals had Latin roots. These words have a very settled look about them today, e.g.

English	French	Latin
desire	désirer	**dēsīderāre**
flowers	fleurs	**flōrēs**
lake	lac	**lacus**
liberty	liberté	**libertās**
misery	misère	**miseria**

Many of these ex-Latin words came to replace earlier English ones, but some have survived alongside the French/Latin imports: *flower* and *blossom*, *liberty* and *freedom*, *misery* and *woe*; others linger in place names, e.g. *mere* (*lake*) in names like Windermere.

Word origins are not always neatly linear, or easily traced. For instance, **discipulus** appears in pre-Norman English as *discipul* and is later reformed as *disciple*. Our word *people* seems to have roots in both Viking *poeple* and, via French, Latin **populus**. The settling of a word in a language is sometimes the result of a combination of sources or influences.

Gender

Puella is a feminine noun and **mūlus** a masculine one. It isn't only nouns like **puella** *girl* that have gender, but all nouns, even inanimate ones such as **silva** *wood* or **aqua** *water*. The gender of a noun helps you link it to an adjective which describes it:

> **mūl<u>us</u> fess<u>us</u> est**
> the <u>mule</u> is <u>tired</u>

> **puell<u>a</u> fess<u>a</u> est**
> the <u>girl</u> is <u>tired</u>

With a few exceptions (e.g. **poēta** *poet*, which is masculine), nouns that end **-a**, such as **puella** or **aqua**, are feminine; and with even fewer exceptions nouns such as **mūlus** (**amīcus**, **discipulus**, **equus**, etc) are all masculine.

Neuter nouns like **vīnum**

There is a third gender: neuter nouns. **Neuter** is the Latin for *neither*, i.e. neither masculine nor feminine. Below is shown **vīnum** (*wine*):

Singular			
Nominative	puell**a**	mūl**us**	vīn**um**
Accusative	puell**am**	mūl**um**	vīn**um**
Ablative	puell**ā**	mūl**ō**	vīn**ō**
Plural			
Nominative	puell**ae**	mūl**ī**	vīn**a**
Accusative	puell**ās**	mūl**ōs**	vīn**a**
Ablative	puell**īs**	mūl**īs**	vīn**īs**

Neuter nouns like **vīnum** have the same endings in the nominative and accusative. This means the ending will never tell you whether it is the subject or the object. That will depend either on other nouns or on common sense …

vīnum mūlus portat (here, **vīnum** = accusative)
the mule carries the wine

> Nouns like **vīnum**
>
> | | | | |
> |---|---|---|---|
> | aurum | *gold* | monasterium | *monastery* |
> | bellum | *war* | oppidum | *town* |
> | crustum | *cake* | ōvum | *egg* |
> | folium | *leaf* | prātum | *meadow* |

PRACTICE 3A

1 **Identify whether the underlined word is nominative or accusative, and then translate the sentence into English:**

  i ōva in sarcinā sunt.

  ii Benedictus crusta et vīnum dēsīderat.

  iii in prātō est aurum.

  iv equus folia nōn amat.

  v monachī bellum nōn dēsīderant.

The story of Augustinus (5)

 03.01 **Benedictus is the monk in charge of cooking. The mule is now struggling under the weight of the shopping.**

> Benedictus coquus est et cum ancillīs in culīnā labōrat. Paulus in culīnā labōrat et etiam in prātō et in bibliothēcā. Paulus enim nōn coquus sed discipulus est. Benedictus, ubi crusta vīnumque dēsīderat, Paulum ad oppidum mittit. hodiē igitur Paulus mūlusque ex oppidō per silvam ad monasterium veniunt. prātum et monasterium longē absunt. sarcina crustīs vīnōque onerōsa est. in sarcinā etiam sunt ōva et oleum et unguenta. mūlus gemit. Benedictus semper unguentum et crusta et vīna dēsīderat sed semper mūlus portat.

ancilla (like puella) *maidservant*
culīna (like puella) *kitchen*
bibliothēca (like puella) *library*
enim *for, indeed, you see*
ubi *when, where*
-que (crusta vinum**que**) *and (cakes and wine)*
mittit *(he/she) sends*
hodiē *today*

ex *from, out of*
per *through, across, along*
longē *far, distant*
absunt *(they) are away, absent*
onerōsa *heavy*
oleum (like vīnum) *oil*
unguentum (like vīnum) *perfume*
gemit *(he/she) groans*

> **LANGUAGE TIP**
>
> **-que** (*and*) is translated <u>before</u> the word it is attached to: **Paulus mūlusque** *Paulus and the mule*

Prepositions

The Latin preposition **cum** (*with*) usually appears when *with* means *together with* or *accompanied by*:

mūlus cum Paulō ambulat
the mule walks with Paulus

If the *with* is introducing, say, a cause (*drunk with wine*), an instrument (*cleaned with water*) or a manner (*spoken with humour*), **cum** will not appear, just the ablative with no preposition, e.g.

sarcina <u>crustīs</u> onerōsa est
the bag is heavy <u>with cakes</u>

Some prepositions are used with the accusative, like **ad** (*to, towards*), others with the ablative (**ā**, **ab**, **ē**, **ex**, etc). The preposition **in** may be used with either the accusative or the ablative, with a slight difference in meaning. When followed by the accusative, **in** means *into* or *on to*: the word in the accusative is the object of some movement. Where **in** is used with the ablative it means simply *in* or *on*, describing a fixed point:

puella in silv<u>am</u> ambulat
the girl walks <u>into</u> the wood

puella in silv<u>ā</u> ambulat
the girl walks <u>in</u> the wood

With a noun in the accusative	With a noun in the ablative
ad *to, towards*	ā or ab[1] *by, from*
in *into, on to*	cum *with, together with*
per *through,*	ē or ex[1] *from, out of*
across, along	in *in, on*
	sine *without*

[1] always **ab** or **ex** before a word beginning with a vowel or 'h'

PRACTICE 3B

1 Add the missing Latin word and translate the sentence into English:

   i ancillae cum _____ (*with Benedictus*) in culīnam veniunt.

   ii Stephanus in _____ (*in the monastery*) labōrat.

  iii puellae cum _____ (*with the students*) in bibliothēcā nōn sunt.

  iv mūlus ē _____ (*out of the wood*) fugit.

   v Paulus per _____ (*through the wood*) ad monasterium ambulat.

  vi monachī in _____ (*into the monastery*) fugiunt.

The story of Augustinus (6)

03.02 The mule is determined to have a rest. A stranger suddenly appears.

hodiē Paulus et mūlus longē ā monasteriō absunt. neque umbrās neque sarcinās amat mūlus. 'heus!' clāmat Paulus, sed mūlus est immōtus. deinde Paulus et mūlus equum audiunt videntque. equus per viam celeriter ad Paulum mūlumque venit. in equō est monachus cucullātus. equus umbrās timet. equus Paulum mūlumque videt et subitō ē viā dēclīnat. monachus ex equō in terram cadit et equus sine monachō celeriter ē viā in silvam fugit. nunc monachus in terrā iacet.

heus!	*hey!*	cucullātus	*hooded*
clāmat	*(he/she) shouts*	subitō	*suddenly*
immōtus	*motionless, immovable*	dēclīnat	*(he/she/it) swerves*
deinde	*then, next*	terra (like puella)	*ground, earth, land*
audiunt	*(they) hear*	cadit	*(he/she) falls*
vident	*(they) see*	sine (+ abl.)	*without*
via (like puella)	*road, track, way*	iacet	*(he/she/it) lies*
celeriter	*quickly*		

> **More verbs**
>
> | | | | |
> |---|---|---|---|
> | audit/audiunt | *hear(s)* | mittit/mittunt | *send(s)* |
> | cadit/cadunt | *fall(s)* | parat/parant | *prepare(s)* |
> | clāmat/clāmant | *shout(s)* | petit/petunt | *seek(s)* |
> | gemit/gemunt | *groan(s), sigh(s)* | sedet/sedent | *sit(s)* |
> | iacet/iacent | *lie(s)* | videt/vident | *see(s)* |

PRACTICE 3C

1 **Identify four prepositions in the story and give the case of the noun(s) with each one.**

2 **Choose the right words and then translate the sentence into English:**

monachus cucullātus ex <u>equum/equō</u> in <u>terram/terrā</u> cadit et in <u>viam/viā</u> iacet.

3 **Add the missing Latin word and translate the sentence into English:**

    i Paulus _____ (*a horse*) in silvā audit.

    ii Benedictus Paulum in _____ (*into the town*) mittit.

   iii equī in _____ (*in the meadow*) iacent.

   iv monachus _____ (*eggs*) in culīnā parat.

    v Paulus semper _____ (*through*) silvam cum mūlō ambulat.

   vi mūlus _____ (*the shadows*) timet sed ē silvā nōn fugit.

  vii Benedictus _____ (*perfumes*) et _____ (*wines*) et _____ (*oil*) semper petit, sed semper mūlus portat.

 viii mūlus gemit quod _____ (*the sacks*) portat.

Caesar

03.03 Gaius Iulius Caesar was born in 100 BC into an old patrician family. In his teens he almost lost his life in the executions ('proscriptions') of the dictator Sulla: his aunt had married the dictator's enemy, Marius. In the 60s he had a scare when for a while he was suspected of supporting Catiline's uprising, which Cicero had put down (see Unit 2).

Caesar emerged a shrewd politician from these experiences. He was generous, charming, approachable, and knew how to make friends, not just with bribes. His soldiers were devoted to him, famously following him across the Rubicon (no general was permitted to lead his army south of this river into what was regarded at the time as Rome's inner domain). His principal military contribution was the conquest of Gaul, roughly modern France and Belgium.

He was regarded as one of the best speakers of his time. Cicero, no close friend, spoke highly of his ability. Little though of this has survived. As a writer he is now known for his record of the Gallic war and a few scattered treatises on style and pronunciation, some written on military campaign. His *Gallic Wars* was published with his political profile in mind: he talks about himself in the third person to add a sense of objectivity and gravitas.

During the campaign Caesar had to contend with Ariovistus, the leader of a Germanic tribe, the Suebi, who had already been recognized in Rome as **amīcī**. Good relations with those beyond the boundary of the empire was important. But now Caesar was extending those boundaries, and expected Ariovistus to adjust from partner to vassal. Before they came to blows, there was the routine exchange of terms for peace, without much expectation of success.

iterum ad eum Caesar lēgātōs cum hīs mandātīs mittit.

Again Caesar sends deputies to him (Ariovistus) *with these terms.*

Gallic Wars 1.35

A conference was proposed. Caesar decided not to go himself but sent two younger officers instead. Ariovistus was angered by this snub, and had the two men put in chains.

cōnantēs dīcere prohibuit et in catēnās cōniēcit.
He (Ariovistus) prevented (them) trying to speak and threw (them) in chains.

Gallic Wars 1.47

They were rescued after the Romans put Ariovistus' army to flight. He escaped, unlike his two wives and two daughters.

utraque in eā fugā periit; duae fīliae: hārum altera occīsa, altera capta est.
Both (wives) perished in that flight; (there were) two daughters: of these one was killed, the other captured.

Gallic Wars 1.53

Others from the Suebi had gathered on the banks of the Rhine and now returned home.

Suēbī, quī ad rīpās Rhēnī vēnerant, domum revertī coepērunt.
The Suebi, who had come to the banks of the Rhine, began to return home.

Gallic Wars 1.54

The conquest of Gaul made Caesar exceptionally rich and powerful, and intensified a power struggle between him and Pompey, from which he emerged victorious in 48 at the battle of Pharsalus in Greece. For the next few years Caesar ruled as dictator until his murder in 44 by, among others, Pompeians whom he had pardoned.

Like **puella**

amīca	*(female) friend*
ancilla	*maid*
bibliothēca	*library*
catēna	*chain*
culīna	*kitchen*
fīlia	*daughter*
terra	*land, earth, ground*
via	*road, track*

Fixed endings

deinde	*then, next*
enim	*for, indeed, the fact is*
etiam	*also, even*
hodiē	*today*
heus	*hey!*
subitō	*suddenly*

Word discovery 3

1 **Which of Caesar's words mean the following?**
   i chains
   ii flight
   iii daughters
   iv banks
   v had come

2 **Identify a Latin ancestor for each of these words which arrived in English via French, e.g.** *desire* **– dēsiderat.**
   i amble
   ii inhabit
   iii labour
   iv porter

3 **The word** via **appears several times in this unit, in both Latin and English. The English word is descended from the Latin noun in a particular case. What is that case?**

Test yourself 3

1 Fill each gap with the missing Latin word and translate the sentence into English:

    i monachī nōn in _____ (*in chains*) labōrant!

    ii monachus in _____ (*on the ground*) iacet et equus ē silvā fugit.

    iii mūlus lentē per _____ (*along the track*) ambulat.

    iv discipulī in _____ (*the library*) et ancillae in _____ (*the kitchen*) labōrant.

    v Ariovistus _____ (*(his) daughters*) videt.

    vi heus! _____ (*eggs*) ē sarcinā in terram cadunt.

    vii puella in _____ (*on the horse*) sedet.

    viii subitō monachus in _____ (*into the water*) cadit.

2 Change the underlined noun to the singular (and the verb if necessary):

    i <u>equī</u> neque in silvā neque in prātō labōrant.

    ii hodiē <u>discipulī</u> in prātō cum ancillīs sedent.

    iii discipulus <u>muscās</u> in vīnō videt.

    iv <u>ōva</u> in terrā iacent.

    v Benedictus <u>crusta</u> petit.

    vi crusta ē <u>sarcinīs</u> cadunt.

    vii <u>ancillae</u> cēnam in culīnā parant.

    viii Ariovistus gemit quod <u>catēnās</u> audit.

3 Which of the following is the correct meaning of **ad lib**?

    a free advertising

    b speak as long as you want,

    c become more left-wing

In this unit you will learn about:
▶ *Latin and English: 'inkhorn' words*
▶ *genitive case*
▶ *Latin questions*
▶ *1st conjugation verbs* (amō, amās, amat)
▶ *sum and* possum
▶ *The story of Augustinus: a hooded horseman*
▶ *Sallust: historian*

Latin and English: 'inkhorn' words

As the Renaissance (a renewed fascination for classical antiquity) took hold in Europe during the middle part of the second millennium, there was an increased demand for translations of Latin and Greek texts, which the recently developed printing presses helped to circulate. Where no equivalent English word was obvious, a translator might keep the original word. If this was repeated enough, the word settled in English, albeit with minor changes to its shape. This borrowing did not limit itself to practical needs but became almost an obsession, a competition even. Scholars and writers engaged in creating new words, modelling them on Latin ones, as an exercise in cleverness. These words became known as inkhorn words. Many survived, some did not: *expede* and *fatigate* did not last, while *expedient*, *impede* and *fatigue* are still with us. A few, like *splendidious*, survive with a change in form (*splendid*).

Native Anglo-Saxon words tend to be closer to the heart of the language: does he who *concurs* really agree with all his heart? Will the person who arrives to a *cordial reception* be as well received as one who gets a warm welcome? One poor soul in the 17th century closed a letter to his superior with 'I *relinquish* to *fatigate* your *intelligence*'. This kind of pomposity inflated by ex-Latin words has not diminished in time. Politics is thick with it: 'we have no *expectation* of a *conciliatory gesture*'. So too is academia: '*contemporary linguistics validates* the *principle*'. And everywhere people busily proclaim that they are '*implementing procedures*' and '*facilitating collaborative projects*'.

The loser here, of course, is Latin. Our impression of the ancient language is inevitably coloured by the way it has been used since. But not all such creations are so dull. The following words are just a few examples of those that now seem irreplaceable: *acute, agile, devious, fatuous, fluctuate, impeccable, impecunious, ingenious, irate, judicious, lucid, odious, speculative.*

The genitive case

You have seen how a noun may be the subject, or object, or tucked away in the ablative telling us where or how. Imagine a police report: *the waitress struck the visitor with a saucepan,* where *saucepan,* if Latin, would be ablative.

If the ablative case is translated with one of the prepositions *in, on, with, by, from,* then the <u>genitive</u> case is translated with the preposition *of*:

> *the waitress struck the chin <u>of the visitor</u> with a saucepan*

Although called the 'of' case, *of* does not always appear in a translation of the genitive; we may instead use the apostrophe:

> *the waitress struck <u>the visitor's</u> chin*

Our apostrophe ending is itself a relic of the genitive case of Old English, one of the few word-endings to have survived. The apostrophe can be used to translate the Latin genitive if it is possessive:

tunica fēminae   *the tunic <u>of the woman</u> (<u>the woman's</u> tunic)*

But not all genitives are possessive. Some describe a quantity:

amphora vīnī   *an amphora <u>of wine</u>*

sarcina ovōrum   *a bag <u>of eggs</u>*

> **LANGUAGE TIP**
> Both in English and in Latin phrases such as The story of Augustinus (**fābula Augustīnī**) could mean either the story Augustinus tells or the story about him.

Singular			
Nominative	puell**a**	mūl**us**	vīn**um**
Accusative	puell**am**	mūl**um**	vīn**um**
Genitive	puell**ae**	mūl**ī**	vīn**ī**
Ablative	puell**ā**	mūl**ō**	vīn**ō**
Plural			
Nominative	puell**ae**	mūl**ī**	vīn**a**
Accusative	puell**ās**	mūl**ōs**	vīn**a**
Genitive	puell**ārum**	mūl**ōrum**	vīn**ōrum**
Ablative	puell**īs**	mūl**īs**	vīn**īs**

> **INSIGHT**
>
> The Latin case system is not quite as pinpoint definitive as we might hope. There are overlaps, e.g. **mūlī** could be genitive singular or nominative plural. The context will help you decide which.

PRACTICE 4A

1 Translate each group of underlined words into one Latin word:

  i the tiredness <u>of the mule</u>

  ii <u>the girl's</u> mother

 iii a barrel <u>of wine</u>

  iv a crowd <u>of girls</u>

  v a fear <u>of woods</u>

  vi a trainer <u>of mules</u>

2 Add the ending and translate into English:

discipulī vīnum Benedict_____ dēsīderant.

The story of Augustinus (7)

 04.01 **The fallen rider is not a monk after all.**

> Paulus ad monachum currit quī nunc immōtus in terrā iacet.
> meherclē! est figūra nōn monachī sed fēminae. oculī fēminae
> sunt opertī, sed fēmina spīrat. Paulus fēminam spectat.
> cucullus feminae est scissus. Paulus fēminam tunicā prōtegit.
> equus intereā, ab umbrīs rāmīsque territus, ē viā in silvam
> fugit. equus folia rāmōsque timet quod ventō crepitant.

currit	*(he/she) runs*	scissus	*torn*
quī	*who*	tunica	*tunic, dress*
meherclē	*by Hercules!*	prōtegit	*(he/she) covers*
figūra (like puella)	*shape*	intereā	*meanwhile*
fēmina (like puella)	*woman*	rāmus (like mūlus)	*branch*
oculus (like mūlus)	*eye*	territus	*scared, terrified*
opertī	*closed*	folium (like vīnum)	*leaf*
spīrat	*breathes, is breathing*	ventus (like mūlus)	*wind*
cucullus (like mūlus)	*hood*	crepitant	*(they) rustle*

PRACTICE 4B

1 What has frightened the horse?

2 What case is fēminae (oculī <u>fēminae</u> sunt opertī, **line 2) and**
   folia **(line 6)?**

3 Add the missing Latin word and translate the sentence into
   English:
   i Paulus _____ (*the eyes*) fēminae spectat.
   ii _____ (*an egg*) in sarcinam cadit.
   iii discipulus sarcinam _____ (*of leaves*) portat.

Questions

A question may be introduced by a question word such as **ubi?**
where?, **quis?/quī?** *who?* or *which?* or **quid?** *what?*. If there is no such
interrogative word to introduce the question, the suffix **-ne** is added to
the first word in the sentence:

monachusne es? *are you a monk?*
valēsne? *are you well?*
ubi habitās? *where do you live?*
quid est? *what is it?*

The suffix **-ne** is sometimes left out, and you then have a statement ending with a question mark. The same happens in English when a question is made obvious by tone of voice, e.g. *You are swimming with a crocodile?*.

cūr? *why?*
quis?/quī? *who? which?*
quid? *what?*
ubi? *where?, when?*

PRACTICE 4C

Translate:

i quis in terrā iacet?
ii quid in sarcinā est?
iii mūlusne equōs amat?
iv cūr discipulī in monasteriō habitant?
v ubi est vīnum?

1st conjugation verbs like **amō, amāre** and **sum, esse**

A verb's ending changes according to the person (*I*, *you*, *he*, *she*, etc). Here are two verbs in the present tense: **amō, amāre** is regular (there are many other verbs like it), while **sum, esse** is irregular, but you will meet it more than any other verb.

amāre	*to love, like*	**esse**	*to be*
amō	*I love*	**sum**	*I am*
amās	*you* (sing.) *love*	**es**	*you* (sing.) *are*
amat	*he/she loves*	**est**	*he/she/it is*
amāmus	*we love*	**sumus**	*we are*
amātis	*you* (pl.) *love*	**estis**	*you* (pl.) *are*
amant	*they love*	**sunt**	*they/there are*

The words **amāre** (*to love*) and **esse** (*to be*) are called infinitives (expressed in English as *to …*).

The verbs here are in the present tense. This means they are happening now or in the current period. The present tense of Latin verbs represents both the present simple and the present continuous of English verbs (*I walk* or *am walking*, *they come* or *are coming*).

Verbs like amō

ambulō	*I walk, am walking*	labōrō	*I work*
amō	*I love, like*	parō	*I prepare*
clāmō	*I shout*	portō	*I carry*
dēsīderō	*I desire, long for*	rogō	*I ask*
equitō	*I ride*	spectō	*I watch*
habitō	*I live*		

PRACTICE 4D

1 Translate:

   i cūr hodiē per silvam ambulās?

  ii monachī in silvā sunt.

 iii quid dēsīderās?

  iv mūlus in silvā nōn habitat.

   v cūr clāmās?

  vi mūlīne in prātō labōrant?

 vii in monasteriō habitāmus.

viii quid ancillae parant?

  ix esne monachus?

   x unguentane semper portat mūlus?

2 Give the Latin infinitives of the verbs like amō **listed above. For example,** amō - amāre.

The verbs listed above have identical endings to **amō**. There are other groups of verbs too, which we will look at later (**audit, gemit, videt,** etc). These different groups are called conjugations. Verbs like **amō** belong to the 1st conjugation.

The story of Augustinus (8)

04.02 **The fallen rider recovers.**

> fēmina iacet immōta. Paulus equum fēminae neque vidēre neque audīre potest. nunc equus ē silvīs ad monasterium fugit. Paulus est sollicitus et mūlus trepidus. Paulus fēminam spectat. 'ēheu!' gemit Paulus. sed fēmina spīrat. 'spīrāsne?' susurrat Paulus. deinde fēmina oculōs aperit.
> 'certē ego spīrō! quis es?'
> 'Deō grātiās, nōn es mortua.'
> 'certē nōn sum mortua. ubi sum? in silvīs?'
> 'ita est.'
> 'ubi est equus?' rogat fēmina. 'ubi sumus?'
> 'lentē, lentē! equus abest. valēsne?'
> 'sīc, sīc, valeō, valeō. ubi est equus?'
> 'aquamne dēsīderās?'
> 'nōn aquam sed equum dēsīderō. ō malum est!' clāmat fēmina.
> 'lentē! quis es? ubi habitās? cūr in silvīs equitās?'

vidēre *to see*	Deō grātiās *thanks be to God*
audīre *to hear*	mortua *dead*
potest *(he/she) is able, can*	susurrō (like amō) *I whisper, murmur*
sollicitus *alarmed, disturbed*	ita (est) *(it is) thus, so, yes*
trepidus *nervous*	lentē *slowly*
ēheu *oh no!, oh dear!, alas!*	abest *(he/she) is absent*
spīrō (like amō) *I breathe*	valeō/valēs *I am/you are well, fine,*
aperit *(he/she) opens*	*healthy*
certē *certainly, for sure*	sīc *thus, so, yes*
ego *I*	malum est *it is bad! damn!*

Absum, adsum and possum

There are one or two verbs like the irregular **sum, esse**: **absum, abesse** (*be absent*) and **adsum, adesse** (*be present*) with one letter different but the opposite meanings.

There is also **possum, posse** (*can, be able*), an old contraction of **pot + sum**. This verb is often followed by an infinitive (*to be able to do something*).

posse   *to be able*

possum   *I can*
potes   *you* (sing.) *can*
potest   *he/she/it can*
possumus   *we can*
potestis   *you* (pl.) *can*
possunt   *they can*

PRACTICE 4E

Translate:

i potesne ambulāre?
  – ita, certē ambulāre possum.
ii ubi est equus?
  – abest. in monasteriō nunc adest.
iii puellane spīrāre potest?
  – ita, Deō grātiās.
iv cūr ancillae nōn in prātō labōrāre possunt?
  – quod semper in culīnā labōrant.
v mūlusne unguenta et ova et vīnum portāre potest?
  – sīc, et fēminam.

Sallust

04.03 For centuries the definition of 'classical' Latin was limited to a handful of authors from the first century BC: Cicero, Caesar and the historian Sallust. The reason such a narrow definition lasted so long was the use of classical Latin as a model for students who had to write extended pieces of Latin. There had to be a definitive standard. During the time lapse between Cicero and Tacitus (over 150 years) the language underwent inevitable changes, which blurred the model. For centuries Cicero, Caesar and Sallust remained the guide for Latin composition. Now, however, with much less requirement in schools for writing Latin, the definition of classical Latin has broadened to include later writers such as Seneca and Tacitus.

Gaius Sallustius Crispus was born in the mid-80s BC. Like Cicero, he was a **novus homo**. He owed some of his social advancement to Caesar, whose cause he supported. He was on less affable terms with Cicero. It has been suggested that he married Cicero's wife Terentia after they divorced in the 40s BC.

Two works of Sallust survive in full: his records of the war against Jugurtha and of the conspiracy of Catiline, along with fragments of other works such as his Histories. He is critical of corruption and the moral decadence of the aristocracy. However, he may not have practised what he later preached. After a stint as provincial governor during Caesar's dictatorship, he faced charges of extortion. Caesar helped him to avoid condemnation, and Sallust used his earnings to develop gardens in Rome and to write his histories at leisure. He died within a couple of years of turning 50.

Sallust shared the view of other ancient commentators that success may breed trouble; in this case the success is the victory over Hannibal's Carthaginians:

> **discordia et avāritia post Carthāginis excidium maximē aucta sunt.**
>
> *Discord and avarice greatly increased after the destruction (**excidium**) of Carthage.*

Histories 1.10

In his record of Catiline's conspiracy Sallust mentions Cicero's speech (see Unit 2). He decides not to quote or summarize it (as he does for others), saying that Cicero has already published it.

> **Catilīna in senātum vēnit. tum Mārcus Tullius cōnsul, sīve praesentiam eius timēns sīve īrā commōtus, ōrātiōnem habuit lūculentam atque ūtilem reī pūblicae.**
>
> *Catiline came into the senate. Then Marcus Tullius (Cicero), the consul, whether fearing (**timēns**) his presence or stirred by anger (**īrā**), gave a brilliant speech, a service to the Republic.*

Conspiracy of Catiline 31

Word discovery 4

1 **In the first sentence of Sallust above (**discordia … sunt**), identify two nouns like** puella.

2 **In the second quotation (**Catilīna … ēdidit**), identify the Latin word (as it appears) for:**
   i presence
   ii stirred
   iii speech

3 **Find Latin ancestors in this unit of** *feminine,* *figurative,* *respirator* **and** *scissors.*

Test yourself 4

1 Fill each gap with the missing word:

   i in monasteriō _____ (*we live*).

   ii mūlīne in prātō _____ (*work*)?

   iii quis nunc in silvā _____ (*is shouting*)?

   iv celeriter cēnam _____ (*of the monks*) parāmus.

   v potesne _____ (*to ride*)?

   vi quis _____ (*the bags*) Benedictī portat?

   vii equus _____ (*of the woman*) in silvā nōn _____ (*is present*).

2 Translate:

   i mūlusne in silvā habitāt?

     – nōn est ita. in silvā nōn habitat sed in prātō.

   ii ubi est fēmina? adestne in silvā?

     – sīc, hodiē in silvīs equitat cucullāta.

   iii discipulīne vīnum Benedictī dēsīderant?

     – sīc, certē vīnum dēsīderant sed ego semper aquam.

   iv coquusne susurrāre potest?

     – ēheu, nōn potest. semper enim clāmat.

3 What does **ad nauseam** mean?

   a follow your nose

   b (travel) by ship

   c to the point of sickness

In this unit you will learn about:
- ▶ *Latin and English: more inkhorn words*
- ▶ *nouns like* magister, puer, *etc*
- ▶ *adjectives like* bonus,-a,-um
- ▶ *vocative case*
- ▶ *The story of Augustinus: Paulus takes Lucia back to the monastery*
- ▶ *Virgil: poet*

Latin and English: more inkhorn words

Latin has been a fruitful source of new adjectives for English, e.g. *conspicuous*, *dubious*, *elegant*, *indignant*, *ridiculous*, etc. Some of these ex-Latin adjectives came to exist alongside much older Anglo-Saxon nouns, for example: *canine* (**canis**) – dog; *domestic* (**domus**) – house; *paternal* (**pater**) – father.

Many inkhorn words were created to replace words which had already settled in English after arriving from Latin via French. The feeling was that these words had lost their Latin purity: thus *compute* from Latin **computāre**, which had already given us *count* via French *compter*. So too *fragile* from **fragilis** although English already had *frail* via French. The new creations which survived did not replace the older words but developed slightly different meanings: we are more likely to speak of a frail aunt and a fragile parcel than a frail parcel and a fragile aunt.

The inkhorn period was a prolific source of new words. From **equus** came *equestrian*, *equitation*, etc. There is another word for horse, **caballus**, more street nag than smart steed, a word you would have heard frequently in spoken Latin. **Caballus**'s descendants are pre-inkhorn, passing into French (*cheval*), Italian (*cavallo*) and Spanish (*caballo*), and in turn English has taken *cavalry*, *chivalry* and *cab* (the descendants of **caballus** have smartened up a bit).

Declensions

All nouns belong to one of five groups or 'declensions'. Nouns like **puella** and **silva** belong to the 1st declension, nouns like **mūlus** and **vīnum** belong to the 2nd declension. In a dictionary or word-list nouns are listed in the nominative *and* genitive so you can identify its declension, for example:

puella,-ae; mūlus,-ī; vīnum,-ī

You need both cases, nominative and genitive, to be sure of the noun's declension. For instance, you will meet other declensions with a nominative ending **-us**.

In vocabularies from here on, all nouns will be listed in their nominative and genitive forms. The gender is usually listed too (m., f. or n.). All the declensions are listed in the Grammar tables at the end of the book.

2nd declension nouns ending **-er**

A few 2nd declension nouns like **mūlus** have an exceptional nominative singular ending **-er** (and vocative – see later in this unit): **puer** (*boy*) is **puer** in the nominative then **puerum** (accusative), **puerī** (genitive), etc. It is as if the noun was once **puerus** and lost its tail.

Likewise **vir** (*man, husband*), which is **virum** in the accusative and **virī** in the genitive.

> **INSIGHT**
>
> There are other words which look like **vir**: **vīrēs** (*strength*) which belongs to the 3rd declension and has a different set of endings, and **vīrus**, which has endings almost identical to **vir** and means *poison* or *slime*. The proximity of **vir** to **vīrus** probably wasn't lost on the ancient world.

Some nouns ending **-er** in the nominative lose the 'e' in the other cases: **magister** (*master*), with an accusative **magistrum**, genitive **magistrī**, etc. Likewise **ager** (*field*), **agrum** in the accusative and **agrī** in the genitive. The genitive form will show whether the 'e' is kept or not: **puer,-erī**; **ager, agrī**; **magister,-trī**, etc.

Like **magister,-trī**		Like **puer,-ī**	
ager, agrī	*field*	presbyter, presbyterī	*priest*
liber, librī	*book*		

Fill each gap with the missing word:

  i quis cum _____ *(with the master)* ambulat?

  ii in sarcinā sunt _____ *(the books)* _____ *(of the boy).*

  iii discipulus cum _____ *(the priests)* in monasteriō, cum mūlō in

        _____ *(in the fields)* labōrat.

The story of Augustinus (9)

 05.01 Paulus and Lucia introduce themselves.

'quis es? ubi habitās?' rogat Paulus.

'in castellō,' inquit fēmina.

'vērō, in castellō? tūne es Egberta, castellī domina?'

'nōn ego Egberta, sed Egbertae fīlia, Lūcia sum. et tū, quis es?'

'sum Paulus, et in monasteriō habitō.'

'es presbyter?'

'nōn presbyter, sed discipulus sum.'

'discipulus epīscopī?'

'nōn epīscopī sed Stephanī.'

'quis est Stephanus? est monachus?'

'vērō, Stephanus est monachus et scholae magister.'

'ēheu! ubi est ille caballus?'

'fortasse est in agrīs cum monasteriī equīs. in mūlum ascendere potes? monasterium nōn longē abest.'

deinde fēmina in mūlum ascendit et mūlus gemit.

---

rogō (like amō) *ask*	schola,-ae (f.) *school*
castellum,-ī (n.) *castle*	ille *that*
inquit *(he/she) says, said*	caballus,-ī (m.) *horse*
vērō *indeed, really, yes*	fortasse *perhaps, probably*
tū *you* (sing.)	ascendere *to climb, get on*
domina,-ae (f.) *mistress, lady*	ascendit *(he/she) climbs, gets on*
fīlia,-ae (f.) *daughter*	
epīscopus,-ī (m.) *bishop*	

Adjectives: **bonus, bona, bonum**

Adjectives describe nouns, giving more detail or colour: *a heavy bag, a tired maid*. Grammatically, an adjective is said to 'agree' with the noun it describes: it will be in the same case, have the same gender and be singular or plural to correspond with the noun:

mūlus sarcinās onerōsās portat
the mule carries the heavy bags

Here are the endings of **bonus** (*good*), an adjective like **onerōsus**. The good news is that you know these endings already. They are identical to those of **mūlus, puella** and **vīnum**.

Singular			
	masculine	feminine	neuter
Nominative	bonus	bona	bonum
Accusative	bonum	bonam	bonum
Genitive	bonī	bonae	bonī
Ablative	bonō	bonā	bonō
Plural			
	masculine	feminine	neuter
Nominative	bonī	bonae	bona
Accusative	bonōs	bonās	bona
Genitive	bonōrum	bonārum	bonōrum
Ablative	bonīs	bonīs	bonīs

An adjective may appear before or after the noun it describes. It may not even be next to its noun:

mūlus cum Paulō ambulat <u>territus</u>
the <u>terrified</u> mule walks with Paulus

mūlus cum Paulō ambulat <u>territō</u>
the mule walks with the <u>terrified</u> Paulus

Some adjectives appear after a verb, typically *to be*, as in English:

mūlus est fessus
the mule is tired

Thus an adjective qualifies a particular noun by matching its ending. When you come across an adjective, look for a noun to pair it with.

> **LANGUAGE TIP**
> A word of warning about matching the endings: they do not always contain the same letters, e.g. **vir bonus** (*a good man*) and **magister bonus** (*a good master*). The endings correspond but their final letters are not identical.

Adjectives like **bonus,-a,-um**

benignus,-a,-um	*kind*	pius,-a,-um	*pious, dutiful*
magnus,-a,-um	*great, large*	prīmus,-a,-um	*first*
malus,-a,-um	*bad, evil*	saevus,-a,-um	*cruel, harsh*
meus,-a,-um	*my*	sānctus,-a,-um	*sacred, holy*
multus,-a,-um	*much, many*	tuus,-a,-um	*your* (sing.)

PRACTICE 5B

1 Identify first the adjective in each sentence, and then the noun it agrees with:

i Paulus est anxius.

ii cūr onerōsae sunt sarcinae?

iii cucullus feminae est scissus.

iv multī equī in agrīs sunt.

2 Put the underlined word into the plural (and change other words if necessary), and then translate the new version of the sentence into English:

i estne <u>epīscopus</u> benignus?

ii mūlus meam <u>sarcinam</u> portat.

iii cūr est <u>fēmina</u> cucullāta?

iv <u>liber</u> magnus in bibliothēcā est.

Nōnne and num

Some questions anticipate the answer 'yes' or 'no'. These begin with **nōnne** (*surely*) if the answer expected is 'yes', and **num** (*surely ... not*) if the reply predicted is 'no':

nōnne epīscopus sānctus est?
surely the bishop is saintly?

num fēmina est mala?
surely the woman is *not* evil?

PRACTICE 5C

Translate:
   i nōnne mūlus tuus aquam dēsīderat?
   ii num ancillae piae vīnum Benedictī dēsīderant?

The story of Augustinus (10)

 05.02 **The journey through the wood continues.**

obscūram per silvam Paulus ad monasterium mūlum dūcit. Lūcia in mūlō sedet. mūlus est lentus. silva est umbrōsa. Lūcia Paulum rogat: 'epīscopusne sānctus in monasteriō adest?'

'sānctus vel saevus epīscopus?'

'nōnne epīscopus est sānctus et benignus?'

'epīscopus est saevus, quod semper presbyterōs iubet verberāre nōs discipulōs vel in bibliothēcā claudere.'

'vōsne discipulī semper estis studiōsī?'

'certē, semper.'

num vōs discipulī semper estis studiōsī? nōnne īgnāvī esse, fortasse malī, etiam somnulentī potestis?

'quid dīcis? malī? īgnāvī? nōs? nōnne iocōsa es?'

'cūr in silvā ambulās? nōnne discipulī in bibliothēcā adesse studiōsī dēbent?'

'Benedictus monasteriī coquus mē iubet per silvam mūlum dūcere. et tū, cūr hīc equitās cucullāta?'

'saepe sōla per silvam equitō vel cum epīscopō vel amīcīs.'

'cum epīscopō? nōn est sānctus epīscopus, sed malus, īgnāvus, saevus, etiam gulōsus, vīnolentus ...'

'ssst, maledīcis. epīscopus saepe apud nōs in castellō manet.

'vērō, ō domina?' Paulus rīdet. 'ecce mūlus saepe apud equōs magnōs manet in agrīs monasteriī, eho mūle?' neque Lūcia neque mūlus rīdet. nunc enim mūlus et Lūciam et sarcinās onerōsās portat. ita per silvās Paulus et Lūcia silentiō veniunt. mox magnōs monasteriī mūrōs vident et ē silvīs in agrōs vādunt.

obscūrus,-a,-um *dark*	dēbent *must, ought*
dūcit (dūcere) *(he/she) leads, brings*	hīc *here*
(to lead, bring)	sōlus,-a,-um *alone, single*
umbrōsus,-a,-um *full of shadows*	gulōsus,-a,-um *greedy*
sānctus,-a,-um *holy, sacred*	vīnolentus,-a,-um *full of wine, drunk*
saevus,-a,-um *cruel, harsh*	*with wine*
iubet *(he/she) tells, orders*	sst *ssh!*
verberāre *to beat*	maledīcis *you slander*
nōs (nom. or acc.) *we/us*	apud (+ acc.) *at the house of*
claudere *to shut, lock*	manet *(he/she) stays*
vōs (nom. or acc.) *you* (pl.)	ecce *see here, behold*
studiōsus,-a,-um *hard-working*	eho *eh, indeed*
malus,-a,-um *bad*	rīdet *(he/she) laughs*
īgnāvus,-a,-um *lazy*	et ... et *both ... and*
somnulentus,-a,-um *sleepy*	silentium,-ī (n.) *silence*
dīcis *you say*	mox *soon, presently*
iocōsus,-a,-um *having a laugh, full*	mūrus,-ī (m.) *wall*
of jokes	vādunt *(they) go, walk*

PRACTICE 5D

1 **What two adjectives does Lucia use to describe the bishop?**

2 **How would the two words change if she were using them to describe herself?**

3 **Does Paulus have anything nice to say about the bishop? Look for adjectives describing good or kindly qualities.**

4 **Choose two adjectives to describe yourself:**

ego sum _____ et _____

Adjectives without nouns

A Latin adjective may appear without a noun as in

est benignus
he is kind

An adjective also may appear with no noun where the noun is obvious (if not immediately to us), and does not need to be spelt out. These missing but unneeded nouns are said to be 'understood':

<u>bonī</u> in agrīs labōrant   (**bonī** = nom. pl. m.)
<u>good (men)</u> work in the fields

When you meet a Latin adjective with no noun, add one which seems to fit, taking into account the case, gender and number (i.e. singular or plural):

<u>multī</u> in agrīs sunt   (**multī** = nom. pl. m.)
there are <u>many (men/people)</u> in the fields

<u>multa</u> dīcit   (**multa** = acc. pl. n.)
he/she says <u>many (things)</u> (i.e. much)

> **INSIGHT**
>
> In English we use adjectives as nouns too, e.g. *The <u>good</u>, the <u>bad</u> and the <u>ugly</u>*. Far more frequently we use nouns as adjectives: *a <u>tennis</u> match*. Newspapers tend to cram together nouns as adjectives in their headlines: 'Pay protest walkout', 'Bank boss exit strategy', 'Vice den corruption probe', etc.

PRACTICE 5E

The Latin for *saints* is an adjective used as a noun. It is also the ancestor of the English word. What is it, in the masculine nominative plural?

The vocative case

Second declension nouns like **mūlus** have a special ending for when they are being spoken to. This is called the vocative case: **mūle** for **mūlus**. It is often preceded by **ō** or **mī/mea** (*my*). Most other vocative forms are the same as the nominative, e.g. **ō Lūcia ...**

PRACTICE 5F

When Caesar is stabbed by his friend Brutus, Shakespeare presents him calling out **Et tū _____**.

Virgil

 05.03 Little is known for certain about the life of Publius Vergilius Maro. There are fewer biographical insights revealed in his poetry than in say Horace or Ovid or Martial. Much of what we know about him has come through a later commentator, Servius, whose reliability is held in question. We can be reasonably sure that Virgil was born in 70 BC in northern Italy (considered Gaul at the time), possibly of Celtic descent or from Romans who had settled there, or a mixture. His father, a farmer, could afford him an education, and Virgil received the traditional schooling in rhetoric, but he did not flourish as a speaker in public. He preferred a more contemplative life out of the limelight, where his talent as a poet blossomed. His work came to the attention of Augustus himself, who encouraged him to write more. His principal works are the *Eclogues*, the *Georgics* and the *Aeneid*.

The *Eclogues*, ten pastoral poems, imagine shepherds conversing in rural seclusion:

> **omnia vincit Amor: et nōs cēdāmus Amōrī.**
> *Love conquers all: let us too yield to Love.*

Eclogues 10.69

The peace of this idyllic landscape was touched with trauma. Virgil's family farm, like others, was exposed to the brutal civil conflicts which had darkened Italy for some decades before this, and which led to widespread relief when Augustus emerged as the single ruler. During the troubles there was the threat of losing land to settlements for soldiers. Octavian himself (as Augustus was then) had given other people's lands to his veterans, and Virgil's farm will have been one of those at risk.

With the *Georgics*, Virgil's second major composition, a poetic manual for farmers and beekeepers in four books, the poet's focus stays in the countryside, offering wise thoughts and practical advice for farmers, mixed with contemporary politics and mythical stories. In the ancient world many instructive or didactic works were written in verse.

fēlīx quī potuit rērum cognōscere causās.
Happy is he who has been able to learn the causes of things.

Georgics 2.490

sed fugit intereā, fugit irreparābile tempus.
But time is escaping meanwhile, irretrievable time is escaping.

Georgics 3.284

The *Aeneid*, Virgil's largest work in 12 books, was started in 29 BC, with encouragement from Augustus and his team to celebrate the new peace. Virgil tells a story from mythical narratives already familiar to many of his readers. Like all Latin poets he draws heavily on Greek stories, especially the two epics of Homer, the *Iliad* (an episode in the war between Greece and Troy) and the *Odyssey* (the return home of the Greek warrior Odysseus): Aeneas, a Trojan prince, escapes from the city now assailed by the Greeks, and after a number of adventures reaches Italy, where his descendants will found the city of Rome.

The *Aeneid* is perhaps the best known Latin poem of all. We may not know for sure many biographical details about the poet, but through his work we know him well: the poem is the man. Sublime, touching, deeply musical, through the medium of myth the *Aeneid* strikes a chord in all our lives.

The poem has its critics too. The idea of a poet obliged to pen lines to satisfy a political leader meets m~~▓▓▓▓▓▓▓▓▓▓▓▓▓▓▓▓▓~~ere is a lingering if perhaps ~~▓▓▓▓▓▓▓▓▓▓▓▓▓▓▓▓▓▓▓▓~~mised by his close ties to Augustus. There are recognizable parallels between the character of Aeneas and the new emperor, each overcoming adversity and (re-)founding Rome. But this poem is not a piece of whitewashed propaganda. The relief expressed by poets at the end of the civil wars was genuine.

During his travels Aeneas is determined to go down to the underworld to meet the soul of his father. He is warned of the challenge ahead:

> **facilis dēscēnsus Avernō:**
> **noctēs atque diēs patet ātrī iānua Dītis;**
> **sed revocāre gradum superāsque ēvādere ad aurās,**
> **hoc opus, hic labor est.**
>
> *The descent to Avernus is easy.*
> *Night and day the door of gloomy Dis (i.e. hell) lies open (**patet**);*
> *but to retrace your step and escape (**ēvādere**) to the air above,*
> *this is the task, this the struggle.*

Aeneid 6.126–9

Having reached Italy Aeneas meets resistance from the local warlord, Turnus. War follows, and Virgil, though known for his gentle humanity and sensitivity to friend and foe, brings the *Aeneid* to the kind of shuddering close you would expect in an amphitheatre: Aeneas stands over the defeated Turnus as he pleads for his life, and catches sight of a spoil of war his stricken foe is wearing, taken from the corpse of Aeneas' young comrade, Pallas. In cold fury Aeneas plunges his sword into his rival, and the poem ends:

vītaque cum gemitū fugit indīgnāta sub umbrās.

And with a groan his life flees resentfully to the shades below.

Aeneid 12.952

Virgil died in 19 BC without revising the poem as he wished, and his orders to destroy the manuscript were overturned by Augustus.

schola,-ae (f.)	*school*	dīcit/dīcunt	*he/she/they say(s)*
umbra,-ae (f.)	*shadow, shade*	dūcit/dūcunt	*he/she/they lead(s)*
vīta,-ae (f.)	*life*	iubet/iubent	*he/she/they order(s)*
epīscopus,-ī (m.)	*bishop*	rīdet/rīdent	*he/she/they laugh(s)*
mūrus,-ī (m.)	*wall*	vincit/vincunt	*he/she/they*
oculus,-ī (m.)	*eye*		*conquer(s)*

Word discovery 5

1 **If** deus **is** *a god*, dominus *a lord* **or** *a master* **and** filius *a son*, **what are the feminine forms of these words, which mean respectively**
   i goddess
   ii lady, mistress
   iii daughter

2 **Identify Latin ancestors of** *mural*, *school*, *umbrella* **and** *vital*.

3 **Think of English adjectives created from** culīna, epīscopus, fīlia, noctēs **and** obscūrus.

4 These adjectives were created from Latin. What do you suspect the Latin nouns in brackets mean?

Example: *domestic* **(domus)** <u>*house, home*</u>

  i ecclesiastical (ecclēsia) _____

 ii lunar (lūna) _____

iii maternal (māter) _____

 iv naval (nāvis) _____

  v solar (sōl) _____

Fixed endings

et … et	*both … and*	nōnne	*surely*
fortasse	*perhaps, possibly*	num	*surely … not*
hīc	*here*	vel	*or, or if you prefer*
mox	*soon, presently*	vērō	*indeed, really, yes*

Test yourself 5

1 Add the word missing from each gap and translate the sentence into English:

  i fēmina nōn est mala, nōn est _____ (*greedy*), nōn est _____ (*cruel*), nōn est _____ (*drunk with wine*).

  ii ō amīcī, cūr Benedictus _____ (*many*) unguenta dēsīderat?

  iii estne tua domina _____ (*kind*)?

  iv estne magister _____ (*harsh*)?

  v discipulīne _____ (*sleepy*) librōs tuōs amant?

  vi ō monache, _____ (*your*) liber est in sarcinā _____ (*my*).

  vii in agrīs sunt _____ (*many men*).

2 Translate:

  i malī discipulī nōn labōrant.
    – num sunt malī, sed fessī?

  ii epīscopus discipulum iubet equum dūcere.
    – sed fugit trepidus equus.

3 What was an **aqueduct**?

  a a pond for ducks

  b a raised channel for water

  c a punishment ducking the culprit in water

In this unit you will learn about:
▶ *Latin and English: Latin words in English*
▶ *dative case*
▶ *2nd conjugation verbs*
▶ *personal pronouns:* **ego, tū, nōs, vōs**
▶ *adjectives like* **miser,-era,-erum**
▶ *The story of Augustinus: in the classroom*
▶ *Horace: poet*

Latin and English: Latin words in English

A few Latin phrases have settled in English, e.g. *in flagrante delicto, non sequitur, status quo.*

A number of single Latin words have settled in their original form, e.g. *agenda, circus, consensus, exit, genius, miser, recipe, referendum, squalor, status, terror, virus.*

These words are sometimes given Latin plurals (e.g. *referendum – referenda*), but this cannot be consistently applied. Words like **recipe** ('take' such and such ingredients – the first word of a cooking instruction) were verbs in Latin and are now nouns in English, while words like **circus** arrived early enough to take on a native English plural (*circuses*). Then there is *agenda*, which is plural in Latin (*agendum*, the singular in Latin, is sometimes used if there is only one thing to be done), but now *agenda* is usually treated in English as singular, with the plural *agendas*.

The pronunciation today of one or two of these words and phrases is not far from how we now assume the ancient version would have sounded, but most have changed, shaped by English speech habits.

The dative case

The dative case represents a kind of object, if an indirect one, for it is often on the receiving end of something. Consider this sentence:

magister historiam narrat
the master relates a story

There is a subject in the nominative (**magister**) and an object in the accusative (**historiam**). We could add a further object here, the people being told the story:

magister historiam <u>discipulīs</u> narrat
the master relates a story <u>to the students</u>

Discipulīs is in the dative case. Verbs followed by a dative often have something to do with giving, telling, showing, serving, i.e. give/show/etc something (accusative) <u>to</u> someone or something (dative):

discipulus unguenta nōn <u>Benedictō</u> sed <u>puellae</u> dat
the student gives the perfumes not <u>to Benedictus</u> but <u>to the girl</u>

Singular			
Nominative	puell**a**	mūl**us**	vīn**um**
Accusative	puell**am**	mūl**um**	vīn**um**
Genitive	puell**ae**	mūl**ī**	vīn**ī**
Dative	puell**ae**	mūl**ō**	vīn**ō**
Ablative	puell**ā**	mūl**ō**	vīn**ō**
Plural			
Nominative	puell**ae**	mūl**ī**	vīn**ā**
Accusative	puell**ās**	mūl**ōs**	vīn**ā**
Genitive	puell**ārum**	mūl**ōrum**	vīn**ōrum**
Dative	puell**īs**	mūl**īs**	vīn**īs**
Ablative	puell**īs**	mūl**īs**	vīn**īs**

You will see more overlaps here. **Mūlō**, for example, may be dative or ablative singular, and **puellae** genitive or dative. On a more positive note, the overlap between the dative and ablative plurals (**-īs**) means fewer endings to learn …

If the genitive is the 'of' case, the ablative the 'by, with, in, on' or 'from' case, we may say that the dative is the 'to' or 'for' case. An exception is 'to' a place in the sense of towards somewhere, which is usually expressed by **ad** and the accusative (e.g. **ad monasterium** = *to(wards) the monastery*). Otherwise 'to' something or someone is represented by the dative:

coquus <u>ancillīs</u> vīnum nōn dat
the cook does not give wine <u>to the maids</u>

PRACTICE 6A

1 **With help from the picture, put each noun into its correct form, and translate:**_____ (*monachus,-ī*) _____ (*domina,-ae*) _____ (*unguentum,-ī*) **dat.**

2 **Complete each sentence with one word:**
  i ancillae crusta _____ (*to the cook*) ostentant.
  ii puella _____ (*to the horses*) aquam dat.
  iii discipulus historiās monasteriī _____ (*to the lady*) narrat.

The story of Augustinus (11)

 06.01 **Students in the monastery classroom are looking at pictures of historical scenes.**

> est merīdiēs. Stephanus, magister scholae, discipulīs librum magnum ostentat. in librō sunt figūrae. discipulī figūrās spectant. magister puerīs historiam Christiānōrum narrat: 'ecce bēstiae et Christiānī in amphitheātrō adsunt. ēheu, Rōmānī multōs Christiānōs in amphitheātrō trucīdant. pāgānī semper saevitiam spectāre dēsīderant,' inquit Stephanus.
>
> 'saevīne pāgānīs umquam Christiānī sunt?' rogat Augustīnus ex discipulīs ūnus.

'fortasse vērum est,' respondet magister. 'ecce Rōmānī
lūdōs in amphitheātrō spectant, etiam doctī, quī eōs putant
esse nōn saevōs sed ineptōs. numquam misericordia est ūlla.
magnī enim opulentōs lūdōs praebent prō suffrāgiīs. sed nunc
monachīs discipulīsque grātī sunt librī, nōn lūdī, eho Paule?'

'Ricardus saevus etiam Christiānus est et nōs saepe
verberat,' gemit Augustīnus. Ricardus alius est ex monachīs
quī discipulōs docent.

'ssst. Paulusne nōbīs recitāre potest? Paule? ubi est Paulus?'

'ō magister, hodiē Paulus in culīnā labōrat,' inquit alius
discipulus.

'quid? cūr Paulus quī hīc adesse in scholā dēbet in culīnā
labōrat? estne discipulus aut ancilla?' et discipulī rīdent.

'Paulus Benedictō semper est servus,' respondet Augustīnus.

'ēheu,' gemit magister.

merīdiēs *midday*	ineptus,-a,-um *foolish*
figūra,-ae (f.) *shape, sketch*	numquam *never*
historia,-ae (f.) *story*	misericordia,-ae (f.) *pity, mercy*
Christiānus,-ī (m.) *Christian*	ūllus,-a,-um *any* (emphatic)
bēstia,-ae (f.) *beast*	lūdus,-ī (m.) *game* (in plural: *public games, shows*)
amphitheātrum,-ī (n.) *amphitheatre*	
Rōmānus,-ī (m.) *Roman*	opulentus,-a,-um *rich, lavish*
trucīdō,-āre (like amō) *slaughter, butcher*	praebent *(they) offer*
	prō (+ abl.) *in return for, in place of, on behalf of*
pāgānus,-ī (m.) *pagan*	
saevitia,-ae (f.) *cruelty*	suffrāgium,-ī (n.) *vote*
umquam *ever*	grātus,-a,-um *pleasing*
ūnus (nom.) *one*	nōbīs (dat.) *to us, for us*
vērus,-a,-um *true, real*	alius (nom.) *another*
respondet *(he/she) replies*	docent *(they) teach*
doctus,-a,-um *learned, educated*	recitō,-āre *recite, read aloud*
eōs (acc.) *them*	aut *or*
putō,-āre (like amō) *think, deem*	servus,-ī (m.) *slave*

PRACTICE 6B

What case is (i) **discipulīs** in line 1 and (ii) the same word in line 8 (**ex discipulīs ūnus**)?

Personal pronouns: **ego, tū, nōs, vōs**

Personal pronouns are *I, me, you, she, he, we, us, they, them*. Here are the 1st and 2nd person pronouns (*I/me, we/us* and *you*):

	I/me	*you* **(sing.)**	*we/us*	*you* **(pl.)**
Nominative	**ego**	**tū**	**nōs**	**vōs**
Accusative	**mē**	**tē**	**nōs**	**vōs**
Genitive	**meī**	**tuī**	**nostrum/-ī**	**vestrum/-ī**
Dative	**mihi**	**tibi**	**nōbīs**	**vōbīs**
Ablative	**mē**	**tē**	**nōbīs**	**vōbīs**

They appear less in the nominative than the other cases, because the verb-endings by themselves indicate the person:

> **cūr mē amās?**
>
> *why do you love me?*

But they do appear for emphasis or if clarification is needed:

> **cūr tū mē amās?**
>
> *why do you love me?*

> **LANGUAGE TIP**
>
> When these pronouns are used in the ablative with the preposition **cum**, the preposition may come after the pronoun, joined to it: **mēcum** = *with me*, **tēcum** = *with you*, etc.

PRACTICE 6C

Complete each sentence with one word, and then translate the sentence into English:

  i magister _____ (*to me*) librum dat.

  ii monachus _____ (*to us*) monasterium ostentat.

  iii _____ (*me*)-ne fēmina amat?

  iv semper _____ (*to you* (sing.)) servus sum.

  v num, ō ancillae, _____ (*you*) coquum amātis?

  vi quis, ō Paule, _____ (*with you*) in silvā ambulat?

2nd conjugation verbs

Here are the endings of the present tense of the 2nd conjugation verb **habeō,-ēre**:

habēre	*to have, hold*
habeō	*I have, hold*
habēs	*you* (sing.) *have, hold*
habet	*he/she/it has, holds*
habēmus	*we have, hold*
habētis	*you* (pl.) *have, hold*
habent	*they have, hold*

2nd conjugation verbs

dēbeō,-ēre	*must, ought*	pāreō,-ēre (+ dat.)	*obey*
doceō,-ēre	*teach*	respondeō,-ēre	*reply*
habeō,-ēre	*have, hold*	rīdeō,-ēre	*laugh (at)*
iaceō,-ēre	*lie*	sedeō,-ēre	*sit*
iubeō,-ēre	*order, tell*	timeō,-ēre	*fear*
maneō,-ēre	*stay, remain*	videō,-ēre	*see*

PRACTICE 6D

1 **What appears to be the principal difference in the endings of 1st and 2nd conjugation verbs in the present tense?**

2 **Complete each sentence with one word, and then translate the sentence into English:**

   i quis vōs _____ (*is teaching*)?

   ii discipulīne in terrā _____ (*are lying*)?

   iii tē sarcinās portāre _____ (*I order*).

   iv cūr tū _____ (*maids*) semper pārēs?

   v in terrā _____ (*we are sitting*) quod fessī sumus.

   vi ō amīce, librum meum _____ (*to see*) dēbēs.

> **LANGUAGE TIP**
>
> One verb listed above has not yet appeared in the story: **pāreō,-ēre**, which means *obey*. This verb is listed '+ dat.', i.e. its object is in the dative, not the accusative. **Pāreō** essentially means 'appear': a slave would appear for or show himself to the person he was serving.

The dative of possession

The dative is used for someone or something on the receiving end of a service, duty, kindness (or cruelty), favour or obligation. It is also used with the verb *to be* to express ownership or association:

sunt mihi multī amīcī
there are many friends to me (I have many friends)

semper mihi benignī sunt
they are always kind to me

> **INSIGHT**
> We might say **multōs amīcōs habeō** for *I have many friends*, but in classical Latin **habeō,-ēre** was usually limited to something you actually possessed, your belongings or property. In later Latin **habeō** corresponds more closely with English *have* in all its uses.

The story of Augustinus (12)

 06.02 **The teacher, Stephanus, returns to the classroom having failed to find Paulus.**

mox Stephanus ē culīnā venit: 'Paulum vidēre nōn possum. nam Paulus nōn in culīnā adest sed in silvīs ambulat.'

'Paulus ex oppidō venit,' inquit Augustīnus, quī Paulī est amīcus. 'Paulus vīna unguentaque ex oppidō portat.'

'unguenta? sed sumus monachī! quis iussit Paulum ad oppidum ambulāre et unguenta vīnaque petere?'

'et oleum et ōva,' inquit Augustīnus.

'et ōva? nōnne hīc multa ōva habēmus?'

'nōn satis Benedictō, ō magister,' inquit Augustīnus. 'Benedictus saepe Paulum iubet ad oppidum mūlum dūcere. Paulus coquō et ancillīs servus est.'

'nōn coquō sed magistrō pārēre dēbet Paulus,' inquit miser magister.

'semper Paulus in culīnā cum ancillīs labōrat,' inquit Augustīnus.

'in culīnā cum ancillīs?'

'etiamne nōs in culīnā labōrāre possumus, magister?'

'sst! ad librōs! vōs sedēre iubeō! ubi eram?'

'in culīnā cum ancillīs!' clāmant discipulī.

'ēheu! ecce in amphitheātrō sumus.'

nam	*for, in fact* (similar to *enim*)		miser (nom.)	*wretched*
iussit	*(he/she) told, ordered*		eram	*I was*
satis	*enough*			

Adjectives: **miser**, **misera**, **miserum**

The adjective **miser, misera, miserum** (*wretched*) is exactly like **bonus, -a,-um**, singular and plural, except for the nominative and vocative masculine singular, which is **miser** for both. Like the noun **puer** it appears to have lost its final syllable in these two cases:

ubi, ō <u>miser</u> discipule, est Lūcia?
where, you <u>wretched</u> student, is Lucia?

> **LANGUAGE TIP**
> One or two adjectives are the same as **miser** but lose the 'e' (like **magister**), e.g.
> **noster, nostra, nostrum** (*our*), **vester, vestra, vestrum** (*your* pl.).

Horace

06.03 Quintus Horatius Flaccus was born in 65 BC in the south of Italy. His father had once been a slave, possibly captured in one of the Italian towns which took arms against Rome early in the first century BC. As a freed man he was able to support his son's education, which, for Latin poets of Horace's time, was exacting: Horace described the challenge of reproducing Greek lyric metres in Latin as his greatest claim to fame.

He took a risk in 42 BC when he lined up at the battle of Philippi with the Republicans and those who had assassinated Caesar. The battle was lost to Mark Antony and Augustus (then Octavian) but there was an amnesty after the battle and he was forgiven. By the age of 30 he was very much a part of Augustus' team, one of the inner circle of poets looked after by Maecenas, whom Augustus entrusted to encourage the arts and literature. Maecenas took a shine to Horace's work, and made sure he wanted for nothing. Many times in his poems Horace thanks friends, his patron, and the gods for his good fortune. He stayed simple in his tastes, so he tells us, and urged others to enjoy similar pleasures. Bring wine, says the poet, and perfume and fresh flowers to a nice spot in the country:

quō pīnus ingēns albaque pōpulus
umbram hospitālem cōnsociāre amant
rāmīs? quid oblīquō labōrat
lympha fugāx trepidāre rīvō?

*For what (purpose) does the lofty pine and white poplar (**pōpulus** – not*
***populus** – is feminine) like to gather together welcoming shade with their*
*branches? Why does the elusive (**fugāx**) water (**lympha**) strive to hurry*
*along its winding (**oblīquō**) course (**rīvō**)?*

Odes 2.3.9–12

Horace had studied the different schools of philosophy. He respects the
Stoics' principle of calm endurance in the face of whatever fortune
may bring:

quisnam igitur līber? sapiēns sibi quī imperiōsus,
quem neque pauperiēs neque mors neque vincula terrent.

Who then (is) free? The wise man who (is) master of himself,
whom neither poverty nor death nor chains frighten.

Satires 2.7.83–4

He was also something of an Epicurean, and praises a life free from stress
and the anxiety of ambition. The live-for-today motif crops up again and
again, famously in the *carpe diem* ode, in which Horace advises a girlfriend
to enjoy the here-and-now (with me please):

sapiās, vīna liquēs, et spatiō brevī
spem longam resecēs. dum loquimur, fūgerit invida
aetās: carpe diem, quam minimum crēdula posterō.

Be wise, decant the wines and to a short period cut back far-reaching hope.
While we are speaking, the unkind hour has slipped away: enjoy the fruit of
(this) day, as little as possible reliant on the one after.

Odes 1.11.6–8

Most of Horace's poems are relatively short. He wrote Satires (in the form
of dialogues) and Epistles (in the form of letters). His Epodes, traditionally
a form of attack and criticism, were in Horace's hands more playful (he has

a go at garlic, for example). And finally his Odes, four books of lyric poems, were considered his greatest achievement. Horace left the business of writing a long epic poem, a pageant of Rome, to his friend Virgil. He says he himself is too much of a lightweight:

nōs convīvia nōs proelia virginum
sectīs in iuvenēs unguibus ācrium
cantāmus.

We (meaning himself) *sing of parties (***convīvia***), we of battles (***proelia***) of fierce girls (***virginum ācrium***) with nails (***unguibus***) scratched (***sectīs***) into young men (***iuvenēs***).*

Odes 1.6.17–19

> **INSIGHT**
>
> ▶ In poetry (particularly in Horace) adjectives may appear at some distance from their nouns (e.g. above: **oblīquō … rīvō**, **virginum … ācrium**).
>
> ▶ The verb *to be* is sometimes left out and 'understood' (e.g. **quisnam igitur līber?**). A word left out (and obviously implied) is called 'ellipsis'.
>
> ▶ **Cantō,-āre**, a verb like **amō,-āre**, means *sing* or *celebrate in song*, with the thing celebrated, the object, in the accusative. The translation suggests there might be a genitive after 'sing <u>of</u>' but the 'of' is wrapped up in the meaning of the Latin verb. The same happens with a number of other verbs which take an object in the accusative despite appearing in English with a preposition, e.g. **cūrō,-āre** (*care for*).

Word discovery 6

1 Magister **has given English** *magistrate***. Identify another English word from** magister, **which arrived much earlier.**

> **INSIGHT**
>
> In classical times a **magister** was usually someone who presided over something, e.g. a teacher, a more formal role than a **dominus** (*boss, lord*) although there is an overlap which increases in later years. **Dominus** is used in the Christian tradition for 'the Lord', i.e. Jesus (AD = **Annō Dominī** *in the year of the Lord*).

2 What one word derived from dominus **is used to describe a person of authority in both a university and the mafia?**

3 Make a two-word phrase current in English for each of the following:

  i vīta,-ae (*life*), curriculum,-ī (*course*)

  ii cēterus,-a,-um (*other, rest*), et

  iii initium,-ī (*beginning*), ab

  iv īnfinītus,-a,-um (*endless*), ad

4 A historia **is a narrative of events, a history, while** fābula **usually has a recognized mythical dimension, a fictitious narrative or tale. Think of an English word from each one.**

bēstia,-ae (f.) *beast*	suffrāgium,-ī (n.) *vote*
fābula,-ae (f.) *story, tale*	opulentus,-a,-um *rich, lavish*
historia,-ae (f.) *story*	grātus,-a,-um *pleasing*
saevitia,-ae (f.) *cruelty*	aut *or*
convīvium,-ī (n.) *banquet*	numquam *never*
incendium,-ī (n.) *fire*	satis *enough*
proelium,-ī (n.) *battle*	umquam *ever*

Test yourself 6

1 Translate:

    i quis in viā iacet?

    ii quis fīlium dominī docet?

    iii cūr tuum dominum cantās?

    iv quis tibi pāret?

    v estne vōbīs historia proeliōrum grāta?

    vi bēstiae in amphitheātrō iacent.

    vii convīvia nōbīs semper sunt opulenta!

    viii coquusne ancillīs miserīs umquam benignus est?

    ix ō domine, multa tibi suffrāgia sunt!

    x domina numquam mē iubet sedēre!

2 Identify the case of the underlined word, and translate:

    i magister <u>amīcīs</u> librōs saepe dat.

    ii nōnne satis <u>vōbīs</u> fābulae bēstiārum sunt?

    iii grātane Rōmānīs est saevitia <u>lūdōrum</u>?

3 Which of the following does **persōna nōn grāta** mean?

    a someone out of favour

    b a priest or parson who has to be paid for his time

    c someone who does not say thank you

Time to review the six cases:

The NOMINATIVE is for the noun 'doing it', the subject of the verb.

Nominative endings: sing./pl.	
1st declension	**puella/puellae**
2nd declension	**mūlus/mūlī**
2nd declension -er	**magister/magistrī**
2nd declension neuter	**vīnum/vīna**

The VOCATIVE is used for addressing people. It is the same as the nominative, except most noticeably for the vocative of 2nd decl. nouns like **mūlus**: **ō mūle!** (*O mule!*).

The ACCUSATIVE is used for the object of a verb, or a target or destination. Neuter nouns have the same form in all three above cases.

Accusative endings: sing./pl.	
1st declension	**puellam/puellās**
2nd declension	**mūlum/mūlōs**
2nd declension neuter	**vīnum/vīna**

coquus <u>ancillam</u> in <u>culīnam</u> mittit
the cook sends <u>the maid</u> into <u>the kitchen</u>

The GENITIVE is the 'of' case. It usually appears with another noun, acting as the owner or source of it.

Genitive endings: sing./pl.	
1st declension	**puellae/puellārum**
2nd declension	**mūlī/mūlōrum**
2nd declension neuter	**vīnī/vīnōrum**

liber <u>magistrī</u>
the book <u>of the teacher</u>

ūnus <u>amīcōrum</u>
one <u>of the friends</u>

For the last example, **ex** + the ablative may be used instead of the genitive: **ūnus ex amīcīs**.

The DATIVE is the 'to' or 'for' case. It can be an indirect object after a verb (*he gives a rose <u>to the lady</u>*); it can show ownership or the interested party; it appears after certain verbs and adjectives (e.g. **pāreō,-ēre**, **grātus,-a,-um**). The dative often expresses one person's power over another: a number of verbs to do with commanding, forgiving, obeying, pleasing or serving have their object in the dative, e.g. **imperō,-āre** (*command*), **pāreō,-ēre** (*obey*), **serviō,-īre** (*serve*).

Dative endings: sing./pl.	
1st declension	**puellae/puellīs**
2nd declension	**mūlō/mūlīs**
2nd declension neuter	**vīnō/vīnīs**

The ABLATIVE case is one that would be used a good deal by detectives trying to solve a mysterious murder:

> He was last seen in <u>the morning</u> by <u>the cook</u> in <u>the kitchen</u> with <u>the vicar</u> and was then struck with <u>a pot</u> …

The ablative case can describe how, where, with what or with whom, (by) how much and when. There are many prepositions which represent this case in English: *in, on, at, with, by, from, out of*.

Ablative endings: sing./pl.	
1st declension	**puellā/puellīs**
2nd declension	**mūlō/mūlīs**
2nd declension neuter	**vīnō/vīnīs**

coquus <u>vīnō</u> ēbrius in <u>prātō</u> cum <u>dominā</u> est
the cook drunk <u>with wine</u> is <u>in the meadow</u> <u>with the lady/his mistress</u>

servus in <u>catēnīs</u> ex <u>agrō</u> fugit
the slave flees <u>in chains</u> out of <u>the field</u>

PRACTICE

1 **List all six cases, singular and plural, of**
  i servus
  ii bēstia
  iii bellum

2 **Adjectives have cases like nouns, singular and plural, and they also have endings for different genders. An adjective agrees with the noun it describes, matching case, gender and number. List all six cases, three genders, singular and plural of grātus,-a,-um.**

3 **You have met the 1st conjugation (verbs like** amō,-āre**) and 2nd conjugation (verbs like** habeō,-ēre**) in the present tense. Write out these verbs in all six persons of the present tense:**

   i narrō,-āre

   ii doceō,-ēre

Word revision

1 **Choose the correct meaning of each Latin word from the words in the box below.**

air/breeze, daughter, god, goddess, gold, husband/man, life, master, mistress, poison/slime, he/she comes, he/she leads, he/she obeys, he/she prepares, he/she says, he/she sees, son, us, way/road, what?, who?, you

aura,-ae _____*air/breeze*   aurum,-ī _____

dea,-ae _____   deus,-ī _____

dīcit _____   dūcit _____

domina,-ae _____   dominus,-ī _____

fīlia,-ae _____   fīlius,-ī _____

nōs _____   vōs _____

quid? _____   quis? _____

venit _____   videt _____

via,-ae _____   vīta,-ae _____

vir,-ī _____   vīrus,-ī _____

parat _____   pāret (+ dat.) _____

2 **Match these 1st conjugation verbs to their meanings.**

Example: **cantō / cantāre** = *I sing / to sing*

   a cantō / cantāre   **i** *I ask / to ask*

   b clāmō / clāmāre   **ii** *I beat / to beat*

   c dō / dare   **iii** *I breathe / to breathe*

d narrō / narrāre	**iv** *I give / to give*
e putō / putāre	**v** *I read aloud / to read aloud*
f recitō / recitāre	**vi** *I shout / to shout*
g rogō / rogāre	**vii** *I sing / to sing*
h spīrō / spīrāre	**viii** *I tell, narrate / to tell, narrate*
i susurrō / susurrāre	**ix** *I think / to think*
j verberō / verberāre	**x** *I whisper / to whisper*

3 Match these 2nd conjugation verbs to their meanings.

Example: **dēbeō / dēbēre** = *I ought, owe / to owe*

a dēbeō / dēbēre	**i** *I fear / to fear*
b doceō / docēre	**ii** *I laugh / to laugh*
c iaceō / iacēre	**iii** *I lie / to lie*
d iubeō / iubēre	**iv** *I order / to order*
e maneō / manēre	**v** *I ought, owe / to owe*
f respondeō / respondēre	**vi** *I stay, remain / to stay, remain*
g rīdeō / rīdēre	**vii** *I reply / to reply*
h sedeō / sedēre	**viii** *I see / to see*
i timeō / timēre	**ix** *I sit / to sit*
j videō / vidēre	**x** *I teach / to teach*

4 Match these verbs to their meanings.

Example: **ascendit** = *he/she climbs*

a ascendit	**i** *he/she climbs*
b cadit	**ii** *he/she conquers*
c carpit	**iii** *he/she falls*
d fugit	**iv** *he/she flees*
e gemit	**v** *he/she goes*
f intellegit	**vi** *he/she groans*
g petit	**vii** *he/she plucks*
h vādit	**viii** *he/she seeks*
i vincit	**ix** *he/she understands*

5 Match these 1st declension nouns to their meanings.

Example: **aqua,-ae** = *water*

a aqua,-ae	**i** *anger*
b avāritia,-ae	**ii** *cause, case*
c catēna,-ae	**iii** *chain*
d causa,-ae	**iv** *dinner*
e cēna,-ae	**v** *greed*

f	fābula,-ae	**vi**	*earth, ground, land*
g	īra,-ae	**vii**	*moon*
h	lūna,-ae	**viii**	*story*
i	terra,-ae	**ix**	*water*

6 Match these 2nd declension nouns to their meanings.

Example: **amīcus,-ī** = *friend*

a	amīcus,-ī	**i**	*cook*
b	caballus,-ī	**ii**	*eye*
c	coquus, -ī	**iii**	*friend*
d	lūdus,-ī	**iv**	*game*
e	mūrus,-ī	**v**	*horse*
f	oculus,-ī	**vi**	*people*
g	populus,-ī	**vii**	*slave*
h	servus,-ī	**viii**	*wall*
i	ventus,-ī	**ix**	*wind*

7 Match these 2nd declension (neuter) nouns to their meanings.

Example: **bellum,-ī** = *war*

a	bellum,-ī	**i**	*banquet*
b	convīvium,-ī	**ii**	*battle*
c	folium,-ī	**iii**	*leaf*
d	oppidum,-ī	**iv**	*meadow*
e	prātum,-ī	**v**	*silence*
f	proelium,-ī	**vi**	*town*
g	silentium,-ī	**vii**	*vote*
h	suffrāgium,-ī	**viii**	*war*

8 Match these adjectives to their meanings.

Example: **doctus,-a,-um** = *learned*

a	doctus,-a,-um	**i**	*blessed*
b	grātus,-a,-um	**ii**	*cruel*
c	obscūrus,-a,-um	**iii**	*dark*
d	opulentus,-a,-um	**iv**	*dutiful*
e	paucus,-a,-um	**v**	*little, few*
f	pius,-a, um	**vi**	*first*
g	prīmus,-a,-um	**vii**	*learned*
h	saevus,-a,-um	**viii**	*pleasing, grateful*
i	sānctus,-a,-um	**ix**	*rich, lavish*
j	vērus,-a,-um	**x**	*true, real*

9 Match these words to their meanings.

Example: **deinde** = *then, next*

a	deinde	**i**	*alas*
b	ēheu	**ii**	*also, even*
c	enim	**iii**	*always*
d	etiam	**iv**	*for, you see, the fact is*
e	hodiē	**v**	*now*
f	igitur	**vi**	*or (as you like)*
g	ita	**vii**	*so, thus, in this way*
h	nunc	**viii**	*then, next*
i	semper	**ix**	*therefore, accordingly*
j	vel	**x**	*today*

10 Which word in exercise 9 is the most similar in meaning to each of the following?

i aut

ii nam

iii sīc

In this unit you will learn about:

▶ *Vulgar Latin*
▶ *3rd declension nouns*
▶ *3rd declension adjectives*
▶ *The story of Augustinus: Paulus and Lucia reach the monastery*
▶ *Ovid: poet*

Vulgar Latin

We know that Romans had their share of rude words but that is not what is meant by Vulgar Latin, even if it was sometimes referred to in a disparaging way. Vulgar Latin was the language spoken by all the people, in contrast to the literary classical Latin of the educated elite. This spoken language did not have the construction or polish of say Cicero or Virgil, and there will have been much variety: habits of speech depended on who was talking, where, when, and what they were talking about. We know there was a tendency to drop case-endings, and that some words which figure in classical Latin were not used in the spoken form, or at least not in the same way: you have seen how the word for *horse* was **caballus** in general speech and **equus** in literature. Similarly a 'head' in classical Latin was **caput** (plural **capita**), while the more colloquial word was **testa** (in classical Latin a 'tile' or 'brick' or 'earthenware pot').

As the empire disintegrated, the different strains of Latin spoken in the divided kingdoms evolved into the Romance languages (French, Italian, Spanish, Portuguese and Romanian). So too a number of dialects and sub-languages have direct roots in Latin, e.g. Occitan in France, Catalan in Spain, Sardinian in Italy and Romansh in Switzerland. In general it is the colloquial words (e.g. **caballus**, **testa**) which lived on in the Romance languages.

3rd declension nouns

3rd declension nouns have their own pattern of endings. However, in the nominative (and vocative) singular you will find all sorts of endings:

	Singular	Plural
Nominative (and Vocative)	various	**-ēs**
Accusative	**-em**	**-ēs**
Genitive	**-is**	**-um**
Dative	**-ī**	**-ibus**
Ablative	**-e**	**-ibus**

Nouns are listed in dictionaries in the nominative and genitive, and nowhere is this more important than with 3rd declension nouns.

> **LANGUAGE TIP**
>
> A quick rule to help recognition: all 3rd declension nouns (and *only* these nouns) have the genitive singular ending **-is**.

In the list below you will see many different nominative forms. Look also at the shape of the genitive. Some take on an additional syllable: **homō … hominis**. It is the genitive, not the nominative, that is the model shape for all cases except the nominative and vocative singular. So taking the stem from the genitive, the accusative of **homō** is **homin + em**, the ablative **homin + e**, the plural **homin + ēs**, etc.

Some 3rd declension nouns

arbor, arboris (f.) *tree*

creātor, creātōris (m.) *creator*

dux, ducis (m.) *leader*

homō, hominis (m.) *man, person*

lēx, lēgis (f.) *law*

mīles, mīlitis (m.) *soldier*

mōns, montis (m.) *mountain*

pater, patris (m.) *father*

regiō, regiōnis (f.) *region*

senātor, senātōris (m.) *senator*

sōl, sōlis (m.) *sun*

urbs, urbis (f.) *city*

uxor, uxōris (f.) *wife*

virgō, virginis (f.) *maiden, young woman*

1 List all six cases, singular and plural, for
   i pater, patris
   ii senātor, senātōris

2 Fill each gap with the missing word:
   i _____ (*the leaders*) semper clāmant.
   ii mīlitēs nōn in _____ (*in the mountains*) sed in _____ (*in the city*) habitant.
   iii quis _____ (*the wife*) _____ (*of the senator*) amat?

There are subpatterns within this declension which will become more obvious the more you meet them, for example, **amor, amōris** (*love, passion*), **arbor, arboris** (*tree*) and **uxor, uxōris** (*wife*) are like **senātor, senātōris**; while **pāx, pācis** (*peace*) and **lūx, lūcis** (*light*) are similar to **dux, ducis**; and **māter, mātris** (*mother*) to **pater, patris; legiō, legiōnis** (*legion*) to **regiō, regiōnis**, and so on.

A few 3rd declension nouns may take an ablative ending **-ī** (i.e., the same as the dative), and a genitive plural **-ium** (for **-um**). Watch out for the genitive plural **-um**, an ending shared with the 2nd declension **mūlum** and **vīnum**.

3rd declension adjectives

Just as there are 1st/2nd declension adjectives (**bonus,-a,-um**) there are adjectives with 3rd declension endings. These adjectives vary in the nominative singular and are then consistent in the other cases. Some end **-is** in the nominative, like **omnis,-e** (*all, every*). There is no difference between the masculine and feminine. The neuter singular ends **-e** (sing.) and **-ia** (pl.) in the first three cases; in the remaining cases it is the same as the other genders.

All genders end **-ī** in the dative and ablative singular.

	Singular		Plural	
	m./f.	n.	m./f.	n.
Nominative/Vocative	omn**is**	omn**e**	omn**ēs**	omn**ia**
Accusative	omn**em**	omn**e**	omn**ēs**	omn**ia**
Genitive	omn**is**		omn**ium**	
Dative	omn**ī**		omn**ibus**	
Ablative	omn**ī**		omn**ibus**	

What could these endings represent (i.e. nom. sing., nom. pl., acc. sing, etc)? For adjectives add the gender.

  i ducī (dux, ducis)
 ii patre (pater, patris)
iii omne (omnis,-e)
 iv magnī (magnus,-a,-um)
  v omnī (omnis,-e)
 vi omnia (omnis,-e)
vii bēstia or bēstiā (bēstia,-ae)
viii suffrāgium (suffrāgium,-ī)
 ix lēgēs (lēx, lēgis)
  x hominum (homō, hominis)

The story of Augustīnus (13)

07.01 Stephanus describes the ancient gods to his students.

Stephanus fābulās deōrum fessīs discipulīs narrāt. 'Iuppiter deus est caelī, Venus amōris, Diāna silvārum et vēnātiōnis, Mars bellī et mīlitum, Apollō sōlis et carminum, Neptūnus aequoris. ōlim erant hominibus multī deī et spīritūs. Rōmānī Bellōnam, Cūrās, Discordiam, Fortūnam, Labōrem, Miseriam, Mortem, et omnēs cēterōs observābant. mehercle, tot deī erant! etiam spīritūs locōrum, silvārum, montium, flūminum, lūnae, sōlis ...'

'nōnne Apollō erat deus sōlis?' rogat Augustīnus.

'ita rēs est. vērō possumus neque omnēs deōs numerāre neque omnia nōmina cognōscere. quis enim in tot deōs crēdere potest?'

'Līberum amō!' susurrat Augustīnus.

'quid dīcis?'

'librum amō, magister.'

'bene. hodiē Fortūna tibi favet: librum exscrībere potes. heu, ubi eram? deī deaeque, quī animās hominum nōn cūrant, mortālibus sunt exempla turpitūdinis. Deus tamen, quī vērus est creātor montium et aequoris et arborum et hominum et bēstiārum et bonōrum omnium, semper nōs omnēs cūrat.'

'quis est malōrum creātor?' rogat Augustīnus. 'num Deus facere malum potest? quis ergō est malōrum creātor?'

'certē Deus nōn est malōrum creātor, Augustīne. nōs sumus omnēs semper cārissimī Deō ...'

'magister, ecce Paulus venit!' ūnus ē discipulīs clāmat.

'... fortasse praeter Paulum. ubi est ille?' inquit Stephanus, et ad fenestram festīnat. 'nihil vidēre possum nisi bovēs ovēsque.'

'Paulus sub arboribus cum virgine ambulat.'

'cum virgine?' Stephanus Paulum et Lūciam cōnspicit. 'ēheu, ecce Paulus et virgō!' et statim omnēs discipulī librōs relinquunt et ad fenestram festīnant. 'ad librōs, ō puerī, ad librōs! scīlicet Paulus in culīnā labōrat! Paulus modo cum ancillīs sedet modo ambulat cum virgine. ō dī immortālēs!'

caelum,-ī (n.) *heaven, sky*	mōns, montis (m.) *mountain*
amor,-ōris (m.) *love*	flūmen,-inis (n.) *river*
vēnātiō,-ōnis (f.) *hunting*	lūna,-ae (f.) *moon*
mīles, mīlitis (m.) *soldier*	erat *(he/she, it, there) was*
sōl, sōlis (m.) *sun*	ita rēs est *that's right, that is so*
carmen,-inis (n.) *song, poem*	numerō,-āre *count*
aequor,-oris (n.) *sea* (lit. *surface*)	nōmina (nom. pl./acc. pl.) *names*
ōlim *once (upon a time)*	cognōscere *to learn, become*
spīritūs (nom.pl./acc.pl.) *spirits*	*familiar with*
Bellōna,-ae (f.) *spirit of war*	crēdere *to believe*
cūra,-ae (f.) *care, anxiety* (with a	Līber,-erī (like puer) *Bacchus*
capital letter:	dīcis *you say*
the spirit of ...)	bene *fine*
discordia,-ae (f.) *discord*	faveō,-ēre (+ dat.) *favour*
fortūna,-ae (f.) *fortune*	exscrībere *to write out, copy*
labor, labōris (m.) *toil, work*	heu *like ēheu, but shorter (oh!)*
miseria,-ae (f.) *distress, suffering*	eram *I was*
mors, mortis (f.) *death*	anima,-ae (f.) *soul*
ceterus,-a,-um *the other, remaining*	cūrō,-āre *care for*
observābant *they used to observe,*	mortālis,-e *mortal* (often used as a
honour	noun)
tot *so many*	exemplum,-ī (n.) *example, model*
erant *they were, there were*	turpitūdō, turpitūdinis (f.) *disgraceful*
locus,-ī (m.) *place*	*behaviour*

tamen *yet, however*	bōs, bovis (m./f.) *ox*
creātor, creātōris (m.) *creator*	ovis, ovis (f.) *sheep*
facere *to do, to make*	sub (+ acc./abl.) *beneath, under*
ergō *so, accordingly, therefore*	cōnspicit *(he/she) catches sight of*
cārissimus,-a,-um *very dear*	statim *immediately*
praeter (+ acc.) *besides, except*	relinquunt *(they) leave, abandon*
ille (nom.) *that (male), he*	scīlicet *for sure* (ironical)
fenestra,-ae (f.) *window*	modo … modo *one minute … the*
festīnō,-āre *hurry, hasten*	*next*
nihil *nothing*	dī *for deī* (nom. pl. of deus)
nisi *unless, except*	immortālis,-e *immortal*

PRACTICE 7C

1 Identify the declension of these nouns which appear above:
   i amōris
   ii silvārum
   iii vēnātiōnis
   iv bellī

2 What case and number is each of the following?
   i sōlis (line 3)
   ii Labōrem (line 5)
   iii virgine (line 29)
   iv arboribus (line 29)?

3 Identify a word from the story above in the dative plural.

4 The preposition sub **can take either the accusative or ablative. With the accusative it means to go beneath something, with the ablative to be under it, similar to** in **(see Unit 3). What would the Latin for** *trees* **be in this sentence:** *I walk out of the villa and beneath the trees***?**

3rd declension neuter nouns

One or two neuter nouns belonging to the 3rd declension appeared in the story above, e.g. **carmen,-inis** (*song, poem*). These nouns have the same endings in the genitive, dative and ablative as other 3rd declension nouns. The accusative (as with all neuters) is the same as the nominative, ending **-a** in the plural:

Singular		
Nominative	**carmen**	**tempus**
Vocative	**carmen**	**tempus**
Accusative	**carmen**	**tempus**
Genitive	**carminis**	**temporis**
Dative	**carminī**	**temporī**
Ablative	**carmine**	**tempore**
Plural		
Nominative	**carmina**	**tempora**
Vocative	**carmina**	**tempora**
Accusative	**carmina**	**tempora**
Genitive	**carminum**	**temporum**
Dative	**carminibus**	**temporibus**
Ablative	**carminibus**	**temporibus**

LANGUAGE TIP

Be careful not to muddle nouns like **mūlus** with 3rd declension neuter nouns like **tempus**. Having learned the ending **-um** to be the object ending of **-us**, you now have **-us** as an object ending.

The variety of nominative forms is characteristic of the 3rd declension. With neuter nouns, the nominative form is also the accusative. A number of these nouns have the nominative/accusative endings **-en** and **-us**. There are others, e.g. **aequor, aequoris** (*sea*); **caput, capitis** (*head*). As with other 3rd declension nouns, the genitive provides the model shape for the other cases. So **caput** (*head*) is **capit-** in all cases other than the nominative, vocative and accusative singular.

Some 3rd declension neuter nouns

corpus, corporis (n.)   *body*

opus, operis (n.)   *work, task*

scelus, sceleris (n.)   *crime, wicked deed*

tempus, temporis (n.)   *time*

nōmen, nōminis (n.)   *name*

carmen, carminis (n.)   *poem, song*

flūmen, flūminis (n.)   *river*

aequor, aequoris (n.)   *sea, surface*

caput, capitis (n.)   *head*

PRACTICE 7D

1 **Write out all six cases, singular and plural, for the following:**
   i opus, operis
   ii flūmen, flūminis
   iii caput, capitis

2 **Complete each sentence with one word:**
   i cūr _____ (*a body*) in terrā iacet?
   ii ego _____ (*the poems*) Catullī dēsīderō.
   iii omnia _____ (*the heads*) numerāre nōn possum.
   iv _____ (*the crimes*) Catilīnae vidēre possum!

The story of Augustinus (14)

 07.02 **A large meal is being prepared in the monastery kitchen.**

in culīnā ancillae strēnuae convīvium parant. nam hodiē Abbas Petrus et Abbātissa Katharīna et Comes Karolus et uxor Comitissa Egberta et aliī prīncipēs in monasteriō adsunt. in culīnā magnum opus est. ancillae pānem et crusta et vīna parant. deinde labōribus fessae in hortō sub arboribus requiēscunt.

'ecce Paulus adest!' clāmat ūna ex ancillīs. 'sed quis est illa?'

'fīlia est Comitis Karolī,' inquit alia, 'nōmine Lūcia.' nunc ancillae abbātissam, quae Lūciam salūtat, vidēre possunt. intereā Benedictus in hortum venit.

'heus, tempus fugit!' clāmat coquus. 'ubi est īlle servus īgnāvus?'

'hīc est puer, nunc Paulus adest.'

'dīcō vōbīs, ille puer īgnāvus cum diabolō ambulat ... quid? Sāncta Marīa! ille ambulat cum abbātissā! quid fit? nunc salūtem dīcit abbātī! meherclē! dīc mihi, nam scīre volō: estne puer miser nunc magnus et abbātissae amīcus? cūr puerum abbātissa laudat?'

'ecce, nunc venit.'

'vidēre est crēdere.'

-ūna ancillārum ad Paulum festīnat. 'age! coquus sarcinās dēsīderat!'

strēnuus,-a,-um *energetic*
abbas, abbātis (m.) *abbot*
Petrus,-ī *Peter*
abbātissa,-ae (f.) *abbess*
Katharīna,-ae *Katharine*
comes, comitis *companion* (class.),
  count (med.)
Karolus,-ī *Charles*
uxor,-ōris (f.) *wife*
comitissa,-ae (f.) *countess*
aliī (nom.pl.) *other*
prīnceps, prīncipis (m.) *leading
  person*
pānis, pānis (m.) *bread*
hortus,-ī (m.) *garden*

requiēscunt *(they) relax*
illa (nom. sing. f.) *that* (female), *she*
alia (nom. sing. f.) *other*
quae (nom. sing. f.) *who*
salūtō,-āre *greet*
ille (nom. sing. m.) *that* (male), *he*
dīcō *I say, tell*
diabolus,-ī (m.) *devil*
quid fit *what is going on?*
salūtem dīcit *(he/she) says hello*
dīc *say, tell*
volō *I want*
scīre *to know*
laudō,-āre *praise*
age! *come on!*

Verbs used with infinitives:
possum, **volō**, etc

A few verbs are used with other verbs in the infinitive, as in English:

ancillae Paulum <u>vidēre</u> <u>possunt</u>
the maids <u>are able</u> <u>to see</u> Paul

dēbeō,-ēre *ought*	parō,-āre *prepare*
iubeō,-ēre *order, tell*	possum, posse *be able*

Another of these verbs is the very irregular **volō, velle** (*want, wish, be willing*):

volō	*I want, wish*
vīs	*you* (sing.) *want, wish*
vult	*he/she wants, wishes*
volumus	*we want, wish*
vultis	*you* (pl.) *want, wish*
volunt	*they want, wish*

scīre <u>volō</u>
<u>*I want*</u> *to know*
puer in culīnā labōrāre <u>vult</u>
the boy <u>is willing</u> to work in the kitchen

1 Identify the infinitive in each sentence, and then translate the sentence into English:

  i coquus puerum in culīnā manēre iubet.

  ii ancillae puerum in culīnam sarcinās portāre iubent.

  iii omnēs puerum in culīnā labōrāre iubent.

  iv puerne cēnam parāre dēbet?

  v voluntne ancillae in culīnā labōrāre?

  vi certē Benedictus in hortō sedēre vult!

  vii puer in bibliothēcā cum discipulīs adesse dēbet.

  viii ō magister, omnēs nōs discipulī in culīnā labōrāre volumus.

2 Add the missing words and translate:

ō domina, estne tibi nihil grātum? nōnne meum _____ (*poem*) audīre
_____ (*you want*)?

Ovid

07.03 The poet Publius Ovidius Naso was born in 43 BC, the year Cicero
was killed. He grew up as calm settled in Italy after the civil wars, and by
his teens Augustus was in control, the sponsor of the new peace.

Ovid was hugely popular as a young poet, playful and fun, taking a fresh
angle on the love poetry of the time: e.g. the *Heroides* (Heroines), letters
from mythological women to absent lovers; the *Amores* (Feelings of love)
about his mistress 'Corinna'; the *Ars Amatoria* (Art of love), a tongue-
in-cheek guide to seduction. His major work was the *Metamorphoses*
(changes in shape), a compendium of ancient myths threaded together
by a transformation in each story, usually caused by resentful gods.
Actaeon, a youth out hunting, is turned into a deer and then eaten by
his own hounds after spotting Diana bathing. He appeals to his dogs:

'Actaeōn ego sum: dominum cognōscite vestrum!'
'I am Actaeon: recognize your master!'

Metamorphoses 3.230

The nymph Echo loses her bodily form because she tries to help Jupiter's girlfriends/victims evade his vengeful wife, the goddess Juno.

inde latet silvīs nūllōque in monte vidētur,
omnibus audītur: sonus est quī vīvit in illā.
From then on she (Echo) hides in the woods and is seen on no mountain,
(but) she is heard by all: there is (only) the sound which lives in her.

Metamorphoses 3.400–1

Echo falls in love with the youth Narcissus who spurns her in favour of an image in the water – of himself:

crēdule, quid frūstrā simulācra fugācia captās?
You gullible fellow, why do you fruitlessly chase elusive images?

Metamorphoses 3.432

Narcissus will waste away pining for his love before turning into a flower. The metamorphosis in the story of Baucis and Philemon is a release at the end of their lives, a boon granted by the gods that they depart the mortal world together (they turn into trees). Jupiter and Mercury, who are dressed as mortals seeking shelter, find a thousand doors closed to them. Only the impoverished Baucis and Philemon show them hospitality. The old couple try and fail to catch their one goose for the gods' supper:

ūnicus ānser erat, minimae custōdia vīllae:
quem dīs hospitibus dominī mactāre parābant.
*There was a solitary goose, the guardian of the tiny homestead, which the owners (**dominī**) were preparing to slaughter (**mactāre**) for their divine guests.*

Metamorphoses 8.684–5

In AD 8 Ovid overran his luck by giving offence to Augustus. Scholars still speculate over the cause, a poem perhaps, or a brilliantly witty if unwise remark. (Ovid himself says it was a poem *and* an error, discreetly veiling the facts in the hope of a pardon.) He was banished with immediate effect, and spent the remaining ten or so years of his life on the Black Sea. His final poems, the *Tristia* (Sorrows) and *Epistulae ex Ponto* (Letters from the Black Sea), are a plea for forgiveness, a longing for his homeland, but they failed to win him a reprieve. In the *Tristia* he recalls his younger, jauntier days, when his father recommended he put poetry aside and take a proper job like his brother, in public speaking and law. Ovid says he tried to drop his versifying, but ...

> **sponte suā carmen numerōs veniēbat ad aptōs,**
> **et quod temptābam dīcere versus erat.**
> *Of its own accord to the right (**aptōs**) rhythms (**numerōs**) came a poem,*
> *and what I was trying to say was a verse.*

Sorrows 4.25-6

Ovid was an inspirational figure through the middle ages and remains so today in both literature and art. He also wrote a play, *Medea*, which was much liked in the years that followed but is now lost. The main difference between a play and a poem was the number of participants: like drama, Latin poetry was presented aloud and performed.

Word discovery 7

1 **What kind of public transport was once named after the Latin for** *for all (people)*?

2 **We might say Ovid's** *Metamorphoses* **was his** *magnum opus*. **What does that mean?**

3 **Find Latin ancestors from this unit for** *custody, hospitality, latent, minimum* **and** *tempt*.

4 **Vulgus,-ī means** *a crowd, throng;* mōbilis,-e **(like** omnis,-e) **means** *easily moved, fickle.* **Unusually for nouns like** mūlus, vulgus **is neuter. So** *a fickle crowd* **is** vulgus mōbile. **What three-letter English word is derived from this Latin phrase?**

bene *fine, well*	scīlicet *to be sure, obviously*
ergō *so, accordingly, therefore*	statim *immediately*
nihil, nīl *nothing*	sub (+ acc./abl.) *beneath, under*
praeter (+ acc.) *except, besides*	tamen *yet, still, however*

Test yourself 7

1 List all six cases, singular and plural, for
   i māter, mātris
   ii arbor, arboris
  iii lēx, lēgis
  iv regiō, regiōnis
   v nōmen, nōminis
  vi corpus, corporis

2 Translate into English:
   i omnēs sub arboribus sedent.
  ii monachus ergō pācem, mīles bellum dēsīderat.
 iii carmina virginis omnibus grāta sunt.
  iv quis est dea amōris? estne Diāna?
   v opera ancillīs sunt multa.

3 Add the missing words and translate:
   i in culīnā labōrāre nōn _____ (*we are able*).
  ii quis _____ (*the body*) per silvam portāre _____ (*is willing*)?
 iii cūr uxor magistrī in _____ (*in the river*) sedet?
  iv scīlicet labōrō cum servīs _____ (*with all*).
   v coquus ancillās convīvium parāre _____ (*orders*).
  vi nōnne deī _____ (*ought*) mortālēs cūrāre omnēs?

4 **Carpe diem** is a phrase made famous by whom?
  a Horace
  b Ovid
  c Virgil

In this unit you will learn about:
- ▶ *late Latin*
- ▶ *3rd, 4th and mixed conjugations*
- ▶ *more 3rd declension adjectives*
- ▶ *The story of Augustinus: Lucia leaves the monastery*
- ▶ *Seneca: philosopher, playwright, Nero's adviser*

Late Latin

The literary language in the centuries following the classical period remained modelled on classical writers. The subject, however, was now largely religious, retelling Christian stories from the gospels or engaging in complex theological debates.

St Jerome completed his translation of the Bible from Hebrew and Greek into Latin in the early fifth century. This was presented in a less literary and more accessible style, like the original, and became known as the Vulgate (*Versio Vulgata*), which lasted in service for more or less a thousand years. **Vulgāta** means *put about*, *shared in public* and hence *published*.

From this period we have the theological and philosophical writings of St Augustine and Boethius. Boethius, who died in AD 524, is regarded as both a late Latin writer and an early medieval one.

3rd, 4th and 'mixed' conjugations

You have met verbs of the 1st conjugation (like **amō, amāre**) and of the 2nd (like **habeō, habēre**). A few verbs from the other three conjugations have already appeared in the story. These are similar to each other:

	3rd	4th	mixed
Infinitive	mitt**ere**	aud**īre**	cap**ere**
	send	*hear*	*capture, take*
I	mitt**ō**	aud**iō**	cap**iō**
you (sing.)	mitt**is**	aud**īs**	cap**is**
he/she/it	mitt**it**	aud**it**	cap**it**
we	mitt**imus**	aud**īmus**	cap**imus**
you (pl.)	mitt**itis**	aud**ītis**	cap**itis**
they	mitt**unt**	aud**iunt**	cap**iunt**

The 5th conjugation is more commonly called the 'mixed' conjugation for it is very close to the 3rd with some characteristics of the 4th.

PRACTICE 8A

1 Match these 3rd conjugation verbs to their meanings.

Example: cadō / cadere = *I fall / to fall*

a	cadō / cadere	**i**	*I leave / to leave*
b	cognōscō / cognōscere	**ii**	*I believe, trust / to believe, trust*
c	crēdō / crēdere (+ dat.)	**iii**	*I conquer, win / to conquer, win*
d	currō / currere	**iv**	*I fall / to fall*
e	dīcō / dīcere	**v**	*I groan / to groan*
f	dūcō / dūcere	**vi**	*I learn / to learn*
g	gemō / gemere	**vii**	*I lead, bring / to lead, bring*
h	mittō / mittere	**viii**	*I run / to run*
i	petō / petere	**ix**	*I say, tell / to say, tell*
j	relinquō / relinquere	**x**	*I seek / to seek*
k	scrībō / scrībere	**xi**	*I send / to send*
l	vincō / vincere	**xii**	*I write / to write*

2 Complete each sentence with one word, and then translate the sentence into English:

i nōs semper _____ (*we are groaning*).

ii ō magister, quid _____ (*are you saying*)?

iii quis mūlum in prātum _____ (*is leading*)?

iv ego ex urbe _____ (*to run*) nōn possum.

v omnēs discipulī in bibliothēcā _____ (*are writing*).

vi domina tibi _____ (*trust*)?

3 **Match these 4th conjugation verbs to their meanings.**

Example: aperiō / aperīre = I open / to open

a	aperiō / aperīre	**i**	I bury / to bury
b	audiō / audīre	**ii**	I come / to come
c	dormiō / dormīre	**iii**	I feel / to feel
d	sciō / scīre	**iv**	I hear / to hear
e	sentiō / sentīre	**v**	I know / to know
f	sepeliō / sepelīre	**vi**	I open / to open
g	veniō / venīre	**vii**	I sleep / to sleep

4 **Match these mixed conjugation verbs to their meanings.**

Example: capiō / capere = I capture / to capture

a	capiō / capere	**i**	I capture / to capture
b	cōnspiciō / cōnspicere	**ii**	I catch sight of / to catch sight of
c	faciō / facere	**iii**	I flee / to flee
d	fugiō / fugere	**iv**	I make, do / to make, do

5 **Complete each sentence with one word, and then translate the sentence into English:**

  i omnēs ancillae in hortum _____ (are coming).

  ii quid _____ (are we doing)?

  iii ō amīce, cūr _____ (are you fleeing)?

  iv discipulusne in silvā _____ (is sleeping)?

  v Lūciane carmen Catullī _____ (to hear) vult?

  vi multāsne bēstiās vēnātiōne _____ (capture) Diāna?

How to tell a conjugation

You can tell the conjugation of a verb from two forms: the 1st person present and the infinitive, e.g.

recitō, recitāre belongs to the 1st conjugation

videō, vidēre to the 2nd

dīcō, dīcere to the 3rd

sciō, scīre to the 4th

cōnspicio, cōnspicere to the mixed

There is a difference in pronunciation of the infinitives of the 2nd and 3rd conjugations (**vidēre** and **dīcere**). Even if the macron is not shown you can still distinguish them by the present: the 2nd conjugation has an **e** before the final **o** (**videō**).

The mixed conjugation has an **i** before the **ō** in the present, like the 4th, but an infinitive ending **-ere**, like the 3rd.

The story of Augustinus (15)

08.01 **Paulus rejoins the other students.**

'cūr igitur sānctōrum sānctārumque opera laudāmus sed tamen nōbīs placet fābulās legere deōrum deārumque crūdēlium?' rogat ūnus ē discipulīs.

'fābulāe iūcundae sunt!' inquit Augustīnus.

'vērō, etiam ūtilēs,' inquit magister. 'nam sānctī exempla virtūtis, pāgānī vitiōrum praebent. nunc opera poētārum magnōrum in monasteriō servāmus exscrībimusque custōdīmusque. fābulās enim legere sīcut allegoriās nōbīs placet. vultisne, ō puerī, carmen Vergiliī recitāre?'

Augustīnus Paulum et virginem per fenestram spectat et *'omnia vincit amor'* susurrat. Augustīnus mūlum fessum videt quī multam aquam bibit. deinde mūlum Paulus in prātum dūcit.

'age,' inquit magister, *'fugit intereā, fugit irreparābile tempus.'* tandem discipulī librōs legere incipiunt.

nec multō post 'adsum, magister,' inquit Paulus.

'Paule? meherclē! nunc ades? cūr studia relinquis? cūr lascīvē in silvīs vādis? ō male discipule, hīc adesse dēbēs! quō fugis? nam volō scīre.'

'magister, erat puella in silvā.'

'scīlicet,' inquit magister.

'saucia erat.'

'saucia, putō, amōre.'

'in terram cecidit, magister, fīlia comitis.'

'unde cecidit, puer?' inquit magister, 'dē caelō? ut pōma dē arboribus sīc virginēs dē caelō cadunt?' aliī discipulī rīdent.

'ex equō cecidit.'

'ō tempora ō mōrēs! putāsne studia esse nūgās?'

'magister, vēra tibi dīcō.'

'vidēsne hunc librum?'

'videō, magister.'

'hodiē librum tōtum exscrībere dēbēs; etiam in noctem.'

'hodiē?'

placet (+ dat.) *it pleases*
legō,-ere *read*
crūdēlis,-e *cruel*
iūcundus,-a,-um *delightful, enjoyable*
ūtilis,-e *useful*
virtūs, virtūtis (f.) *virtue*
vitium,-ī (n.) *vice*
praebeō,-ēre *offer*
poēta,-ae (m.) *poet*
servō,-āre *keep*
custōdiō,-īre *guard*
sīcut *just as, as if*
allegoria,-ae (f.) *allegory*
omnia … amor see Unit 5
bibō,-ere *drink*
age *come on!*
fugit … tempus see Unit 5
irreparābilis,-e *irretrievable*
tandem *at last*
incipiō,-ere *begin*

nec multō post *not long after*
studium,-ī (n.) *study*
lascīvē *wantonly*
vādō,-ere *go, walk*
quō *to where*
saucius,-a,-um *wounded, smitten*
putō,-āre *think, suppose*
cecidit *he/she fell*
unde *from where*
dē (+ abl.) *from, down from*
ut *as*
pōmum,-ī (n.) *fruit*
aliī (nom. pl. m.) *other*
ō tempora ō mōrēs see Unit 2
mōs, mōris (m.) *custom, habit, manner*
nūgae,-ārum (f.) *trifles, nonsense*
vēra n. pl. of vērus,-a,-um
tōtus,-a,-um *entire, whole*
nox, noctis (f.) *night*

PRACTICE 8B

1 Identify the conjugation of each of the following:

   i cognōscō,-ere (*learn*)
   ii cūrō,-āre (*care for*)
  iii custōdiō,-īre (*guard*)
   iv faveō,-ēre (+ dat.) (*favour*)
   v incipiō,-ere (*begin*)
   vi legō,-ere (*read*)
  vii praebeō,-ēre (*offer, furnish*)
 viii salūtō,-āre (*greet*)
   ix servō,-āre (*keep*)
   x vādō,-ere (*go, walk*)

2 Identify the 3rd person singular (*he/she …*) and 3rd person plural (*they …*) in the present tense of each verb in no.1.

Words for loving, liking and wanting

Amō,-āre means *like* or *love, be fond of*, sexual and otherwise. **Dēsīderō,-āre** means *want very much* or *long for*, like its English descendant *desire*.

Volō, velle is the most common word for *want* or *wish*, generally used with the infinitive of another verb (*want to do* …). There are one or two other words for wanting or liking which have not yet appeared, such as **cupiō,-ere** (*want, desire*), and **dīligō,-ere** (*love, esteem, value*). **Volō, velle** is used for wishes which are thought about, **cupiō,-ere** for more natural or emotional desires.

Another word for *like* is **placet** (from **placeō,-ēre**) which means *it is pleasing, acceptable, agreeable*. This 'impersonal' verb (i.e. 3rd person singular *it* …) usually appears with an infinitive, with the person(s) pleased in the dative:

> **<u>vōbīsne</u> <u>placet</u> carmen <u>recitāre</u>?**
> *<u>is it pleasing</u> <u>to you</u> <u>to read aloud</u> the poem?*
> (i.e. *are you happy to read aloud the poem?*)

The story of Augustinus (16)

08.02 Paulus and Augustinus are working through their punishment.

abbātissa et Lūcia prope portam monasteriī stant, ubi raedam exspectant. mox duo famulī equōs et raedam ē stabulō ad viātōrēs dūcunt. Lūcia tamen nōn equitāre potest quod convalēscit. itaque Lūcia cum abbātissā in raedā sedet. nunc epīscopus ad raedam venit et in equum ascendit. omnēs ē monasteriō lentē discēdunt et sub arborēs vādunt.

intereā in bibliothēcā Paulus et Augustīnus adhūc scrībunt. puerōs enim Stephanus rēgulam monachōrum exscrībere iussit. nunc viātōrēs quī monasterium relinquunt Augustīnus ē fenestrā cōnspicit: 'tua virgō ē monasteriō discēdit. vīsne eam vidēre?'

'opus perficere dēbēmus,' inquit Paulus. 'librum fīnīre volō.'

'scrībere mihi nōn placet. hodiē est lentum et difficile: *nam vigilāre leve est, pervigilāre grave est*, ut dīcit poēta Martiālis. ecce illa virgō: est abbātis abbātissaeque amīca; etiam, putō, opulenta. et tū, Paule, scientiam vel pecūniam habēre vīs? vel amōrem?'

'sst! nunc scrībere dēbēmus.'

'quis librōs philosophōrum vel theologōrum legere vult? est ille fēlīx quī potuit rērum cognōscere causās, ut dīcit poēta Vergilius?'

'sst.'

'ille profectō est fēlīx quem domina dīligit opulenta.'

'ssssst.'

prope (+ acc.) *near*
porta,-ae (f.) *gate*
stō,-āre *stand*
raeda,-ae (f.) *carriage*
exspectō,-āre *wait for*
famulus,-ī (m.) *attendant, servant*
stabulum,-ī (n.) *stable*
viātor,-ōris (m.) *traveller*
convalēscō,-ere *recover, regain health*
itaque *and so*
ascendō,-ere *climb on to, mount*
discēdō,-ere *depart*
adhūc *still, as yet*
rēgula,-ae (f.) *rule* (medieval Latin used the singular where we might say *rules*)
iussit *he/she ordered*
eam (acc.) *her*
perficiō,-ere *complete, finish*

fīniō,-īre *finish, end*
difficilis,-e *difficult*
nam … grave est see Unit 9
vigilō,-āre *be awake*
levis,-e *light, unimportant*
pervigilō,-āre *be awake all night*
gravis,-e *heavy, serious*
Martiālis,-is *Martial*
illa (nom. sing. f.) *that* (female), *she*
scientia,-ae (f.) *knowledge*
pecūnia,-ae (f.) *money*
philosophus,-ī (m.) *philosopher*
theologus,-ī (m.) *theologian*
fēlīx … causās see Unit 5
fēlīx (nom. sing. m.) *happy, fortunate*
profectō *truly, indeed*
quem (acc. sing. m.) *whom*
dīligō,-ere *esteem, value, love*

PRACTICE 8C

1 **Identify three infinitives in the story above.**

2 **Identify the conjugation of the following:**
   i ascendō,-ere (*climb on to, mount*)
   ii bibō,-ere (*drink*)
   iii cupiō,-ere (*want, desire*)
   iv custōdiō,-īre (*guard*)
   v dīligō,-ere (*esteem, value, love*)
   vi discēdō,-ere (*depart*)
   vii fīniō,-īre (*finish, end*)
   viii stō,-āre (*stand*)
   ix perficiō,-ere (*complete, finish*)
   x putō,-āre (*think*)

Adjectives like **omnis,-e**

Here are some more adjectives like **omnis,-e** (see the endings in Unit 7):

brevis,-e	*brief, short*	levis,-e	*light, superficial*
cīvīlis,-e	*civil*	mīrābilis,-e	*wonderful, extraordinary*
crūdēlis,-e	*unfeeling, cruel*	mollis,-e	*soft*
difficilis,-e	*difficult*	mortālis,-e	*mortal*
dulcis,-e	*sweet, charming*	nōbilis,-e	*noble*
facilis,-e	*easy*	omnis,-e	*all, every*
fortis,-e	*brave, strong*	terribilis,-e	*terrible*
gravis,-e	*heavy, serious*	trīstis,-e	*sad, gloomy, grim*
humilis,-e	*humble, insignificant*	turpis,-e	*disgraceful*
irreparābilis,-e	*irretrievable*	ūtilis,-e	*useful, suitable*

<u>dulce</u> et <u>breve</u> est carmen!

the poem is <u>charming</u> and <u>short</u>!

Remember that adjectives are sometimes used as nouns:

omnēs <u>nōbilēs</u> erant fortēs?

were all the <u>nobles</u> brave?

PRACTICE 8D

1 Add the word missing from each gap and translate:

   i estne tempus _____ (*irretrievable*)?

   ii pervigilāre _____ (*serious*) est, sed tēcum vigilāre _____
     (*charming*) est.

   iii cūr puerī _____ (*sad*) sunt?

   iv Fortūna _____ (*brave men*) favet.

   v _____ (*easy*) sunt opera!

   vi quid _____ (*humble men*) petunt?

2 Add the word missing from each gap and translate:

hodiē Augustīnō nōn placet rēgulam _____ (*grim*)

exscrībere sed carmen _____ (*sweet*) recitāre.

More 3rd declension adjectives: **fēlīx** and **ingēns**

These 3rd declension adjectives, **fēlīx** (*fortunate, happy*) and **ingēns** (*huge*), are similar to **omnis,-e**:

Singular					
	m./f.	n.		m./f.	n.
Nom./Voc.	fēl**īx**	fēl**īx**		ing**ēns**	ing**ēns**
Acc.	fēl**īcem**	fēl**īx**		ing**entem**	ing**ēns**
Gen.	fēl**īcis**			ing**entis**	
Dat.	fēl**īcī**			ing**entī**	
Abl.	fēl**īcī**			ing**entī**	
Plural					
Nom./Voc.	fēl**īcēs**	fēl**īcia**		ing**entēs**	ing**entia**
Acc.	fēl**īcēs**	fēl**īcia**		ing**entēs**	ing**entia**
Gen.	fēl**īcium**			ing**entium**	
Dat.	fēl**īcibus**			ing**entibus**	
Abl.	fēl**īcibus**			ing**entibus**	

There are other adjectives like these (e.g. **fugāx, fugāc-** *fleeing*, **īnfēlīx, īnfēlīc-** *unfortunate*, **sapiēns, sapient-** *wise*).

Seneca

 08.03 Lucius Annaeus Seneca was born in the final years of the first century BC, into a wealthy family in Cordoba in Spain, and moved to Rome early in his life. His name crops up in a variety of contexts and stories. Let's first say who he was not: his father was also called Seneca, known today as Seneca the Elder, author of rhetorical dialogues and some other writings now lost.

Seneca the Younger was known for being hugely rich, rich enough – according to the historian Cassius Dio – to lend the ancient Britons 40 million sesterces (not much change, if any, from a billion dollars), as a part of the customary process of imperial acquisition: conquer, invest, enjoy the returns. However, the British seemed none too clear on the repayment part of the deal, and Cassius Dio tells us that Seneca insisted on a return of interest or capital, which the British failed to provide. The trouble that followed blew up into the rebellion by the British queen, Boudicca.

Seneca is perhaps best remembered as an exponent of Stoic philosophy, a doctrine of self-restraint acquired through the pursuit of knowledge: simple virtue is more likely to achieve happiness than any number of luxuries. All his writing, his moral essays and letters, his plays, are infused with this thinking, and his aphorisms on the benefits of a simple, unambitious lifestyle have been much quoted since. For us the irony is hard to miss, in light of his extraordinary wealth. But he wasn't the only rich Roman drawn to Stoicism, for it reminded those with much to lose that they might lose it, and offered consolation for tough times which money could not fix.

Seneca had some influence on later traditions of European drama. His own plays were reworked from Greek stories and plays, which he composed for recitation rather than stage performance, although there was a certain level of performance in any reading or recitation. The most obvious difference was the venue and scale of production. Seneca's plays were written for private dinner parties, not rough noisy theatres.

Seneca was also tutor to the young Nero, and then an adviser during the first part of his reign. With contacts like this it is not difficult to imagine how he accumulated his great wealth. But this high seat was close to the precipice. In AD 59 Seneca was still at hand when Nero had his own mother killed. In 65 Seneca himself was implicated in a plot against the emperor and forced to take his own life. The Stoic outlook, braced against the unpredictability of *Fortuna*, must have served him well.

nōn quī parum habet, sed quī plūs cupit, pauper est.
*A poor man (**pauper**) is not the man who has too little (**parum**) but he who craves more (**plūs**).*

Moral Epistles 1.2.6

quī nīl potest spērāre, dēspēret nihil.
He who can hope for nothing should despair of nothing.

Medea (a tragedy) 163

facilius est sē ā certāmine abstinēre quam abdūcere.
*It is easier to keep (**sē** = oneself) out of a quarrel than (**quam**) to withdraw from one.*

On Anger 3.8.8

honesta quaedam scelera successus facit.

*(Their) success makes some (**quaedam**) crimes honourable (**honesta**).*

Phaedra (a tragedy) 598

quī peccāre sē nescit, corrigī nōn vult.

He who is unaware that he does wrong is unwilling to be corrected.

Moral Epistles 3.28.9

Word discovery 8

Find Latin ancestors in this unit of *abduct, arboretum, diligent, fabulous, impecunious, regular, relinquish* and *total*.

Test yourself 8

1 Translate the following into English:

i nam quī sarcinam ingentem portāre potest nōn est homō sed caballus.
– ego nōn sum caballus, sed humilis mūlus.

ii fēlīx est quī cum ancillīs in hortō sedet.
– īnfēlīcēs sumus quī in bibliothēcā labōrāmus.

iii scīlicet Fortūnae pervigilāre placet. cūr mihi illa semper est crudēlis?
– sed nōnne etiam tibi favet?

iv sunt tot verba! gemō!
– scrībis ergō gemis!

v puer semper ancillīs sed numquam coquō pārēre vult.
– dulcēs sunt ancillae, coquus crūdēlis.

2 Put the underlined word into the plural, change other words where necessary, and translate the new version into English. The conjugation of the verb in each sentence is in brackets:

i <u>magister</u> puerōs docet. (2nd)

ii ō <u>puer</u>, mihi crēdis? (3rd)

iii <u>ancilla</u> puerum ad oppidum mittit. (3rd)

iv <u>mīles</u> turpis sub arborēs fugit. (M.)

v semper <u>ego</u> librum exscrībō. (3rd)

vi cūr <u>uxor</u> gemit? (3rd)

3 **Nēmō mē impūne lacessit** (originally a motto of Scottish royalty) is inscribed on a British pound coin and means which of these?

a No one harms me and gets away with it.

b Go on, trample all over me – the economy is a mess.

c No one gets rich but me.

9

In this unit you will learn about:
▶ *Medieval Latin*
▶ *the perfect tense*
▶ *present participles*
▶ *The story of Augustinus: extra duties in the library*
▶ *Martial: poet*

Medieval Latin

In classical times, **dux, ducis** was a *leader* and **comes, comitis** a *companion*. In the Middle Ages these words were used as titles: *Duke* and *Count* (companion to a king). **Prīnceps, prīncipis** is a *leading person*, high in rank. In ancient Rome it was a word used for *emperor* (the first man).

For all but the last few hundred years Latin remained the common language of Europe. Students of European history will not get far before they come upon Latin in histories, letters, poems, stories, charters, laws and other fragments of evidence which reflect the rich variety of writing thoughout the medieval era. Latin was the shared language of law, church liturgy and a variety of other written records. Histories and poems continued to be composed in Latin, and hymns and songs were sung in churches. However, it was no longer a first language.

Some scholars consider that Medieval Latin cannot be defined as a single distinct language because of the broad variance of usage in the scattered centres of medieval Europe. Similarly we might regard English if it were used around the world but only as a second language with no native speakers: with all the diverging strains it would be very challenging to set down a 'correct' version. But medieval Latin never lost sight of the classical model, even if the focus was at times hazy. There was a broad mixture of output, from careful imitations to more spontaneous Latin influenced by local habits and the emerging vernacular languages. A number of efforts were made to improve the Latin taught in schools. In the eighth century

Charlemagne commissioned a scholar and poet from England, Alcuin, to raise the standard of Latin in classrooms.

Medieval Latin was closely linked with the church. From its early use as the language of the gospels, the more challenging Latin of Christian intellectuals, the hymns, the liturgy, the chants of monks, Latin had a deeply religious flavour. But the association did not end there. Monasteries looked after secular Latin too, where manuscripts of classical and other writings were copied and stored. If you wanted a desk job in the medieval world you joined the church, for the clergy performed almost all administrative and 'clerical' tasks, and were behind most schooling initiatives. The schools that Charlemagne supported were in the first place set up in cathedrals. Alcuin himself was a bishop.

The perfect tense

The perfect tense in Latin is represented in English either by the simple past (*he loved, he took*) or the present perfect (*he has loved, he has taken*). In Latin there are the usual six endings for each person, and – good news – these endings are the same for *all* verbs. There is a but. The endings may be consistent, but not so all the stems (the past tense of English has something similar, e.g. *take* to *took*, and *see* to *saw*).

Perfect endings

-ī *I* ...
-istī *you* (sing.) ...
-it *he/she/it* ...
-imus *we* ...
-istis *you* (pl.) ...
-ērunt *they* ...

Most 1st conjugation verbs have a regular perfect stem:

amō, amāre	**amāv-ī** (*I loved or I have loved*)
laudō, laudāre	**laudāv-ī**
parō, parāre	**parāv-ī**
etc	

PRACTICE 9A

Put each of the following into one Latin word:
 i he loved
 ii they praised
 iii we have prepared

2nd conjugation verbs have regular-ish perfect stems:

habeō, habēre	**habu-ī** (*I had* or *I have had*)
dēbeō, dēbēre	**dēbu-ī**
doceō, docēre	**docu-ī**

except for verbs like

iubeō, iubēre	**iuss-ī**
rīdeō, rīdēre	**rīs-ī**
videō, vidēre	**vīd-ī**

PRACTICE 9B

Put each of the following into one Latin word:
 i they laughed
 ii you (sing.) have taught
 iii she saw

Verbs of the 3rd conjugation are a rule unto themselves ...

cadō, cadere	**cecid-ī** (*I fell* or *I have fallen*)
dīcō, dīcere	**dīx-ī**
dūcō, dūcere	**dūx-ī**
mittō, mittere	**mīs-ī**
petō, petere	**petīv-ī**
relinquō, relinquere	**relīqu-ī**
scrībō, scrībere	**scrīps-ī**
vincō, vincere	**vīc-ī**

PRACTICE 9C

Put each of the following into one Latin word:
 i they led
 ii she said
 iii we have sent

4th conjugation verbs have a reasonably regular stem. The **v** is sometimes left out:

audiō, audīre	**audīv-ī (audi-ī)**
custōdiō, custōdīre	**custodīv-ī (custōdi-ī)**
dormiō, dormīre	**dormīv-ī (dormi-ī)**
fīniō, fīnīre	**fīnīv-ī (fīni-ī)**
sepeliō, sepelīre	**sepelīv-ī (sepeli-ī)**

PRACTICE 9D

Put each of the following into one Latin word:
i I have finished
ii he has slept
iii they guarded

Mixed conjugation verbs, being most like the 3rd, are not very uniform:

capiō, capere	**cēp-ī**
cōnspiciō, cōnspicere	**cōnspex-ī**
faciō, facere	**fēc-ī**
fugiō, fugere	**fūg-ī**

PRACTICE 9E

Put each of the following into one Latin word:
i we have captured
ii you (pl.) have made
iii they fled

INSIGHT

One pattern to emerge is the lengthening of a short vowel in the present to a long one in the perfect (facit > **fēcit**; fugit > **fūgit**; venit > **vēnit**; videt > **vīdit**). With **fugit** and **venit** the spelling is the same in both tenses, and it is the change in sound that distinguishes the two. Compare this with English 'read', which on the page can be present or past but with different sounds.

The story of Augustinus (17)

Lūcia et abbātissa monasterium relīquērunt. Augustīnus dē virgine adhūc cōgitat: 'tua amīca nōbilis monasterium relīquit, ō Paule, et ex oculīs ēvānuit.'

'illa mihi nōn est amīca,' inquit Paulus.

'nōn tua vērō? bene. fortasse mea? iō! illamne salūtāre in silvā dēbeō, cadēns dē equō vel mūlō? deinde *nōs cēdāmus Amōrī!*'

'age, Augustīne, tuum opus nōn perfēcistī.' hodiē Paulō nōn placet amīcum audīre.

'*sapiās, vīna liquēs, et spatiō brevī / spem longam resecēs.*'

'ō satis poētārum, Augustīne. meherclē, tū nōndum scrībere incēpistī!'

'vix scrībere possum. nam mē Cupīdō īnflammāvit amōre.'

'nunc tū opus incipere dēbēs, sī tibi placet, silentiō.'

'īgnōsce sī tibi molestus sum.' Augustīnus librum spectāvit et 'num tōtum librum exscrībō?' rogāvit.

'tōtum,' inquit Paulus. 'Stephanus nōs verba omnia exscrībere iussit.'

'omnia?' tandem Augustīnus scrībere incēpit:

I - Dominum Deum diligere. II - Non occidere. III - Non adulterare. IV - Non facere furtum. V - Mortuum sepelire. VI - Iniuriam non facere. VII - Inimicos diligere. VIII - Non falsum testimonium dicere. IX - Nudum vestire. X - Infirmum visitare. XI - Non esse superbum. XII - Invidiam non exercere. XIII - Castitatem amare. XIV - Non esse vinolentum ...

'Et tū Benedicte?' susurrāvit Augustīnus.

---

dē (+ abl.) *concerning, about; down (from)*	illam (acc. sing. f.) *that (female), her*
cōgitō,-āre, cōgitāvī *think, ponder, reflect*	cadēns *falling* (the person falling is the subject of dēbeō)
ēvānēscō,-ere, ēvānuī *vanish, disappear*	adiuvō,-āre, adiūvī *help, assist*
mihi possessive dative *(my)*	nōs ... Amōrī *see Unit 5*
amīca,-ae (f.) *girlfriend*	perficiō,-ere, perfēcī *complete, finish*
iō! *hurrah!, yes!, oh!*	sapiās ... resecēs *see Unit 6*
	spatium,-ī (n.) *space, extent*
	satis *enough*

nōndum *not yet*	occīdō,-ere, occīdī *kill*
incipiō,-ere, incēpī *begin*	furtum,-ī (n.) *theft*
vix *scarcely, hardly, barely*	iniūria,-ae (f.) *harm*
Cupīdō,-inis (m.) *Cupid* (god of love)	inimīcus,-ī (m.) *enemy*
īnflammō,-āre, īnflammāvī *inflame*	nūdus,-a,-um *naked*
īgnōsce *forgive (me), sorry*	vestiō,-īre, vestīvī *clothe, dress*
molestus,-a,-um *troublesome*	īnfirmus,-a,-um *sick*
verbum,-ī (n.) *word*	visitō,-āre, visitāvī *visit*
iubeō,-ēre, iussī *order*	superbus,-a,-um *proud*
DOMINUM ... VINOLENTUM *adapted from*	invidia,-ae (f.) *grudge, jealousy*
the Rule of St	exerceō,-ēre, exercuī *practise*
Benedict	castitās,-tātis (f.) *chastity*
(I = 1, II = 2, etc)	

PRACTICE 9F

Identify the equivalent forms in the present tense of each verb:
 i relīquit (line 2)
 ii īnflammāvit (line 10)
 iii iussit (line 15)

Present participles

A participle is created from a verb:

Stephanus Paulum in silvā <u>ambulantem</u> vīdit
Stephanus saw Paulus <u>walking</u> in the wood

You can see that **ambulantem** is not the main verb (which is **vīdit**), but it functions like an adjective, agreeing with **Paulum**.

The present participle in English can be translated by adding *-ing* to the verb it is created from and treating it as an adjective:

discipulus <u>dormiēns</u> nōn scrībit
the <u>sleeping</u> student is not writing

Present participles have the same endings as the adjective **ingēns** (see Unit 8). 1st conjugation verbs have their characteristic **a** in the ending (**am<u>ā</u>ns**), while all the others end **-<u>ē</u>ns**:

amāns	*loving*
habēns	*having*
mittēns	*sending*

| | **audiēns** | | hearing | |
| | **capiēns** | | capturing | |

	Singular		Plural	
	m./f.	n.	m./f.	n.
Nom./Voc.	**-ns**	**-ns**	**-ntēs**	**-ntia**
Acc.	**-ntem**	**-ns**	**-ntēs**	**-ntia**
Gen.	**-ntis**		**-ntium**	
Dat.	**-ntī**		**-ntibus**	
Abl.	**-ntī /-nte**		**-ntibus**	

Sometimes it may feel more natural to translate a present participle with one or two additional words, like *while*, *who* or *as*:

Stephanus Paulum in silvā <u>ambulantem</u> vīdit

Stephanus saw Paulus <u>walking</u> in the wood

Stephanus saw Paulus <u>who was walking</u> …

Stephanus saw Paulus <u>as/while he was walking</u> …

PRACTICE 9G

1 Complete the sentence with a participle, and then translate the sentence into English:

ego ancillās in culīnā _____ (*working*) vīdī.

2 Complete each sentence with a participle:
  i ego puellam dē caelō _____ (*falling*) numquam vīdī.
  ii Paulus ad amīcum in terrā _____ (*lying*) festīnāvit.

3 Turn the underlined words into the plural (changing other words as necessary), and translate your answer into English:
  i poēta <u>fēminam</u> in raedā sedentem amat.
  ii tūne <u>hominem</u> in silvā susurrantem audīvistī?
  iii ego <u>ōvum</u> dē arbore cadēns vīdī.
  iv servus cum <u>mūlō</u> gementī labōrat.

The story of Augustinus (18)

 09.02 Augustinus is still in the library, copying out the rules of the monks.

iam Paulus opus perfēcit abiitque et Augustīnum relīquit in bibliothēcā adhūc scrībentem: ... XXVII – DIEM IUDICII TIMERE. XXVIII – NIHIL AMORI CHRISTI PRAEPONERE. XXIX – HONORARE OMNES HOMINES. XXX – DOLUM IN CORDE NON TENERE. XXXI – CONTENTIONEM NON AMARE ... mox Augustīnus obdormiit.

'dormīsne, Augustīne?' clāmāvit Stephanus dormientem discipulum vidēns excitānsque ē somnō. 'ubi sunt pāginae?'

'īgnōsce mihi, ō domine, sed nōn dormiō.'

'nōn nunc fortasse. sed tē in mēnsā iacentem vīdī. nōnne opus perfēcistī?'

'prope perfēcī, magister.'

'eho, quid est?' Stephanus et Augustīnus clāmōrem horrendum audiērunt. 'quis magnā vōce clāmat? estne vōx ululantis hominis aut bēstiae?' Stephanus fenestram adiit, ubi Theodōrum monachum ē monasteriō currentem cōnspexit. 'ecce, Theodōrus in silvam ēvānuit ululāns. quid Theodōrus timuit?' et Stephanus celeriter bibliothēcam relīquit.

iam *now, already*	somnus,-ī (m.) *sleep*
abeō, abīre, abiī *go away*	pāgina,-ae (f.) *page, leaf*
diem (acc.) *day*	īgnōsce (+ dat.) *forgive*
iūdicium,-ī (n.) *judgment*	mēnsa,-ae (f.) *table*
Christus,-ī (m.) *Christ*	prope can be an adverb (*almost,*
praepōnō,-ere, praeposuī *put before*	*nearly*) or a preposition (*near* something)
honōrō,-āre, honōrāvī *honour*	clāmor,-ōris (m.) *shout, cry*
dolus,-ī (m.) *deceit*	horrendus,-a,-um *dreadful*
cor, cordis (n.) *heart*	vōx, vōcis (f.) *voice, cry, sound*
teneō,-ēre, tenuī *hold, keep*	ululō,-āre, ululāvī *howl*
contentiō,-ōnis (f.) *dispute, controversy*	adeō,-īre, adiī *go to, approach*
obdormiō,-īre, obdormiī *fall asleep*	cōnspiciō,-ere, cōnspexī *catch sight of*
excitō,-āre, excitāvī *wake, arouse*	

eō, īre (*go*)

The verb **eō** (infinitive **īre**) is about as irregular as a verb can be. (English 'go' has its oddities too: *go, gone, went, been*.) The perfect stem is barely visible: **i-ī** (occasionally **īvī, īvistī**, etc; likewise in the compounds **abīvī**, etc). This verb often appears in compound form (e.g. **abeō, abīre, abiī** *go away* and **adeō, adīre, adiī** *go to, approach*).

Present	Perfect
eō	iī
īs	īstī
it	iit
īmus	iimus
ītis	īstis
eunt	iērunt

PRACTICE 9H

Put each of the following into one Latin word:
- **i** she is going
- **ii** he went
- **iii** they have gone away
- **iv** we are going away
- **v** you (pl.) are approaching

Martial

 09.03 Like Seneca, the poet Marcus Valerius Martialis was born in Spain. The two families were probably known to each other, and Seneca may have helped when in AD 64 Martial (now in his 20s) came to Rome to seek his fame and fortune. But any support from Seneca came to an abrupt halt the following year when Nero forced him to take his own life.

Of the other poets whose work survives, Martial is perhaps most like Catullus: short poems written in the first person, clever expressions of feeling (annoyance mostly) at life around him. His patrons are a constant target. As a 'client' you were expected to rally round and support your 'patron', and in return you would receive your patron's favours. Martial teases, criticizes and ridicules these benefactors: he might walk a few miles for a formal visit and on arrival find his patron not at home, or worse, avoiding him. These and other indignities are recorded in witty succinct verses. The targets of his irritation are named, but how many names are substitutes is not entirely clear (a poetic practice at least as old as 'Lesbia' for Catullus' Clodia). Many of his friends and acquantainces are addressed personally. A character called Fidentinus gets repeated stick for attempting to pass off Martial's poems as his own:

nostrīs versibus esse tē poētam,

Fīdentīne, putās cupisque crēdī?

By our (my) verses you to be a poet, Fidentinus, you think and desire to be believed?

Epigrams 1.72.1–2

Martial's poetry engages with the day-to-day realities of life in Rome, and less so larger themes framed in mythological stories. For that reason his poems are more accessible than the works of Horace, Ovid or Virgil in which mythical characters and places crop up all the time:

nōn hīc Centaurōs, nōn Gorgonās Harpyiāsque

inveniēs: hominem pāgina nostra sapit.

You will not find Centaurs here or Gorgons or Harpies:

*our (my) page offers a flavour of (**sapit**) human (life).*

Epigrams 10.4.9–10

Martial lends detail and colour to our picture of life in Rome in the first century AD. He is direct and to the point; for instance, to the schoolteacher who yells at his pupils early in the morning, whom he offers whatever the pupils pay him just to shut him up:

vīcīnī somnum nōn tōtā nocte rogāmus:

nam vigilāre leve est, pervigilāre grave est.

*We neighbours (**vīcīnī**) do not ask for sleep all night long: for to be awake is no matter (**leve**) but to lie awake the whole night is serious.*

Epigrams 9.68.9–10

Some of his work would challenge censors today for its explicit sexual content. Here he responds to a critic who complains that his verses cannot be read in a classroom:

nec castrāre velīs meōs libellōs.

gallō turpius est nihil Priāpō.

Do not wish to emasculate my little books.

*There is nothing more disgusting (**turpius**) than a eunuch Priapus.*

(Priapus: a hugely-endowed spirit of fertility; Gallus: not a Gaul here, but a eunuch priest of the goddess Cybele)

Epigrams 1.35.14–15

Martial may poke fun at his patrons and others, but the emperor Domitian is treated more carefully. The poet asks him to look lightly upon his work and assures him of his own good conduct:

lascīva est nōbīs pāgina, vīta proba.

Our (my) page is lewd, (my) life is upright.

Epigrams 1.4.8

Word discovery 9

1 **Identify English words from** mōs, pāgina **and** somnus.

2 **Find Latin ancestors in this unit of** *dormant*, *judicial*, *lascivious*, *levity* **and** *vicinity*.

3 **The irregular French verb** *aller* (*go*) **has forms as diverse as** *vais*, *allez* **and** *irai*. **Can you identify the three different Latin verbs (for** *go* **or** *walk*) **which are ancestors of these forms?**

pāgina,-ae (f.) *page*	dē (+ abl.) *down from, about, concerning*
pecūnia,-ae (f.) *money*	iam *now, already*
porta,-ae (f.) *gate*	itaque *and so, therefore*
raeda,-ae (f.) *carriage*	nam *for, in fact*
somnus,-ī (m.) *sleep*	nec (neque) *and not, but not*
mōs, mōris (m.) *habit, custom, manner*	nisi *unless, except*
vōx, vōcis (f.) *voice, cry, sound*	sī *if*
inimīcus,-a,-um *hostile*	tandem *at last, finally*
superbus,-a,-um *proud, arrogant*	ut *as (and other meanings)*
	vix *scarcely, hardly, barely*

Test yourself 9

1 Write out the perfect tense (all six persons) of the following :
    i parō, parāre, parāvī (*prepare*)
    ii occīdō, occīdere, occīdī (*kill*)
   iii incipiō, incipere, incēpī (*begin*)

2 Translate the following into English:
    i cūr monachus iam in silvam fūgit?
   ii quis monachum gementem audiit?
  iii dux vēnit, vīdit, abiit.
   iv ancillae rīdentēs mē cēnam parāre docuērunt.
    v monachī ancillās ad coquum in terrā iacentem adīre iussērunt.

3 Put each underlined verb into the perfect tense, and then translate your answer into English:
    i coquus mē numquam <u>laudat.</u>
   ii quis in raedā <u>rīdit?</u>
  iii tōta verba <u>scrībis?</u>
   iv tandem fēmina raedam <u>relinquit.</u>
    v vōbīs pecūniam <u>mittimus.</u>

4 Fill each gap with the missing word:
    i nōnne illa tē _____ (*she loved*)?
       – _____ (*she went away*) et mē in hortō _____ (*sitting*) relīquit.
   ii ō amīce, _____ (*did you conquer*) aut _____ (*did you flee*)?
       – _____ (*I came*) _____ (*I saw*) _____ (*I laughed*).
  iii ubi est magister?
       – magister cum discipulō _____ (*who is asleep*) in bibliothēcā adest.

5 **In flagrante dēlictō** means which of the following?
   a having a delicious hot meal
   b profiting from a crime
   c caught in the act

In this unit you will learn about:
- ▶ *a dying language*
- ▶ *the imperfect tense*
- ▶ *gerundives and imperatives*
- ▶ *4th declension nouns*
- ▶ *The story of Augustinus: a death in the monastery*
- ▶ *Tacitus: historian*

A dying language

Two significant events happened in the middle part of the second millennium which helped to push Latin into the museum of discontinued languages: the Reformation and the Renaissance.

For a thousand years and more Christianity had been the principal religion of Europe, with a powerful figure at the top of a very political hierarchy, the Pope. Throughout medieval times secular rulers conformed to papal authority. If a medieval monarch fell out of line he would be denied communion (excommunicated) and so suffer politically by losing the support and respect of allies and subjects. And then there was the administrative and educational role of the clergy – a ministry of information upon which secular rulers depended. A break with the church came at a cost.

However, the break did come in some parts of Europe, as leaders in the north became less and less willing to submit to the authority of Rome. Many of these politicians were opportunists engaged in a power struggle, but the Reformation's footsoldiers were more genuine, frustrated by the machinery of the church, its hypocrisy and the distraction from the principal source of belief, the Bible. The first move by Reformers was to translate the Bible into their own vernacular languages. That was followed by liturgy, hymns and other religious texts. Newly invented printing presses made their work a good deal easier, for they no longer relied upon traditional scribes in the churches.

Latin was a casualty of this religious conflict. That is not to say that all Protestants considered it tainted – Elizabeth I of England was one who was taught to read, write and even speak Latin. But its days as the primary language of religious belief were numbered, at least in the Reformist countries. In Catholic countries Latin continued to be used until the 1960s.

The other event, the Renaissance, was broadly concurrent. This was an upsurge of interest in classical antiquity, the arts as well as literature. One symptom of this was the inkhorn taste for creating English words on Latin models: 'splendidious felicitations', etc (see Unit 4). Latin and Greek authors were read, translated – and printed – more widely than ever before.

It is an irony that this renewal of interest helped to push Latin into the glass case where it lies today. The appetite for recreating the ancient language and the pursuit of more rigorous classical standards sucked what life was left out of the spontaneous Latin of the time. The desire for ancient polish and renewed accuracy accelerated the end of the living language: Latin was embalmed with fixed prescriptive linguistic rules only possible in a language standing still.

The imperfect tense

The perfect tense describes a past action completed relatively quickly. The imperfect tense, on the other hand, describes a past event which was repeated or which lasted for a while:

discipulī in bibliothēcā semper <u>cantābant</u>
the students always <u>used to sing</u> / <u>would sing</u> / <u>sang</u> in the library

Augustīnus carmina Catullī <u>legēbat</u>
Augustine <u>was reading</u> / <u>used to read</u> / <u>would read</u> the poems of Catullus

You can translate the imperfect as a simple past (e.g. *sang* above), but first check whether one of *was/were* … , *used to* … or even *would* … may make a better translation.

> **INSIGHT**
> We say *would* … to express the past imperfect, as in *she <u>would</u> visit her aunt every Tuesday*. This is a different use of *would* from the hypothetical one: *if she were ill she <u>would</u> stay in bed*.

PRACTICE 10A

If you were to put the sentence below into Latin, one verb would be imperfect and the other perfect. Which is which?

Clare <u>was reading</u> the paper when the detective <u>entered</u>.

The imperfect is about the most recognizable of all the tenses. Endings are common to all verbs (except **sum, esse** and its compounds below).

Imperfect endings

    -bam   *I was...*

    -bās   *you* (sing.) *were...*

    -bat   *he/she/it was...*

    -bāmus   *we were...*

    -bātis   *you* (pl.) *were...*

    -bant   *they were...*

1st conjugation verbs have the customary **a** (**amābam**) while the others end **-ēbam** (or **-iēbam**): **amābam**, etc; **habēbam**, etc; **mittēbam**, etc; **audiēbam**, etc; **capiēbam**, etc.

PRACTICE 10B

Translate each of the following into the imperfect:

  i she was sending
  ii they used to take/capture
  iii we used to have
  iv he was hearing

Irregular verbs in the imperfect: **adsum** (**aderam**), **absum** (**aberam**) and **possum** (**poteram**) have the same imperfect endings as **sum**:

    eram   *I was*

    erās   *you* (sing.) *were*

    erat   *he/she/it was*

    erāmus   *we were*

    erātis   *you* (pl.) *were*

    erant   *they were*

Other irregular verbs have the usual imperfect endings:

volēbam, volēbās, etc *I wanted, was willing*, etc

ībam, ībās, etc *I was going*, etc

1 Complete the sentence and then translate it into English:

monachusne mīlitēs in silvā susurrantēs audīre _____ (*was able*)?

2 Put the underlined verbs into the imperfect and then translate the sentence into English:

 i ō Paule, ubi <u>es</u>?
 ii fīlia magistrī mē <u>amat</u>.
 iii cēnam semper <u>parāmus</u>.
 iv discipulī <u>dormiunt</u>.
 v ego Theodōrum vidēre <u>possum</u>.
 vi quis <u>adest</u>?

3 Complete each sentence with a verb in the imperfect tense:

 i corpus monachī in terrā _____ (*was lying*).
 ii discipulus mūlum per silvam _____ (*was leading*).
 iii ego in monasteriō _____ (*was writing*).
 iv ō virgō, tū in silvā _____ (*were present*)?
 v cūr Theodōrus in silvam _____ (*was fleeing*)?
 vi monachī corpus _____ (*were burying*).

The story of Augustinus (19)

 10.01 **The funeral of Theodorus.**

post Theodōrī mortem — fortuītam, ut dīxit abbas, sed quis potest scīre? — multae erant lacrimae. Theodōrus enim, monachus pius, omnium amīcus fuerat.

discipulī trīstēs in bibliothēcā dīligenter labōrābant. Stephanus tremēns magnum librum Novī Testāmentī tenēbat recitābatque historiam Lazarī: '*Iēsus autem ēlevātīs sūrsum oculīs dīxit: Pater, grātiās agō tibi quoniam audīstī mē. ego autem sciēbam quia semper mē audīs...*'

Paulus per fenestram silvās spectāns dē morte Theodōrī cōgitābat: quis eum occīdere voluit? monachus mortuus omnibus discipulīs monachīsque semper benignus erat. rūmor erat. Dānī? num Dānī Theodōrum occīdērunt? nūllī Dānī in regiōne multōs annōs vīsī erant.

Stephanus adhūc historiam recitābat '... *vōce magnā clāmāvit: Lazare, venī forās!* et dēsiit quod campanam per monasterium resonantem audīre poterat. 'nunc, ō puerī,' inquit magister, 'corpus Theodōrī sepeliendum est,' lacrimāsque per genās fundēns bibliothēcam relīquit.

nec multō post Paulus ē bibliothēcā per pluviam exsequiās Theodōrī spectābat. Stephanus cum aliīs monachīs corpus Theodōrī ex ecclēsiā portābat abbāsque exiguam pompam dūcēbat. discipulī librōs relīquērunt et cum Paulō pompam spectābant. 'ecce,' inquit ūnus, 'Theodōrum sepeliunt prope arborem ubi nōbīs fābulās narrābat.'

'cūr nōn omnēs adsunt monachī? cūr eum tam celeriter sepeliunt?' rogāvit alter.

'quis Theodōrum occīdit?' rogāvit tertius.

'ecce, nunc corpus in terram dēmittunt,' inquit Paulus. mox discipulī vōcem Stephanī iterum iterumque gementem audiēbant.

'*nox est perpetua ūna dormienda,*' inquit Augustīnus, Catullī versum recitāns.

HIC IACET

THEODORUS

MONASTERII HUIUS

MONACHUS

QUI IN ANNO TRICESIMO

ET

QUINTO MORTUUS NUNC

CUM DEO IN PACE

REQUIESCIT

post (+ acc.)   *after, behind*
fortuītus,-a,-um   *accidental*
lacrima,-ae (f.)   *tear*
fuerat   *(he/she/it) had been*
dīligenter   *attentively*
tremō,-ere, tremuī   *tremble*
Novum Testāmentum,-ī (n.)   *New Testament*
Lazarus,-ī   Jesus brings him back to life a few days after he dies (John, 11.41–3)
Iēsus (nom.)   *Jesus*
autem   *indeed, but, yet*
ēlevātus,-a-um   *raised*
sūrsum   *upwards*
grātiās agō (+ dat.)   *I thank*
quoniam   *for the reason that*
audīstī   for audīvistī
quia   *because, that*
eum (acc.)   *him*
voluit   perfect of volō, velle, voluī
rūmor,-ōris (m.)   *rumour, gossip*
nūllus,-a,-um   *no, not any*
Dānus,-ī (m.)   *Dane, Scandinavian*
multōs annōs   the accusative is used to express a period of time
vīsī erant   *(they) had been seen*
venī forās!   *come out!*

dēsinō,-ere, dēsiī   *stop*
campana,-ae (f.)   *bell*
resonō,-āre   *resound*
sepeliendum est   *(it) has to be buried*
gena,-ae (f.)   *cheek*
fundō,-ere, fūdī   *pour*
pluvia,-ae (f.)   *rain*
exsequiae,-ārum (f.)   *funeral*
aliīs (abl. pl.)   *other*
ecclēsia,-ae (f.)   *church*
exiguus,-a,-um   *slender, small*
pompa,-ae (f.)   *procession*
tam   *so*
alter   *another, the next*
tertius,-a,-um   *third*
dēmittō,-ere, dēmīsī   *lower*
iterum   *again*
nox …   from Catullus, Poem 5 (see Online Support)
perpetuus,-a,-um   *unending*
ūna (nom. f.)   *one*
dormiendus,-a,-um   *to be slept*
versum (acc.)   *verse, line of verse*
huius (gen., all genders)   *this*
annus,-ī (m.)   *year*
trīcēsimō et quīntō (abl.)   *35th*
pāx, pācis (f.)   *peace*
requiēscō,-ere, requiēvī   *rest*

Gerundives

The girl's name Amanda comes from the Latin for *to be loved* in the nominative feminine singular:

mea amīca amanda est
my girlfriend is to be loved (i.e. *should be loved*)

This is called a 'gerundive'. There is usually a sense of obligation attached to a gerundive (i.e. *should be …*).

Gerundives are adjectives created from verbs with the endings
-ndus, -nda, -ndum (like **bonus,-a,-um**).

The noun it agrees with is the thing 'to be done':

cēna <u>paranda</u> est
the dinner is <u>to be prepared</u> (i.e. should be prepared)

Gerundives from 1st conjugation verbs end **-<u>a</u>ndus**, the others -**<u>(i)</u>endus**:

amandus,-a,-um

habendus,-a,-um

mittendus,-a,-um

audiendus,-a,-um

capiendus,-a,-um

PRACTICE 10D

What do these mean?

  i meus dominus laudandus est.
 ii mea pecūnia est custōdienda.
iii opus perficiendum est.
 iv carmina sunt audienda.

Gerundives are adjectives (be careful to distinguish them from participles!), and like other adjectives sometimes appear without a noun:

Lūcia <u>agenda</u> nōn perfēcit
Lucia did not finish <u>the things to be done</u> / <u>the things she had to do</u>

Agenda (from **agō,-ere**) is in the accusative neuter plural of the gerundive, as the object of **perfēcit**.

LANGUAGE TIP

Gerundives are <u>passive</u>, i.e. the noun it agrees with is done to, not the doer.
Present participles are <u>active</u>: the noun they agree with is doing it:
puella amanda
a girl to-be-loved (i.e. she is the one loved)
puella amāns
a girl loving (i.e. she is doing the loving)

The gerundive is sometimes used in an 'impersonal' way, like **placet** (*it is pleasing*) – see Unit 8. If so, the gerundive appears in the neuter with no noun attached:

nunc est <u>mittendum</u>

now it is <u>to be sent</u> (it is time to send/ now we should send)

The person who should be doing it will either appear as a pronoun in the dative (not the ablative, which you might expect as it means *by* ...), or is obvious and doesn't need to be said:

ō amīcī, nunc (<u>vōbīs</u>) est fugiendum

friends, now it must be fled by <u>you</u> (it's time to leg it / <u>you</u> should ...)

The imperative

A gerundive may be used to hurry someone up ('*this must be done now*', etc), although the imperative is the usual word for a command or plea. The most common forms are in the 2nd person, i.e. addressed to 'you', with a singular for just one 'you' and a plural for more:

	Singular	Plural	
1st conjugation	am**ā**	am**āte**	*love!*
2nd conjugation	hab**ē**	hab**ēte**	*have!*
3rd conjugation	mitt**e**	mitt**ite**	*send!*
4th conjugation	aud**ī**	aud**īte**	*hear!*
Mixed conjugation	cap**e**	cap**ite**	*take!*

PRACTICE 10E

1 Complete the sentence with the imperative of festīnō,-āre:

ō miserī, _____!

2 Fill each gap with the correct imperative:

   i ō Caesar, _____ (*come!*) _____ (*see!*) _____ (*conquer!*)

   ii ō amīcī, _____ (*drink!*) _____ (*laugh!*), _____ (*sleep!*)

The story of Augustinus (20)

 10.02 The abbot celebrates mass in the church.

nec multō post Theodōrī exsequiās, multī aderant in ecclēsiā candēlīs incēnsōque odōrātā. abbas ipse cum omnibus monachīs missam celebrābat. Lūcia iuxtā mātrem in prīmō subselliō sedēbat.

abbas ad āram in veste purpureā splendēns stābat et magnā vōce '*in nōmine Patris et Fīliī et Spīritūs Sānctī* ōrābat. monachī discipulīque post āram in chorō cantābant.

'Pater noster, quī es in caelīs...' cantābat abbas. omnēs discipulī cantābant praeter Augustīnum, quī dormiēbat quod Stephanus eum per tōtam noctem epistulās Sānctī Paulī ad Corinthiōs exscrībere iusserat. Augustīnus poenās dabat quod in scholā nōn epistulās Sānctī Paulī sed versūs Catullī legēbat. nunc Paulus amīcum stertentem audīre poterat voluitque ē somnō excitāre. frūstrā.

'*et nē nōs indūcās in tentātiōnem, sed līberā nōs ā malō,*' abbas cantābat. Lūcia ipsa dormientem spectābat et Paulum cāsū cōnspiciēns oculōs dēiēcit.

Egberta Lūciae 'quis est ille puer quī tē spectat?' susurrāvit rīsitque. Egberta tamen rīdēre dēsiit quod Benedictum sē ipsam spectantem cōnspexit. 'monachī īnsolentissimī sunt!' susurrāvit Egberta, et Karolus coniūnx strepitum audiēns 'Egberta, valēsne?' rogāvit.

intereā Stephanus Augustīnum dormientem spectābat. itaque Paulus 'cavē, Augustīne!' metū susurrāvit, 'nunc est cantandum!'

'ēheu!' Augustīnus gemitū respondit 'nōnne est ūna nox dormienda? ego cupiō dormīre!'

'*ōrā prō nōbīs peccātōribus,*' inquit abbas manūs ad caelum tendēns.

nec multō post	here used as a preposition + acc. (i.e. *not long after* the exsequiās)	ipse (nom. sing. m.)	*himself* (emphasizing)
		missa,-ae (f.)	*mass*
		celebrō,-āre, celebrāvī	*celebrate*
candēla,-ae (f.)	*candle*	iuxtā (+ acc.)	*next to*
incēnsum,-ī (n.)	*incense*	subsellium,-ī (n.)	*bench, pew*
odōrātus,-a,-um	*scented*	āra,-ae (f.)	*altar*

ad āram   *at the altar*
vestis,-is (f.)   *clothing*
purpureus,-a,-um   *purple*
splendeō,-ēre   *be bright, shine*
spīritūs (gen.)   *spirit (nouns ending
                  -ūs and -ū follow
                  after this passage)*
ōrō,-āre, ōrāvī   *in classical Latin
                  speak, plead,
                  entreat; ancient
                  Romans used ōrō
                  for please, i.e. I
                  entreat (you); in
                  church Latin:
                  I pray*
chorus,-ī (m.)   *choir*
noster, nostra, nostrum   *our*
caelīs   translate as singular
eum (acc.)   *him*
epistula,-ae (f.)   *letter*
Sānctus Paulus   *Saint Paul*
Corinthiī,-ōrum (m.)   *Corinthians*
iusserat   *(he/she) had ordered*
poenās dabat   *(he/she) was paying
                  the penalty, i.e.
                  being punished*
versūs (acc. pl.)   *verses*
stertō,-ere   *snore*

frūstrā   *in vain, to no purpose*
nē indūcās   *do not lead (not
              imperative but
              subjunctive, with a
              similar sense)*
tentātiō,-ōnis (f.)   *temptation*
līberō,-āre,-āvī   *free, deliver*
ipsa (nom. f.)   *herself*
cāsū (abl.)   *accident, chance*
dēiciō,-ere, dēiēcī   *lower*
sē ipsam (acc.)   *her herself*
īnsolentissimus,-a,-um   *very/most
                          insolent*
coniūnx, coniugis (m./f.)   *husband,
                            wife
                            (spouse)*
strepitum (acc.)   *noise*
valeō,-ēre, valuī   *be well*
caveō,-ēre   *be careful*
metū (abl.)   *fear*
est cantandum   *it is to be sung (i.e.
                  we must sing)*
gemitū (abl.)   *with a groan*
respondeō,-ēre, respondī   *reply*
peccātor,-ōris (m.)   *sinner,
                      wrongdoer*
manūs (acc. pl.)   *hands*
tendō,-ere   *stretch*

PRACTICE 10F

Identify in the story above (i) an imperative and (ii) a gerundive.

> **INSIGHT**
> A handful of adjectives have forms very like **bonus,-a,-um**, except for the genitive
> singular (**-ius**, all genders) and dative singular (**-ī**, all genders). These include **nūllus,-
> a,-um** (*not any, no, none*); **sōlus,-a,-um** (*alone, only, single*); **tōtus,-a,-um** (*whole, all*);
> **ūllus,-a,-um** (*any*); **ūnus,-a,-um** (*one*). Similar to these is **alius, alia, aliud** (*other*)
> which differs only in the neuter singular, ending **-ud** instead of **-um**.
> In the plural all endings follow the model of **bonī,-ae,-a**.

4th declension nouns

These nouns end **-us** in the nominative and **-um** in the accusative, as do 2nd declension nouns like **mūlus**. But there the similarity ends. The **-us** ending, in fact **-ūs**, reappears in the genitive singular and both the nominative and accusative plural:

	Singular	Plural
Nom. & Voc.	spīrit**us**	spīrit**ūs**
Accusative	spīrit**um**	spīrit**ūs**
Genitive	spīrit**ūs**	spīrit**uum**
Dative	spīrit**uī**	spīrit**ibus**
Ablative	spīrit**ū**	spīrit**ibus**

Some 4th declension nouns
cāsus,-ūs (m.)   *accident, chance*
domus,-ūs[1] (f.)   *house, home*
exercitus,-ūs (m.)   *army*
gemitus,-ūs (m.)   *groan*
lacus,-ūs (m.)   *lake*
manus,-ūs (f.)   *hand*

metus,-ūs (m.)   *fear*
spīritus,-ūs (m.)   *spirit*
strepitus,-ūs (m.)   *noise*
versus,-ūs (m.)   *verse, line of verse*
vultus,-ūs (m.)   *face*

[1]Declension hybrid: **domus** (*house, home*) has one or two endings from the 2nd declension: the genitive could be **domūs** or **domī**, the dative **domuī** or **domō**, and the ablative was always **domō**. In the plural all endings were as for **spīritus** (4th declension), except the accusative plural which was sometimes **domōs** instead of **domūs**.

PRACTICE 10G

Fill each gap with a single word and translate:

  i potesne _____ (*verses*) Augustīnī audīre?

 ii coquus ad vīnum _____ (*his hands*) tendēbat.

iii adsuntne Dānī cum _____ (*with an army*)?

 iv _____ (*because/out of fear*) fugiēbāmus.

  v _____ (*by accident*) tē vīdī in _____ (*in the lake*).

 vi tūne _____ (*the noise*) _____ (*and the groans*) in silvā audīre
      _____ (*could you*)?

Tacitus

10.03 Publius Cornelius Tacitus was born in the mid-50s AD, like Seneca and Martial outside Italy, to a wealthy 'Gallo-Roman' family in Gaul. As time rolls on, prominent characters emerge from more distant parts of the empire – the concept of 'Roman' gradually broadened.

Tacitus was known to be a brilliant lawyer, and it shows in his historical narratives. In his *Annals*, a record of Rome under the early emperors, he claims to write **sine īrā et studiō** (without resentment and favour). One read of his work and you may wonder who he is trying to fool. It is Tacitus who is behind the suggestively dark portraits of Roman emperors as whimsical autocrats, jealous and cruel.

Nearly twenty years before the *Annals* appeared, just before the end of the first century AD, Tacitus wrote an 'encomium' (eulogy) of his father-in-law, Gnaeus Julius Agricola, who governed the province of Britain from 77 to 85. In an encomium, some **īra** (at the now-dead emperor, Domitian) and **studium** (for his father-in-law) were expected. Domitian had been bumped off in 96, hated by senators and those immediately beneath him. Tacitus, himself a senator, may have felt a little uneasy, for both he and Agricola had enjoyed enough favour from Domitian for their careers to prosper. In Agricola's case, says Tacitus, he had talent and ability which the state could not do without, and his success was in spite of the man at the top. Agricola was modest enough to stay out of the limelight, and so survive Domitian's jealousy, who is the target here:

> **proprium hūmānī ingeniī est ōdisse quem laeserīs.**
>
> *It is a characteristic of human nature to hate (a person) whom you have injured.*

Agricola 42

When Tacitus came to write his *Annals*, he wanted recognition as an impartial historian. No doubt by then his sharp judgements and suggestive writing were well known, and his claim **sine īrā et studiō** at the start of the work was a reminder that he was a neutral observer, if an opinionated one.

Seneca's suicide at Nero's prompt is described in full, including the attempt by his wife to die with him, though she changed her mind halfway through and survived. Seneca's veins were cut, and the old man's blood flow was slow, so he asked for hemlock, following the example of the Greek thinker Socrates (and when that too took its time Seneca was put in a bath where he suffocated):

ōrat prōvīsum prīdem venēnum.

He asks for the poison anticipated well in advance.

Annals 15.64

The story of Nero having his mother Agrippina murdered is chillingly told. After her death he was scared to return to Rome, and only did so in the manner of a triumphant general to orchestrated popular joy. Then, his mother out the way, Nero …

sēque in omnēs libīdinēs effūdit.

And he indulged (lit. *poured himself out into, wasted himself in*)
his every desire.

Annals 14.13

Tacitus is an important source for what we know about Roman Britain. Boudicca's rebellion of AD 60–1 is carefully chronicled: a furious and savage uprising which followed Roman abuse of Boudicca and her daughters. It was checked with some difficulty – but the rebellion died with its leader:

Boudicca vītam venēnō fīnīvit.

Boudicca ended her life with poison.

Annals 14.34

Tacitus' *Dialogue on Oratory*, a discussion of rhetoric, was published a few years after the *Agricola*:

fāma et laus cuius artis cum ōrātōrum glōriā comparanda est?

What practice has the reputation and high standing to stand comparison with the renown of public speakers?

Lit.: *of what practice* (**cuius artis**) *is the reputation and high standing* (**fāma et laus**) *to be compared with the renown* (**glōriā**) *of …*

Dialogue on Oratory 7

The trouble with the schools of rhetoric, argues a character in the *Dialogue*, is their students talk only about sport. And they're not the only ones:

nē praeceptōrēs quidem ūllās crēbriōrēs cum audītōribus suīs fābulās habent.

Not even the teachers have any stories (they share) more frequently with their pupils.

Dialogue on Oratory 29

Word discovery 10

1 **Identify the gerundive from these verbs, and an English word derived from gerundive:**
   i **dīvidō,-ere** (*divide, distribute*)
   ii **propāgō,-āre** (*propagate*)
   iii **addō,-ere** (*add*)
   iv **agō,-ere** (*do, perform*)

2 **Which one of these girls' names is** *not* **derived from Latin:** *Amanda*, *Brenda* **or** *Miranda*?

3 **The English word** *recipe* **is derived from what form of** recipiō,-ere?

4 **Identify a 4th declension noun which is an ancestor of**
   i casual
   ii domestic
   iii manual

5 **Identify an English word each from** frūstrā **and** iuxtā.

---

autem   *indeed, but, yet*
frūstrā   *in vain, to no purpose*
iuxtā (+ acc.)   *next to*
post (+ acc.)   *after, behind*
quia   *because, that*

Test yourself 10

1 Put each underlined verb into the imperfect, and then translate the sentence into English:

   i quis in lacū <u>est</u>?

   ii Lūcia Paulusque cāsū in silvam <u>vādunt</u>.

   iii Stephanus corpus sepeliendum ex ecclēsiā <u>portāt</u>.

   iv discipulī gemitūs Stephanī audīre in tōtō monasteriō <u>possunt</u>.

   v multōs annōs nōs omnēs metū Dānōrum silvās <u>timēmus</u>.

   vi ēheu, Benedictus <u>vult</u> tōtum vīnum bibere sōlus!

2 Identify the right form of **ōrō,-āre** in each case:

   i ō domina, _____ (*please!*), cantā mēcum.

   ii ō amīce, _____ (*pray*) prō nōbīs.

3 Translate:

   i numquam venēnum ūllum bibī!

   ii monachus vultū trīstī sedet sub arbore.

   iii ō dea, dā mihi dēsīderanda.

   iv cūr Dānī sunt timendī?

4 **Caveat emptor** means which of the following ?

   a the space must be sold empty

   b there is no food left

   c the buyer should be cautious

In this unit you will learn about:
▶ *ecclesiastical Latin*
▶ *5th declension nouns*
▶ *the future tense*
▶ *pronouns:* **ille, hic, is, ipse, sē**
▶ *The story of Augustinus: Augustinus wakes in church*
▶ *Suetonius: biographer of emperors*

Ecclesiastical Latin

Latin was finally dropped from Catholic liturgy in the 1960s, ending an unbroken line of Latin from the Church's earliest days, though hymns, prayers and chants are still sung in some churches. In the centuries before printing presses, churches were the centres of learning where books were copied and kept, and churchmen found pleasure in classical Latin literature; but the primary use of the language was to observe the ritual and get the Christian message across to the local brethren. Each region of the Christian domain had its own mix of Latin and local speech habits, evolving over many centuries. The pronunciation will have varied from country to country and priest to priest. In 1912 Pope Pius X, frustrated by the disparate sounds of Latin across Europe, encouraged the clergy everywhere to adopt what was then the Italian pronunciation of Latin. Hence 'Yaysoos' and 'chaylum' for **Jesus** and **caelum**. The Italian sound of church Latin you hear sung today has no earlier provenance.

5th declension nouns

The fifth and last declension. There are not many of these nouns, but they appear often enough: **rēs** corresponds to many of our meanings of *thing*. It can be abstract, as in 'the <u>thing</u> is', or something more concrete 'keep your <u>things</u> safe'. Translate as *thing, matter, affair* or *issue*.

	Singular	Plural
Nom. & Voc.	**rēs**	**rēs**
Accusative	**rem**	**rēs**
Genitive	**reī**	**rērum**
Dative	**reī**	**rēbus**
Ablative	**rē**	**rēbus**

> **INSIGHT**
> With the adjective **pūblicus,-a,-um**, **rēs** means *the government*, and in the era before emperors, *the Republic*:
>
> **Caesar <u>rem pūblicam</u> tenet**
> *Caesar controls <u>the government</u>*

Some 5th declension nouns
rēs, reī (f.)   *thing, matter*
diēs, diēī (m./f.)   *day*
faciēs, faciēī (f.)   *face, shape, appearance*
fidēs, fideī (f.)   *faith, trust, confidence*
spēs,-eī (f.)   *hope*

> **LANGUAGE TIP**
> **fidēs,-eī** means *faith, trust, confidence*. It can be the confidence you have in something, or the quality that someone has for you to have confidence in them. To have faith in someone, to trust their word, is **fidem habēre** + dat.

PRACTICE 11A

Translate:

i quis fidem mīlitibus habet?
ii Paulus faciem virginis in terrā iacentis spectāvit.
iii mīles spem fidemque in armīs pōnit.
iv nōnne nōs omnēs fidem habēmus monachīs?

The future tense

The future tense expresses what is to happen in the future, usually translated with *shall* or *will*. We also use what appears to be an English present tense to represent the future, e.g., *I am leaving tomorrow*.

The future endings of the first two conjugations are similar and the other three likewise. Here is the future tense of the 1st and 2nd conjugations:

	1st	2nd
I shall…	am**ābō**	hab**ēbō**
you (sing.) *will…*	am**ābis**	hab**ēbis**
he/she/it will…	am**ābit**	hab**ēbit**
we shall…	am**ābimus**	hab**ēbimus**
you (pl.) *will…*	am**ābitis**	hab**ēbitis**
they will…	am**ābunt**	hab**ēbunt**

Note how similar (and possibly confusing) is the future tense of these two conjugations to the imperfect (-**bat**, -**bant**, etc).

hodiē cantāb<u>imus</u>

today we shall sing

hodiē cantāb<u>āmus</u>

today we were singing

PRACTICE 11B

1 Write out all six persons of the following:
 i the future of **parō,-āre**
 ii the future of **videō,-ēre**
 iii the imperfect of **amō,-āre**

2 Complete each sentence with one word:
 i imperātor virtūtem _____ (*will praise*).
 ii discipulōs carmina recitāre _____ (*I shall order*).
 iii ancillae in hortō _____ (*will sit*).

The future tense of the 3rd, 4th and mixed conjugations is as follows:

	3rd	4th	mixed
I shall…	mitt**am**	aud**iam**	cap**iam**
you (sing.) *will…*	mitt**ēs**	aud**iēs**	cap**iēs**
he/she/it will…	mitt**et**	aud**iet**	cap**iet**
we shall…	mitt**ēmus**	aud**iēmus**	cap**iēmus**
you (pl.) *will…*	mitt**ētis**	aud**iētis**	cap**iētis**
they will…	mitt**ent**	aud**ient**	cap**ient**

The 3rd, 4th and mixed conjugations are different from the first two and similar to each other: note the **e** throughout, except for the 1st person -**am**. To avoid confusing these 3rd, 4th and mixed future endings with, say, the 2nd conjugation present (**hab<u>et</u>**) you will need to know which conjugation a verb belongs to.

PRACTICE 11C

1 Write out all six persons of the following:
  i the future of **faciō,-ere**
  ii the future of **dīcō,-ere**
  iii the future of **veniō,-īre**

2 Complete each sentence with one word:
  i numquam tuōs versūs _____ (*I will hear*)!
  ii quis mē _____ (*will guard*)?
  iii mīlitēs nōn nōs _____ (*will conquer*).

The future tense of irregular verbs

Irregular verbs have broadly regular future endings with the one major exception of **sum, esse** and its compounds **possum, posse, adsum, adesse**, etc.

erō *I shall be*
eris *you* (sing.) *will be*
erit *he/she/it will be*
erimus *we shall be*
eritis *you* (pl.) *will be*
erunt *they will be*

The future of **adsum** (*I am present*) is **aderō, aderis**, etc; the future of **absum** (*I am absent*) is **aberō, aberis**, etc; and the future of **possum** (*I am able*) is **poterō, poteris**, etc.

Here are the future endings of **eō, īre** (*go*) and **volō, velle** (*want*):

eō, īre: **ībō, ībis, ībit, ībimus, ībitis, ībunt**

volō, velle: **volam, volēs, volet, volēmus, volētis, volent**

PRACTICE 11D

Complete each sentence with one word:

  i quis _____ (*will be present*)?
  ii quid facere _____ (*they will want*)?
  iii Lūcia cum mātre in raedā _____ (*will go*).
  iv quis nōs per silvam _____ (*will lead*)?

The story of Augustinus (21)

nunc in ecclēsiā abbas manūs tollēbat: 'hīc, in ecclēsiā, ubi
sedēmus, ubi ōrāmus, ubi Dominum laudāmus, est vestra
sēcūritās. hīc fidem habētis. hīc Dominus vōbīscum est et
semper erit. sī igitur mūnīmentum quaeritis, circumspicite.
ecce tēctum! ecce magnī mūrī! hīc in ecclēsiā vōs cūrāvimus,
nunc vōs cūrāmus, et post mortem animās vestrās semper
cūrābimus. centum annōs monasterium hīc stetit et hīc stābit
annōs mīlle! hīc sunt omnia tūta. quod vestrās animās illud
vestrās rēs custōdīre potest. iterum vōbīs dīcō: in ecclēsiā
sunt tūtae nōn sōlum animae sed etiam rēs. rūmōrēs enim
audīvimus quōsdam, nōn quidem cōnfirmātōs, sed tamen
referendōs. nihil nōs vīdimus. aliēnī in silvīs aderant? quis
scit? vīditne aliēnōs in silvā miser Theodōrus? quis nunc dīcere
potest? Theodōrus saltem in caelō cum angelīs requiēscit. crās
ergō, sī volētis esse sēcūrī, vestrōs bovēs ovēsque equōsque
mūlōsque in monasteriī agrōs addūcētis. sī vōbīs placēbit, etiam
pōnite rēs vestrās atque pecūniam in nostrō monasteriō. vel
autem, ut vultis, rēs vestrās tenēte apud vōs, sed cavēte.'

bombam vōcem abbātis Paulus nōn audiēbat sed faciem Lūciae
contemplābat. 'quam amābilis es,' gemuit. 'mēcum certē sēcūra
eris.' subitō Lūcia eum spectāvit surrīsitque.

tollō,-ere *raise*	tūtus,-a,-um *safe*
vester, vestra, vestrum *your* (pl.)	quod … illud *that which … that …*
sēcūritās,-tātis (f.) *security, peace of mind*	rēs here *material possessions*
mūnīmentum,-ī (n.) *protection*	nōn sōlum *not only*
quaerō,-ere *seek*	quōsdam (acc. m. pl.) *certain, unspecified*
circumspicite imperative of circumspiciō,-ere (*look around*)	quidem *indeed*
	cōnfirmātus,-a,-um *confirmed*
tēctum,-ī (n.) *ceiling*	referō, referre *report, repeat, announce*
mūrus,-ī (m.) *wall*	aliēnus,-ī (m.) *stranger*
centum *hundred*	saltem *at least*
stō,-āre, stetī *stand*	angelus,-ī (m.) *angel*
mīlle *thousand*	crās *tomorrow*

sēcūrus,-a,-um *free from care*
addūcō,-ere, addūxī *lead to, bring to*
pōnō,-ere, posuī *put, place*
atque *and*
bombus,-a,-um *droning*

contemplō,-āre,
contemplāvī *consider, gaze at*
quam *how*
amābilis,-e *lovely, attractive*
gemō,-ere, gemuī *groan, sigh*
surrīdeō,-ēre, surrīsī *smile*

3rd person pronouns: **hic, ille, is**

1st and 2nd person pronouns were introduced in Unit 6. Revisit and review these.

A number of different words act as 3rd person pronouns (*he*, *she*, *it* and *they*). As subjects they are only used for emphasis or clarification, as the pronoun is implied in the verb's ending:

quid dīc<u>it</u>?

what is <u>he/she</u> saying?

The 3rd person pronouns **hic** and **ille** are used to point people out, meaning *this man here* (**hic**) and *that man there* (**ille**); **is** is less demonstrative, meaning *this* (or *that*) *man*. All three are used to mean *he, she* or *it*, and in the plural *they*.

> **LANGUAGE TIP**
>
> It is easy to confuse the pronoun **hic** with the adverb **hīc** (*here*), especially in texts where macrons are not shown. An adverb is a word which qualifies a verb (many end *-ly* in English) or an adjective or another adverb: *he entertained us <u>lavishly</u> … he was <u>lavishly</u> rich … she walked <u>extremely</u> quickly.*

PRACTICE 11E

With the help of the Grammar tables at the end of the book identify the case and number of each underlined pronoun, and translate:

  i quis <u>eum</u> occīdere voluit?
 ii quis est <u>illa</u>?
iii vīsne <u>eam</u> vidēre?
 iv numquam <u>eōs</u> vīdī.
  v cūr <u>eum</u> tam celeriter sepeliunt?
 vi <u>ego</u> <u>illam</u> salūtābō.

All three pronouns also act as adjectives, in other words appear with and agree with nouns (**hic** = *this*, **ille** = *that*, **is** = *this* or *that*).

Identify the case, gender and number of each underlined pronominal adjective, and translate:

  i <u>ille</u> puer īgnāvus cum diabolō ambulat.

 ii suntne Dānī in <u>hāc</u> silvā?

iii <u>illa</u> virgō in ecclēsiam venit.

 iv <u>illae</u> vōcēs erant Dānōrum.

  v quis est <u>ille</u> puer quī tē spectat?

 vi cūr in <u>hōc</u> locō ades?

Reflexive pronoun **sē** and emphatic pronoun **ipse**

The pronoun **sē** has only four cases: accusative, genitive, dative and ablative. It has no nominative, for it cannot be a subject: **sē** refers to a subject already mentioned, as in *he washed <u>himself</u>*.

There are only four forms, in fact three, as the ablative and accusative are the same: **sē** (acc.), **suī** (gen.), **sibi** (dat.) and **sē** (abl.). These cases represent all three genders and both singular and plural:

> **Lūcia in aquā <u>sē</u> videt**
> *Lucia sees <u>herself</u> in the water*

> **Paulus <u>sē</u> videt**
> *Paulus sees <u>himself</u>*

> **monachī <u>sē</u> vident**
> *the monks see <u>themselves</u>*

The pronoun **ipse** is an emphatic form of **is**, usually translated as *himself*, *herself*, etc. Note the difference between an emphatic pronoun and a reflexive one: *he <u>himself</u> spoke* and *he talked to <u>himself</u>*.

PRACTICE 11G

1 **With help from the Grammar tables and from the pictures below, complete each sentence with the correct form of** ipse **or** sē, **and then translate the sentence into English:**

i _____ virgō in stāgnō natāvit.

ii mūlus _____ vidēre poterat.

2 **With the help of the same table, identify the case of each underlined pronoun, and translate:**
  i Lūcia <u>ipsa</u> cēnam parābat.
  ii Lūcia vōcem abbātis <u>ipsīus</u> audīvit.
  iii Paulus mūlum <u>sēcum</u> in silvam dūxit.
  iv Egberta Benedictum <u>sē ipsam</u> spectantem cōnspexit.

The story of Augustinus (22)

 11.02 **The abbot is still preaching, and Augustinus is still asleep.**

in ecclēsiā Paulus abbātis gravem vultum et monachōs et Augustīnum adhūc dormientem et Lūciam cum nōbilibus sedentem spectābat. abbas adhūc praedicābat:

'nōs monachī, quī in monasteriō habitāmus, nōn sōlum vītās animāsque sed etiam scientiam artēsque custōdīmus et semper custōdiēmus. Deō volente, nōs vigilantēs etiam rēs

vestrās cūrābimus. iterum dīcō vōbīs: hoc monasterium tūtum est. hīc vōbīs intrā hōs mūrōs est spēs salvātiōnis in caelō et in terrā sēcūritātis. crās igitur, sī dormīre sine cūrā vultis ...'

'dormīre?' inquit Augustīnus. 'ego certē dormīre sine cūrā volō.'

'sst.' susurrāvit Paulus. 'vīsne alium librum exscrībere? vel verbera?'

'dīc mihi: quid novī est?'

'Dānī prope monasterium vīsī sunt.'

'nōn crēdō!' inquit Augustīnus. 'cuius est ille rūmor?'

'Stephanī. fortasse enim Theodōrus ante mortem Dānōs in silvīs vīdit.' Augustīnus Paulum nōn audīvit sed Lūciam in prīmō subselliō spectābat:

'dā mī bāsia,' inquit.

'quid?'

'dā mī bāsia mīlle.'

'sssst!'

'deinde usque altera mīlle.'

'scīlicet tibi bāsia dabō nūlla,' rīdēbat Paulus.

'ēheu!' gemuit Augustīnus, 'illa tē sōlum spectat, tē sōlum amābit.'

tandem abbas praedicāre dēsiit et rediit ad āram. 'Deō grātiās,' respondērunt omnēs.

---

praedicō,-āre, praedicāvī *preach*
ars, artis (f.) *art, skill, practice*
Deō volente *with God willing*
intrā (+ acc.) *within*
salvātiō,-ōnis (f.) *salvation*
verber,-is (n. 3rd decl.) *blow* (pl.: *beating*)
dīc imperative of dīcō,-ere (like fac from faciō,-ere, it has lost the final -e)
quid novī est *what's new?, what's up?* (lit. *what of a new thing is there?*)

vīsī sunt *(they) were / have been seen*
cuius *whose*
ante (+ acc.) *before, in front of*
bāsium,-ī (n.) *kiss* (from Catullus, Poem 5)
usque *without interruption*
altera (n. pl.) *another*
sōlus,-a,-um *alone, only*
redeō,-īre, rediī *come back, return*

PRACTICE 11H

Identify the equivalent forms in the future tense of each verb:

 i praedicābat
 ii vīs
 iii audīvit
 iv rediit

Suetonius

11.03 Gaius Suetonius Tranquillus was born around AD 70 and still going possibly 60 years later and beyond. He wrote his *Lives of the Caesars* (biographies of Julius Caesar, Augustus and the following 10 emperors) in the first years of the second century AD. Biography was one of the few genres which the Romans themselves developed without an obvious Greek model. It fitted well with Roman interest in personality (for example, compare the individualized sculptured portraits of Romans with dreamy idealized images of Greeks). Another biographer, Plutarch, was in fact a Greek who wrote in Greek, but he was a near contemporary of Suetonius and was writing for a Roman readership.

Suetonius' *Lives* are hugely readable and full of insights into their subjects. The ancients considered biography as something distinct from history for it focused on the little details, on personal habits and defects, not on the great events which they believed history was made for. Now Suetonius remains along with Tacitus an important historical source for the first century AD; even if not all he says can be accepted as fact.

Suetonius was trained in the rhetorical schools, as all the writers had been, and his biographies are carefully divided into good points first, bad ones after. It is no surprise which had the lengthier treatment in the lives of emperors like Nero and Domitian. But Suetonius seems to have had no hidden purpose or sense of wrong to right. In giving us insights into each of the characters, he wanted to tell all the good stories he had heard. Strange and remarkable events are included, which for the superstitious Romans invariably carried religious significance – like this one which happened just before Augustus fought a sea-battle:

piscis ē marī exsilīvit et ad pedēs iacuit.

A fish leapt out of the sea and lay at his feet.

Life of Augustus 96

Domitian's decline into cruelty and avarice was finally brought to an end by those close to him:

tandem oppressus est amīcōrum lībertōrumque intimōrum cōnspīrātiōne, simul et uxōris.

Eventually he was done in by a conspiracy of friends, of inner-circle freedmen and even his wife as well.

Life of Domitian 14

Not all emperors grew into tyrannical psychopaths. Domitian's father, Vespasian, was a practical man with a humorous twinkle, who seemed none too bothered by his relatively humble origin. Vespasian was born in a village outside Rome, and grew up speaking the local accent. After he became emperor, an adviser by the name of Mestrius Florus tried to improve his pronunciation of 'au' (which the emperor pronounced 'ō', a sound too rural, too street-level, for Florus). The word in question was 'wagons' (from **plaustrum,-ī**):

Mestrium Flōrum cōnsulārem, admonitus ab eō plaustra potius quam plōstra dīcenda, posterō diē Flaurum salūtāvit.

*He greeted Mestrius Florus, a man of consular rank – on the day after he had been advised by him that **plaustra** rather than **plōstra** should be said – as 'Flaurus'.*

Life of Vespasian 22

Word discovery 11

1 Identify Latin ancestors in this unit of:
   i bomb
   ii creed
   iii inquire
   iv percentage
   v referendum

2 How is the Latin phrase id est commonly expressed in English, and what does it mean?

atque   *and*
centum   *hundred*
mīlle   *thousand*

quam   *how*, *as*, *than* (can also be the acc. f. sing. of the word for *who, which*)
sōlus,-a,-um   *alone, single* (neuter form sōlum is used as an adverb
                 meaning *only*)

Test yourself 11

1 Complete each sentence and then translate into English:
    i ō mūle, in silvīs umbrās _____ (*you will see*).
    ii versūsne tibi, ō domina, centum meōs _____ (*I shall recite*)?
    iii Caesar _____ (*will come*), _____ (*will see*), _____ (*will conquer*).
    iv tē numquam _____ (*I shall leave*).
    v tūne sōla mē semper _____ (*you will love*)?

2 Identify the case of each underlined word, and then translate the sentence:
    i in <u>hāc</u> culīnā tē manēre iubeō.
    ii numquam <u>illa</u> carmina audīvī.
    iii mūlus in aquā <u>sē</u> cōnspexit.
    iv hīc iacet Lūcius Agrippa urbis <u>huius</u> dux.
    v Clōdia <u>eius</u> carmina sed nōn poētam <u>ipsum</u> amat.

3 Whose poems are they?
    i Fabullus dominam amat sed nōn carmina eius.
    ii Fabullus dominam amat sed nōn carmina sua.

4 Diana was the goddess of hunting and also of which of the following ?
    a love
    b childbirth
    c health and safety

In this unit you will learn about:
- ▶ *past participles*
- ▶ *principal parts*
- ▶ *the pluperfect and future perfect tenses*
- ▶ *the ablative absolute*
- ▶ *The story of Augustinus: winter passes, summer comes*
- ▶ *Juvenal: poet*

Final word

After the fall of the Roman empire, the gap between spoken (Vulgar) and literary Latin widened. The Latin spoken in the kingdoms of fragmenting western Europe evolved under local influences into the Romance languages: Italian, French, Portuguese and Spanish. The literary language kept its Latin identity and survived for a thousand years in the churches and their schools. The liturgy and school texts were in Latin, and people wrote and sang and even joked in Latin. This language was a mixed bag, some laboured, some light and impish, some echoed the beauty of ancient models. Classical authors were the secular inspiration and classical Latin the model style. But despite recurring attempts to pull the language back to classical norms, medieval Latin inevitably reflected the wear and tear of a living language and 'failed' to live up to its past. Forms and idioms were influenced by Vulgar Latin and by the vernacular languages, and the church added a number of new words and new meanings to classical ones. Latin's role as a vocal language, apart from recitals and songs in churches, was diminishing all the time. It was a learned person's second language, largely confined to the page – but still alive.

From the seventeenth century onwards, Latin's role grew ever narrower, confined to academia and the Catholic Church. This 'dead' language offered rich pickings for scientists, lawyers and others who wanted definitive names or phrases which would be unlikely to spill into wider use and so lose their exclusive meanings. Latin was a fruitful source for botanists to name their plants, for ornithologists, for medics, for motto writers. To get into a university or become a doctor or join the ranks of the learned in just about any discipline, Latin remained a *sine qua non* until well into the twentieth century. By then other disciplines were emerging, in both humanities and sciences, and classics teachers who had never had to fight their corner started to lose students to history, English, modern languages and other disciplines.

But Latin has survived. People are pulled in, curious about its history and antiquity, its prodigious influence on English and other languages, and the world it reveals, the lives of ancients, their stories, followed by successive eras each of which in some way has adopted, reworked or translated classical models.

The influence of Latin, both written and spoken, is immense. As a dead language it still has great value; it is there for us to scrutinize on the cold slab, picking over the detail, analysing inflexions, shuffling words, exploring influence and heritage, reading historical texts. A rounded study of Latin will also pursue the living language, to recapture the moment, a language rising and falling, its songs and histories, the thoughts and feelings of peoples like our ourselves and yet different.

Past participles

Participles were introduced in Unit 9. Like the present participle, the past participle is an adjective formed from a verb. Unlike the present one, the past participle has endings like **bonus,-a,-um** (the present participle ends **-ēns**, or **-āns**), and it is passive. In other words the noun it agrees with is not the doer but the done-to:

carmen <u>audītum</u>
the (having been) <u>heard</u> poem

raeda <u>parāta</u>
the (having been) <u>prepared</u> carriage

The reason why the past participle is *past* is because by the time you read it, it has already happened (i.e. the poem in the example above has been listened to, and the carriage preparation done).

See how the past participle below (**vīsum**) has happened before the main verb (**excitāvit**), i.e. the master saw him first, and then woke him:

magister discipulum in ecclēsiā <u>vīsum</u> excitāvit
the master woke the student (having been) <u>seen</u> in the church

The present participle on the other hand may be still going on – or at least still going on as the action of the main verb unfolds:

magister discipulum in ecclēsiā <u>dormientem</u> vīdit
the master saw the student <u>sleeping</u> in the church

Principal parts

The link between past participle **vīsus,-a,-um** (*seen*) and its verb **videō,-ēre** is not immediately obvious. This is true of others too, e.g. **doctus,-a,-um** and **doceō,-ēre** (*teach*), **scissus,-a,-um** and **scindō,-ere** (*tear*). So the past participle has to be remembered in its own right, and is included in vocabulary lists as the fourth of a verb's four 'principal parts':

videō, vidēre, vīdī, <u>vīsum</u>   *see*

To know a verb is to know these four principal parts: the present (**videō**), the present infinitive (**vidēre**), the perfect (**vīdī**) and the past participle (**vīsum** – always listed in the neuter).

PRACTICE 12A

Look up these verbs in the general vocabulary at the end of the course and identify all four principal parts and the meaning of each verb:

 i amō,-āre; parō,-āre; spectō,-āre
 ii doceō,-ēre; habeō,-ēre; iubeō,-ēre; teneō,-ēre
 iii dīcō,-ere; dūcō,-ere; mittō,-ere; relinquō,-ere; scrībō,-ere; vincō, -ere
 iv audiō,-īre; custōdiō,-īre; veniō,-īre
 v capiō,-ere; faciō,-ere; fugiō,-ere

Past participles with **sum, esse**

A past participle with the verb *to be* becomes a full verb, in the past passive:

equus <u>vīsus</u> <u>est</u>
the horse <u>was seen</u> (or <u>has been seen</u>)

INSIGHT

With **est** or **sunt** the past participle creates the perfect passive and is usually translated *was …* or *has been …*, where you might expect *is …* or *are …* . There is some logic behind this. For example, **cēna est parāta** could be translated as *the dinner has been prepared* (describing the action in the past) or *the dinner is prepared –* i.e. *ready* (describing the current condition).

When used with **est** or **sunt** (or other part of **esse**) as a verb in the perfect passive, the past participle agrees with the subject, and so is always nominative (singular or plural, masculine, feminine or neuter):

<u>Lūcia</u> vīs<u>a</u> est
Lucia was / has been seen

<u>carmen</u> est audī<u>tum</u>
the poem was/ has been heard

Ā or **ab** is used with the ablative to show *by whom* something was done (called the ablative of agent).

carmen <u>ā Lūciā</u> audītum est
the poem was heard <u>by Lucia</u>

PRACTICE 12B

1 **Identify the past participle in each sentence, and then translate the sentence into English:**
   i estne ille rūmor cōnfirmātus?
   ii domina mihi dīxit manibus ēlevātīs.
   iii monachus territus ē silvā fūgit.
   iv omnēs carmen audītum laudāvērunt.
   v tunica fēminae est scissa.

2 **Complete the sentence with the correct form of** audiō,-īre:

vōx abbātis ab omnibus praeter Augustīnum _____ est.
(*was heard*)

The story of Augustinus (23)

mēnsēs lentē trānsībant. hiems erat sevērissima et frīgus monasterium invāsit. Paulus Lūciam vidēre sōlam nōn poterat, quod illa semper cum mātre ambulābat aut in ecclēsiā ōrābat. discipulus īnfēlīx per longās gelidāsque noctēs in cellā iacēbat per fenestram stellās spectāns.

mox nātālis Christī diēs ā monachīs celebrātus est. Karolus et Egberta et Lūcia ad missās audiendās advēnērunt et posteā domum cum epīscopō abbātissāque discessērunt. in monasteriō multae vīnī amphorae exhaustae, multī ānserēs dēvorātī sunt. post cēnam fābula ab Augustīnō cēterīsque discipulīs ācta est: Iōsēphus et Marīa ā tabernīs multīs reiectī stabulum inveniunt. omnēs monachī ā fābulā Augustīnī sunt exhilarātī praeter abbātem quī eam putābat esse iocōsiōrem. sīc paucōs diēs cūrae omnēs aberant.

monachī enim multōs mēnsēs anxiī fuerant, populus incertus. hominēs mediā in hieme Dānōs nōn exspectābant propter frīgus atque mare turbulentum; itaque rēs suās apud sē tenēbant. vēre tamen veniente rēs in monasterium adductae sunt. primō thēsaurus in ecclēsiā modicus erat, sed post paucōs diēs fictilia, fībulae, scūta, lintea et alia in monasterium trādita sunt; sīc thēsaurus gradātim crēscēbat.

mēnsis,-is (m.) *month*
trānseō,-īre,-īvī (-iī), trānsitum *go by, pass*
hiems, hiemis (f.) *winter*
sevērissimus,-a,-um *very severe, hard*
frīgus,-oris (n.) *cold, chill*
invādō,-ere,-vāsi,-vāsum *enter*
gelidus,-a,-um *cold*
cella,-ae (f.) *cell, room*
stella,-ae (f.) *star*
nātālis,-e *natal, of birth*
Christus,-ī (m.) *Christ*
posteā *afterwards*

discēdō,-ere, discessī *withdraw, depart*
amphora,-ae (f.) *jar, pitcher*
exhauriō,-īre, exhausī, exhaustum *drain, empty*
ānser,-is (m./f.) *goose*
dēvorō,-āre,-āvī,-ātum *consume*
agō,-ere, ēgī, āctum *do, perform*
Iōsēphus,-ī (m.) *Joseph*
Marīa,-ae (f.) *Mary*
taberna,-ae (f.) *inn*
reiciō,-ere, reiēcī, reiectum *reject, refuse*
stabulum,-ī (n.) *stable*

inveniō,-īre, invēnī, inventum   *come upon, find*

exhilarō,-āre,-āvī,-ātum   *cheer, gladden*

eam   *her* (or *it* if representing a feminine (inanimate) noun)

iocōsiōrem (acc.)   *too flippant*

paucus,-a,-um   *little, few*

paucōs diēs, multōs

mēnsēs   i.e. periods of time

fuerant   *(they) had been*

incertus,-a,-um   *uncertain*

medius,-a,-um   *mid-, middle of*

propter (+ acc.)   *because of*

mare,-is (n.)   *sea*

turbulentus,-a,-um   *stormy*

suus,-a,-um   *his, her, their own*

vēr,-is (n.)   *spring*

thēsaurus,-ī (m.)   *store*

modicus,-a,-um   *modest, small*

fictilia,-ium (n.pl.)   *earthenware*

fībula,-ae (f.)   *brooch*

scūtum,-ī (n.)   *shield*

linteum,-ī (n.)   *linen cloth*

alia (n.pl.)   *other*

trādō,-ere, trādidī, trāditum   *hand over*

gradātim   *little by little, gradually*

crēscō,-ere, crēvī, crētum   *grow*

The pluperfect tense

The pluperfect is a further step back into the past than other past tenses, always translated with *had*, e.g. *Lucia <u>had seen</u> those men before.*

The endings are the same for all verbs, added to the perfect stem. The endings are identical to the imperfect of **sum, esse:**

I had ...	amāv**eram**	vīd**eram**	fu**eram**
you (sing.) had ...	amāv**erās**	vīd**erās**	fu**erās**
he/she/it had ...	amāv**erat**	vīd**erat**	fu**erat**
we had ...	amāv**erāmus**	vīd**erāmus**	fu**erāmus**
you (pl.) had ...	amāv**erātis**	vīd**erātis**	fu**erātis**
they had ...	amāv**erant**	vīd**erant**	fu**erant**

To recognize the pluperfect you will need to know the perfect stem of a verb, which is shown as the third of the four principal parts, e.g.

mīs-eram (*I had sent*)
mittō, mittere, <u>mīs-ī</u>, missum

The pluperfect in the passive is formed by the past participle and the imperfect of **sum, esse:**

virgō in silvā <u>vīsa erat</u>
the young woman <u>had been seen</u> in the wood

The future perfect tense

The future perfect is another (and the last!) Latin tense to recognize. It imagines a point in the future when an action has been completed:

this time next week <u>you will have finished</u> this course

Like the pluperfect, it has the perfect stem, and whereas pluperfect endings are like the imperfect of **sum**, future perfect endings are the same as the future of **sum**, except **-erint** in the 3rd person plural for **erunt** (*they will be*):

I shall have ...	mīs**erō**	cēp**erō**	fu**erō**
you (sing.) will have ...	mīs**eris**	cēp**eris**	fu**eris**
he/she/it will have ...	mīs**erit**	cēp**erit**	fu**erit**
we shall have ...	mīs**erimus**	cēp**erimus**	fu**erimus**
you (pl.) will have ...	mīs**eritis**	cēp**eritis**	fu**eritis**
they will have ...	mīs**erint**	cēp**erint**	fu**erint**

The future perfect tends to appear in 'if' or 'when' clauses, and then often translated into English as if present:

sī mīlitēs <u>vīderō</u>, domum veniam

if I <u>see</u> (<u>shall have seen</u>) soldiers, I shall come home

The future perfect in the passive is formed by the past participle and the <u>future</u> of **sum, esse**:

sī liber <u>exscrīptus erit</u>, quid faciam?

if the book <u>is copied out</u> (<u>will have been</u> ...), what shall I do?

PRACTICE 12C

1 **Fill each gap with the verb in the future perfect, and translate:**
   i ego sī tuum librum _____ (legō,-ere, lēgī, lēctum), dormiam.
   ii Ricardus sī tē dormientem _____ (videō,-ēre, vīdī, vīsum), verberābit.
   iii sī illī mīlitēs magistrum _____ (capiō,-ere, cēpī, captum), quis nōs docēbit?

2 **Translate each verb into the pluperfect tense:**
   i she had slept
   ii we had guarded
   iii they had captured
   iv I had seen
   v he had beaten
   vi you (sing.) had read

The ablative absolute

This is the name of a phrase which includes a participle and appears in the ablative. An ablative absolute sits in a sentence almost detachable from it, neither subject nor object of the verb, and is often translated as a separate clause (a word-group with its own verb):

Benedictus <u>crustīs dēvorātīs</u> discessit
Benedictus <u>with the cakes having been consumed</u> departed
(Benedictus departed <u>after he had consumed the cakes</u>)

nōs omnēs <u>magistrō veniente</u> tacuimus
<u>with the master coming</u> we all hushed
<u>as the master was coming</u> we all hushed

The story of Augustinus (24)

 12.02 Summer returns, and Paulus and the mule are off again through the wood. This time they take a detour to see Lucia's home. It's hot. Paulus takes a dip in a pond.

hodiē discipulī versūs omnēs exscrīpserant et omnia studia in bibliothēcā perfecta erant. nunc aestāte veniente Paulus ad oppidum sub arborēs mūlum dūcēbat per viam īnsolitam; nam diū voluerat Lūciae vīllam vidēre. mox Paulus ē silvīs vēnit et poterat magnum castellum vidēre in quō Lūcia cum mātre Egbertā et patre Karolō, virō nōbilī, habitābat. Paulus tamen castellum adīre timuit quod sē putābat discipulum esse humilem. mūlō dīxit 'sī inierō, illa mē agnōscēs?' mūlus tamen eum nōn audīvit quod multōs mūlōs labōrantēs in agrīs prope castellum cōnspexerat. subitō mūlus rudīvit. 'ēheu, tacē!' clāmāvit Paulus habēnās rapiēns, et mūlum celeriter in silvam dūxit.

prope silvam Paulus stāgnum vīderat quod nunc adiit cum mūlō tacitō. hīc multam aquam mūlus sitiēns bibit. 'hodiē est aestuōsum!' gemuit Paulus. deinde, habēnīs mūlī arborī ligātīs, Paulus ad stāgnum revēnit et veste dēpositā in aquam frīgidam sē immersit: sub aquam natāvit et rediēns ad aequor exhālāvit. 'hīc manēre volō per tōtum diem,' suspīrāvit Paulus, et ōtiōsus in aequore innābat caelum contemplāns. nec multō post mūlum iterum rudentem audīvit. 'quid est tibi, mūle? tacē!'

perficiō,-ere, perfēcī,
    perfectum *complete*
aestās,-ātis (f.) *summer*
īnsolitus,-a,-um *unusual,*
             unfamiliar
diū *for a long time*
vīlla,-ae (f.) *villa, country-house*
in quō (abl.) *in which*
ineō, inīre, iniī *go in*
agnōscō,-ere, agnōvī,
    agnitum *recognize*
rudō,-ere, rudīvī, rudītum *bray*
taceō,-ēre, tacuī, tacitum *hush,*
              be quiet
habēna,-ae (f.) *rein*
rapiō,-ere, rapuī, raptum *snatch*
stāgnum,-ī (n.) *pond*
quod not *because* but *which*
    (referring to stāgnum)
sitiēns (like ingēns) *thirsty*

bibit present or perfect (bibō,-
    ere, bibī)
aestuōsus,-a,-um *hot*
ligō,-āre,-āvī,-ātum *tie*
reveniō,-īre, revēnī *come back*
dēpōnō,-ere, dēposuī,
    dēpositum *put down*
frīgidus,-a,-um *cool*
immergō,-ere, immersī,
    immersum *dip, immerse*
natō,-āre,-āvī,-ātum *swim*
rediēns present participle of
      redeō,-īre
aequor,-is (n.) *surface*
exhālō,-āre,-āvī,-ātum *exhale*
suspīrō,-āre,-āvī,-ātum *sigh*
ōtiōsus,-a,-um *idle*
innō,-āre,-āvī,-ātum *swim, float*
quid est tibi? *what's the matter*
          with you?

PRACTICE 12D

Identify three ablative absolutes in the story above.

Juvenal

12.03 Decimus Iunius Iuvenalis is not as widely read in schools as say
Virgil or Ovid, but a writer of unique talent and temperament all the same.
He was the last of the poets in what we broadly call the classical period.
He was a satirist, not only because he wrote 'saturae', for other Romans did
that, but he adopts a keenly critical voice of the world around him. Like
a modern satirist, he seeks to expose vice, greed and other flaws within
society.

Not much is known about his life, or when he was born or died. The
evidence shows that he wrote his Satires (16 poems) in the early part of
the second century AD, roughly when Tacitus was writing his Annals and
building work on Hadrian's Wall first started. The Roman empire was close
to its height, and Rome was the master of everywhere that most people
knew existed. Such times of overwhelming political self-belief are ripe for
writers like Tacitus and Juvenal:

difficile est saturam nōn scrībere.

It is difficult not to write satire.

Satire 1.30

The eighth Satire argues that aristocratic credentials are nothing without personal qualities. Nero was descended from emperors, Seneca was not, but …

lībera sī dentur populō suffrāgia, quis tam
perditus ut dubitet Senecam praeferre Nerōnī?

If a free vote were given to the people, who would be so depraved
*(**perditus**) as to hesitate to prefer Seneca to Nero?*

Satire 8.211–2

Satire 14 tackles a broader theme on inheritance, the vices we pick up from our parents. Juvenal raises two specific examples of bad parental influence, rather odd ones it has to be said, the first to do with the inherited habit of building lavish villas, and the other about how Jewish sons adopt their father's practice of keeping the Sabbath, not eating pork, and circumcision. It is one of the few mentions of Jewish or Christian traditions in ancient pagan literature:

Rōmānās autem solitī contemnere lēgēs
Iūdaicum ēdiscunt et servant ac metuunt iūs,
trādidit arcānō quodcumque volūmine Moyses.

*But accustomed (**solitī**) to scorn Roman laws*
*they learn by heart, keep and revere the Jewish code (**iūs**),*
*and whatever (**quodcumque**) Moses passed on in the mystic scroll.*

Satire 14.100–2

Several well-known Latin sayings come from these Satires. Satire 10 takes on the folly of ambition and the things we pray for:

ōrandum est ut sit mēns sāna in corpore sānō.

*It should be prayed that (for us) there may be (**sit:** subjunctive form of **est**,*
*after **ut**) a healthy mind in a healthy body.*

Satire 10.356

A century or so before Juvenal the people of Rome lost the right to vote for magistrates (after the autocratic government of emperors had taken over such appointments). The people, he says, are easily distracted:

(populus nunc) duās tantum rēs anxius optat, pānem et circēnsēs.

(Now the people) hope anxiously for two things only: bread and circuses.

Satire 10.80–1

Perhaps Juvenal's most famous line is in fact not universally accepted by textual scholars as his:

quis custōdiet ipsōs / custōdēs?

Who will guard the guardians themselves?

Satire 6.347–8

This is now aimed at people in authority who monitor the ethical standards of the rest of us (government, police, judiciary, etc). Juvenal himself was worried about **custōdēs** who watched a wife's bedroom to check that she did not get up to mischief with another party (or indeed with the guards themselves).

Word discovery 12

1 **Identify Latin ancestors which appear in this unit of:**
   i exhaust
   ii frigid
   iii trade

2 **Many Latin past participles have descendants in English. Can you identify from each verb (a) the past participle and (b) an English derivative from that participle (e.g.** rīdeō,-ēre **(a)** rīsum **(b)** *derision*):
   i audiō,-īre
   ii dīcō,-ere
   iii invādō,-ere
   iv narrō,-āre
   v parō,-āre
   vi salūtō,-āre
   vii scrībō,-ere
   viii stō, stāre

Test yourself 12

1 Identify the participle in each sentence and translate:
    i vīdistīne discipulum in bibliothēcā scrībentem?
    ii tōtum crustum ā coquō dēvorātum est.
    iii vīdistīne monachum in silvā occīsum?
    iv multa opera ā discipulīs perfecta sunt.
    v audīvistīne carmen ā Catullō recitātum?
    vi ancillās cēnam parantēs audīvī.

2 Identify the ablative absolute in each sentence, and translate:
    i hīs dictīs Stephanus ex ecclēsiā iit.
    ii mūlus Paulō natante rudīvit.
    iii discipulī magistrō audītō tacuērunt.
    iv Benedictus crustīs dēvorātīs vīnum dēsīderāvit.

3 **Tē moritūrī salūtāmus** means which of the following?
    a Let's hang around and greet each other
    b We who are about to die salute you
    c We are safe with you dead

The story of Augustinus (25)

 R.01 **Lucia comes across Paulus swimming in the pond. They see armed strangers approaching, and the two of them hide in the pond. You can hear a continuous reading of the whole story so far at track 14 of the audio. Thereafter the story continues at www. lingua.co.uk/latin/get-started.**

intereā Lūcia vēnātiōne fessa per silvam veniēbat sine ūllā praedā. equus eius quoque erat calidus fessusque lentusque. illa igitur in stāgnō natāre cōnstituerat et nunc per silvam stāgnum adībat. rudentem tamen mūlum audiit et 'heus, ecquis adest?' inquit. nūllō respondente ex equō dēscendit et sagittā ē pharetrā ēreptā equum lentē ad sonitum dūxit. in silvā mūlum Paulī agnōvit et arcum sagittamque manū tenēns stāgnum fūrtim adiit.

Paulus, quī mūlum ipse audierat, adhūc caelum contemplābat. subitō vōcem 'tolle manūs tuās!' audiit.

'qu... qu... quis es?' metū balbus rogāvit, 'quid vīs?'

'tūne anas?' inquit Lūcia rīdēns et cum arcū sagittāque ex arboribus vēnit.

'Lūcia! ego Paulus.'

'Paulus?'

'ita vērō. vīsne natāre? ōrō, sagittam dēpōne.'

'cūr hīc ades?'

'natāre voluī. sī tibi placet, arcum dēpōne.'

'arcum semper teneō,' respondit illa.

'tu es sagittāria?' rogāvit ille.

'sīc. et tū, quō vādis?'

'ad oppidum. in quid arcum intendis?'

'in arborem illam,' inquit Lūcia, arborem dēmōnstrāns in rīpā ulteriōre.

'illam numquam percutiēs!' Paulus rīsit. sagitta tamen
per aurās strīdēns in arborem adhaesit quam Lūcia
dēmōnstrāverat.

'est incrēdibile!' clāmāvit Paulus. 'tū vēra es vēnātrīx.
bēstiāsne trucīdās multās?'

'nōn multās,' inquit Lūcia circum stāgnum vādēns ad sagittam
recuperandam. 'hodiē tamen nihil cēpī.'

'nisi mē!' rīsit Paulus.

'nisi tē. sed bēstiās vīdī multō saeviōrēs quam tē.'

'ego bēstiās amō.'

'quid?'

'eās mihi nōn trucīdāre placet. omnēs enim vīvimus sub caelō,
hominēs bēstiaeque ...'

'ssst, quis est ille?' inquit Lūcia. 'vōcēs audīre īgnōtās possum.
ecce hominēs stāgnum adeunt cum armīs.'

'quī sunt illī?' rogāvit Paulus.

'nesciō.'

'ōcius, in aquam, ōcius!'

Lūcia sē immersit in aquam et ambō inter calamōs sē cēlāvērunt.

praeda,-ae (f.) *gain, game*	anas,-atis (f.) *duck*
eius gen. of the pronoun is, ea, id	ita vērō *indeed so, yes*
quoque *also, too*	sagittāria,-ae (f.) *archeress*
calidus,-a,-um *warm, hot*	intendō,-ere, intendī,
cōnstituō,-ere, cōnstituī,	intentum *aim*
cōnstitūtum *decide*	dēmōnstrō,-āre,-āvī,-ātum *point out*
adībat imperfect of adeō, adīre	rīpa,-ae (f.) *bank*
ecquis? *who?*	ulterior (ulteriōre: abl.) *far*
dēscendō,-ere, dēscendī,	percutiō,-ere, percussī,
dēscēnsum *get down*	percussum *strike, hit*
sagitta,-ae (f.) *arrow*	per aurās translate as singular
pharetra,-ae (f.) *quiver*	(*through the air*)
ēripiō,-ere, ēripuī, ēreptum *take*	strīdeō,-ēre, strīdī *hiss, whistle*
out, snatch	adhaereō,-ēre, adhaesī,
sonitus,-ūs (m.) *sound, noise*	adhaesum *stick*
arcus,-ūs (m.) *bow*	quam here acc. f. *which, whom* (a
fūrtim *stealthily*	few lines later *than*)
tolle imperative of tollō,-ere	incrēdibilis,-e *incredible*
balbus,-a,-um *stammering*	vēnātrīx,-īcis (f.) *huntress*

circum (+ acc.) *around*

recuperō,-āre,-āvī,-ātum *recover*

nisi *except*

multō saeviōrēs quam *much more savage than*

vīvō,-ere, vīxī, vīctum *live*

īgnōtus,-a,-um *strange*

arma,-ōrum (n.) *arms, weapons*

nesciō,-īre *do not know*

ōcius *quick!, hurry!*

ambō *both*

calamus,-ī (m.) *reed*

cēlō,-āre,-āvī,-ātum *hide*

FINAL PRACTICE

1 In the story above, identify the case of
  i vēnātiōne (line 1)
  ii respondente (line 5)
  iii manūs (line 10).

2 Identify an ablative absolute.

3 Identify a verb in each of the following:
  i imperfect
  ii perfect
  iii pluperfect

4 Identify the past participles of these verbs:
  i dēscendō,-ere
  ii doceō,-ēre
  iii dūcō,-ere
  iv incipiō,-ere
  v iubeō,-ēre
  vi mittō,-ere
  vii occīdō,-ere
  viii scindō,-ere
  ix taceō,-ēre
  x videō,-ēre

5 Identify the principal parts of a verb (appearing in this revision unit) whose past participle is an ancestor of the following. For example, *demonstration***:** dēmōnstrō,-āre, dēmōnstrāvī, <u>dēmōnstrātum</u>.
  i adhesive
  ii immersion
  iii intention
  iv percussion

6 A number of compound verbs have appeared in the course. If you know the simple forms, the meanings are often guessable (a compound verb is a verb with a word added to the front – typically a preposition). What are the simple verbs behind these compound forms? For example, absum, abesse (*be away, absent*): sum, esse (*be*). Prepositions are listed below.

   i addūcō,-ere *lead to*
  ii adeō,-īre *go to, approach*
 iii adsum, adesse *be at hand, present*
  iv dēpōnō,-ere *put down*
   v discēdō,-ere *withdraw apart, depart*
  vi ēvādō,-ere *go out, come out*
 vii incipiō,-ere[1] *take in hand, begin*
viii ineō,-īre *go in*
  ix invādō,-ere *enter*
   x inveniō,-īre *come upon, find*
  xi perficiō,-ere[1] *make thorough, complete*
 xii pervigilō,-āre *be awake throughout*
xiii reveniō,-īre *come back*
 xiv surrīdeō,-ēre[2] *smile*
  xv praepōnō,-ere *put before*
 xvi trānseō,-īre *go by, pass*

[1] The first syllable of a few simple verbs is weakened when compounded (e.g. **capiō/incipiō**).

[2] In certain combinations the prefix may change shape (**surrīdeō = subrīdeō**).

PREPOSITIONS

ā, ab (+ abl.) *by, from*
ad (+ acc.) *to, towards*
ante (+ acc.) *before, in front of*
apud (+ acc.) *at the house of*
circum (+ acc.) *about, around*
contrā (+ acc.) *against*
cum (+ abl.) *with, together with*
dē (+ abl.) *concerning, about, down (from)*
ē, ex (+ abl.) *from, out of*
in (+ abl.) *in, on*
in (+ acc.) *into, on to*

intrā (+ acc.)   *within*
iuxtā (+ acc.)   *next to*
per (+ acc.)   *through, across, along*
post (+ acc.)   *after, behind*
praeter (+ acc.)   *besides, except*
prō (+ abl.)   *in return for, in place of, on behalf of*
prope (+ acc.)   *near*
propter (+ acc.)   *because of*
sine (+ abl.)   *without*
sub (+ acc./abl.)   *beneath, under*
trāns (+ acc.)   *across, over*

7 A **popīna** was which of the following?
   a an illegitimate daughter of a pope
   b a small Romanian poppy grown for medicinal purposes
   c an ancient foodshop, a place to 'pop in' for a snack

Next steps

So far you have seen all the declensions of nouns, all regular conjugations of verbs (and many irregular ones) in the active tenses, and made inroads into the passive ones, particularly passive tenses in the past (e.g. **ductus est** = *he was led*, as opposed to **dūxit** (active) = *he led*). The active tenses you have studied here are called 'indicative', as opposed to 'subjunctive', which are a pleasure to come. The subjunctive typically deals with hypothetical and potential actions rather than actual facts. One or two subjunctives are still visible today. For example, the indicative **requiēscit** means *he/she rests*, whereas the subjunctive means *may he/she rest* (**requiēscat**). Likewise **stat** means *he/she* or *it stands*, while the subjunctive **stet** is *let it stand* (a proofreader's comment for a correction to be ignored). The subjunctive of **cavet** (*he/she is careful*) has become a noun in English (**caveat** = *may he/she be careful*).

You can pursue these topics in a number of courses in the Teach Yourself series and elsewhere. My own *Complete Latin Course* (Routledge 2014) may prove a helpful source of revision and further development. In this course you read passages selected from classical texts, which illustrate points of grammar and also tell the story of the history and culture of ancient Rome. It presents the challenge (and reward) of reading the ancient authors themselves.

In the meantime you may wish to see how things work out for **mūlus** and his friends in the continuation of The story of Augustinus at www.lingua. co.uk/latin/get-started.

As for the ancient authors introduced here, all are available in translations published by Penguin, Oxford World Classics and others. And I should say a word for those writers who have *not* appeared, such as Plautus, Terence, Lucretius, Livy, Tibullus, Propertius, Petronius and Pliny. Their details and works are only a click away in the global electronic libraries.

Congratulations for getting this far. I hope it has whet your appetite for more!

The Sound of Latin

You will find here an introduction to the pronunciation of classical Latin. You may prefer to explore the theory after some practical work listening to the audio where you can choose passages or quotations for repetition.

HOW DO WE KNOW THE SOUND OF LATIN?

A recording of Cicero making a speech or Virgil reciting his poetry would be a fine thing. The best we can do twenty centuries later is tentatively reconstruct the sound of Latin, letter by letter, syllable by syllable, from various bits and pieces of evidence. There are areas left to interpretation, but scholars have established some fairly solid foundations, particularly the sounds of individual letters. We can be reasonably confident about Latin verse, for this comes with such a tight set of conventions the instructions are almost written for you. Of course there are uncertainties and different modes of practice; but that can be said of many other languages we routinely recreate, such as Shakespearean English.

We would be hard put to identify one model pronunciation in any case. Latin was the first language of the empire of Rome, which lasted for half a millennium, and stretched from the Crimea to Spain, Edinburgh to Egypt. Latin speech habits will have varied according to period, region, social and ethnic background, as in any language.

Evidence comes in many forms: what contemporaries and later writers wrote about the language; what has survived in inscriptions or graffiti, or in puns, or habitual spelling errors; what can be deduced from transliteration into and out of Greek; what evolved in Latin's offspring languages; and, not least, the metrical framework of poetry, which tells us much about individual letters.

LONG AND SHORT VOWELS

Each of the five vowels (and **y**) has a long and a short version. Long vowels carry macrons (**ā, ē, ī, ō, ū**). You will find macrons marked in this course, but not in standard texts of Latin literature. A long vowel has a more lingering sound than a short one, not necessarily said with extra stress or weight. The length of a vowel (long or short) is called its 'quantity'.

PRONUNCIATION GUIDE

The guide here is for native speakers of English, and gives a broad description of the sound of classical Latin, composed in the first centuries BC and AD:

a	short 'a' sound, between the 'u' in _cup_ and the 'a' in _cap_; as in _ă-ha!_
ā	long as in _father_
ae	somewhere between _pine_ and _pain_; the latter was the sound in spoken Latin, certainly after the classical period and probably before it; scholars do not entirely agree over the classical sound
au	as in _house_; in speech a tendency towards Latin ō
b	as in English (bs and bt are pronounced 'ps' and 'pt')
c	as in _cat_ (not _chair_ or _ceiling_)
ch	like English 'k', with a sharper expulsion of breath
d	as in English
e	(short) as in _pet_
ē	(long) as in _pay_
ei	can be two syllables, e.g. de-ī, or a diphthong (where two vowels together create a single syllable), e.g. deinde
eu	usually two syllables, as in _meus_; in a few words, a diphthong (_heus_)
f	as in English, always soft
g	similar to a hard English 'g' (never as in _George_); in certain words less closure: a fading sound in magister, fugit, ego and others
gn	at the beginning of a word as 'n' (the g is soundless like English 'k' in _know_); in the middle of a word between _hangnail_ and _Bolognese_
h	as in English, although there was a tendency to ignore an initial h in speech
i	a short vowel, as in _lip_
ī	a long vowel, as in _keep_
i	a consonant (sometimes written as a 'j') like English 'y'
l	as in English
m	as in English at the beginning or in the middle of words; a final 'm' is a fading sound which should be pronounced with the lips open, as a nasalization of the preceding vowel
n	as in English, except below
nf	a preceding vowel is always long (_inferō_) and the n reduced to little more than a nasalization of that vowel
ng	as in _anger_ (not _banger_)
ns	a preceding vowel is always long (_insula_) and the n reduced to little more than a nasalization of that vowel
o	as in _not_
ō	as in _note_ (as pronounced by Scots and Welsh)
oe	as in _boil_ or as a Scot might say _oy!_
p	as in English but with quicker completion and less 'h'
ph	as in 'p', with a sharper expulsion of breath
qu	closer to _queen_ than _quarter_
r	trilled with the tip of the tongue
s	as in _gas_ (never voiced as in _has_)
t	as in English but with quicker completion and less 'h'

th	as in 't', with a sharper expulsion of breath
u	as in p_u_ll
ū	as in p_oo_l
ui	usually two syllables (e.g. grad_ui_, f_uī_); in a few words, a diphthong like French 'oui' (e.g. h_ui_c, c_ui_)
v	in the first century BC close to an English 'w' (Cicero, Catullus, Virgil, etc); developed to a 'v' sound in the first century AD
x	as in English
y	a short vowel as in French t_u_ (closer to 'i' towards the end of the classical period)
ȳ	a long vowel as in French s_u_r
z	as in English

For double letters extend the sound of the repeated consonant:

a_nn_us, i_ll_a, mi_tt_it, po_ss_e

SYLLABLES

You have seen how a vowel may be long or short. Confusing as it may seem at first, a syllable is also long or short. In an attempt to steer clear of this confusion, some have renamed long and short syllables as 'heavy' and 'light'. But this has not caught on, partly because these replacements suggest weight and stress, which is misleading. A better solution is to keep 'long' and 'short' syllables, and perhaps rename vowels to 'lingering' and 'rapid'. Syllable length (or quantity) is something you may wish to study more closely to understand the principles behind Latin verse – essentially an arrangement of words and their long and short syllables in metrical lines. For now you need a broad idea of it to master basic stress.

What makes a syllable 'long'?

▷ Any syllable containing a long vowel is itself long (**amāre**).

▷ A syllable with a diphthong (two vowels together creating one sound, e.g. **puell_ae_**) is long. But not all pairs of vowels are run together: these two vowels of **puellae** form _two_ syllables.

▷ A syllable is also long if a short vowel is followed by two consonants (**pue_ll_ae**), except:

 ▷ where the second consonant is **l** or **r**: the syllable may be long or short, e.g. **pa_tr_ēs** (but double letters, **ll** or **rr**, always make a syllable long);

 ▷ **qu**, **ch**, **ph**, **rh** and **th** are treated as single consonants.

▷ A syllable ending **-x** is always long (treated as 'ks').

STRESS

Latin had a stress accent similar to English: the second last (penultimate) syllable of a word is stressed if it is long:

dormíre   puéllae   dīxḗrunt

but if it is short, then the one before (third last, or antepenultimate) is stressed:

pópulus   dóminus   ómnibus   mílitēs   díxerant

A word of only two syllables will have the first syllable stressed, even if short (if lightly, e.g. **erat**).

In Latin conversation there will have been a tendency to understand the difference between, say, **dīxḗrunt** and **dīxerant** from the stress rather than the sound of the different letter.

MEDIEVAL LATIN

Different strains of pronunciation emerged in the various regions of the sub-Roman world. As early as the fifth century the **c** appears to have softened before the letters **i** or **e** (in Italy 'ch', in France 's', etc), and likewise the **g**. The diphthong **ae** was reduced and treated as a single **e**. Other changes include an 'f' sound for **ph**. For ecclesiastical Latin, see Unit 11.

Classical Latin verse used poetic metres borrowed from Greek poetry, which depended on the arrangement of long and short syllables (quantity). Virgil, Horace and other classical Latin poets were at the mature end of a process of harnessing these Greek quantities to the natural stresses of their own language.

Post-classical Latin of the spontaneous sort came to disregard long and short syllables, and in poetry quantity was ignored in favour of a rhythm of stress only (similar to that in English). There were more studied imitations of classical works, which reproduced quantitative metres, but few recovered the easy and natural interplay of quantity and stress which we hear in the rhythms of their classical models. For more on poetic metres see the online supports.

Grammar index

These grammatical terms are explained in the units as listed (R = Revision Unit). They also appear in the grammar guide in the online support: www.lingua.co.uk/latin/get-started

Grammar tables

Conjugations: active tenses

Present active

	1st	2nd	3rd	4th	Mixed
Infinitive	amāre	habēre	mittere	audīre	capere
	love	have	send	hear	take
I	amō	habeō	mittō	audiō	capiō
you (sing.)	amās	habēs	mittis	audīs	capis
he/she/it	amat	habet	mittit	audit	capit
we	amāmus	habēmus	mittimus	audīmus	capimus
you (pl.)	amātis	habētis	mittitis	audītis	capitis
they	amant	habent	mittunt	audiunt	capiunt

FUTURE ACTIVE

I	amābō	habēbō	mittam	audiam	capiam
you (sing.)	amābis	habēbis	mittēs	audiēs	capiēs
he/she/it	amābit	habēbit	mittet	audiet	capiet
we	amābimus	habēbimus	mittēmus	audiēmus	capiēmus
you (pl.)	amābitis	habēbitis	mittētis	audiētis	capiētis
they	amābunt	habēbunt	mittent	audient	capient

IMPERFECT ACTIVE

I	amābam	habēbam	mittēbam	audiēbam	capiēbam
you (sing.)	amābās	habēbās	mittēbās	audiēbās	capiēbās
he/she/it	amābat	habēbat	mittēbat	audiēbat	capiēbat
we	amābāmus	habēbāmus	mittēbāmus	audiēbāmus	capiēbāmus
you (pl.)	amābātis	habēbātis	mittēbātis	audiēbātis	capiēbātis
they	amābant	habēbant	mittēbant	audiēbant	capiēbant

PERFECT ACTIVE

I	amāvī	habuī	mīsī	audīvī[1]	cēpī
you (sing.)	amāvistī	habuistī	mīsistī	audīvistī	cēpistī
he/she/it	amāvit	habuit	mīsit	audīvit	cēpit
we	amāvimus	habuimus	mīsimus	audīvimus	cēpimus
you (pl.)	amāvistis	habuistis	mīsistis	audīvistis	cēpistis
they	amāvērunt	habuērunt	mīsērunt	audīvērunt	cēpērunt

FUTURE PERFECT ACTIVE

I	amāverō	habuerō	mīserō	audīverō[1]	cēperō
you (sing.)	amāveris	habueris	mīseris	audīveris	cēperis
he/she/it	amāverit	habuerit	mīserit	audīverit	cēperit
we	amāverimus	habuerimus	mīserimus	audīverimus	cēperimus
you (pl.)	amāveritis	habueritis	mīseritis	audīveritis	cēperitis
they	amāverint	habuerint	mīserint	audīverint	cēperint

PLUPERFECT ACTIVE

I	amāveram	habueram	mīseram	audīveram[1]	cēperam
you (sing.)	amāverās	habuerās	mīserās	audīverās	cēperās
he/she/it	amāverat	habuerat	mīserat	audīverat	cēperat
we	amāverāmus	habuerāmus	mīserāmus	audīverāmus	cēperāmus
you (pl.)	amāverātis	habuerātis	mīserātis	audīverātis	cēperātis
they	amāverant	habuerant	mīserant	audīverant	cēperant

[1] or without the 'v' throughout

IRREGULAR VERBS

	esse	posse	īre	velle
	be	be able	go	want

PRESENT

I	sum	possum	eō	volō
you (sing.)	es	potes	īs	vīs
he/she/it	est	potest	it	vult
we	sumus	possumus	īmus	volumus
you (pl.)	estis	potestis	ītis	vultis
they	sunt	possunt	eunt	volunt

FUTURE

I	erō	poterō	ībō	volam
you (sing.)	eris	poteris	ībis	volēs
he/she/it	erit	poterit	ībit	volet
we	erimus	poterimus	ībimus	volēmus
you (pl.)	eritis	poteritis	ībitis	volētis
they	erunt	poterunt	ībunt	volent

IMPERFECT

I	eram	poteram	ībam	volēbam
you (sing.)	erās	poterās	ībās	volēbās
he/she/it	erat	poterat	ībat	volēbat
we	erāmus	poterāmus	ībāmus	volēbāmus
you (pl.)	erātis	poterātis	ībātis	volēbātis
they	erant	poterant	ībant	volēbant

IRREGULAR VERBS

	esse	posse	īre	velle
	be	be able	go	want

PERFECT

I	fuī	potuī	iī (īvī)	voluī
you (sing.)	fuistī	potuistī	īstī	voluistī

etc

FUTURE PERFECT

I	fuerō	potuerō	ierō	voluerō
you (sing.)	fueris	potueris	ieris	volueris

etc

PLUPERFECT

I	fueram	potueram	ieram	volueram
you (sing.)	fuerās	potuerās	ierās	voluerās

etc

Imperatives

Singular	Plural	
amā	amāte	love!
habē	habēte	have!
mitte	mittite	send!
audī	audīte	hear!
cape	capite	take!

Participles

Present (active)	Past (passive)
amāns *loving*	amātus *loved*
habēns *having*	habitus *had, held*
mittēns *sending*	missus *sent*
audiēns *hearing*	audītus *heard*
capiēns *capturing*	captus *captured*

Gerundives

amandus,-a,-um *to-be-loved*
habendus,-a,-um *to-be-had*
mittendus,-a,-um *to-be-sent*
audiendus,-a,-um *to-be-heard*
capiendus,-a,-um *to-be-captured*

1st and 2nd declension nouns

	1st decl.	2nd decl.	
	girl	mule	wine
Sing.			
Nom.	puella (f.)	mūlus (m.)	vīnum (n.)
Voc.	puella	mūle	vīnum
Acc.	puellam	mūlum	vīnum
Gen.	puellae	mūlī	vīnī
Dat.	puellae	mūlō	vīnō
Abl.	puellā	mūlō	vīnō
Pl.			
Nom.	puellae	mūlī	vīna
Voc.	puellae	mūlī	vīna
Acc.	puellās	mūlōs	vīna
Gen.	puellārum	mūlōrum	vīnōrum
Dat.	puellīs	mūlīs	vīnīs
Abl.	puellīs	mūlīs	vīnīs

3rd declension nouns

	father	leader	maiden	wife
Sing.				
Nom.	pater (m.)	dux (m.)	virgō (f.)	uxor (f.)
Voc.	pater	dux	virgō	uxor
Acc.	patrem	ducem	virginem	uxōrem
Gen.	patris	ducis	virginis	uxōris
Dat.	patrī	ducī	virginī	uxōrī
Abl.	patre	duce	virgine	uxōre
Pl.				
Nom.	patrēs	ducēs	virginēs	uxōrēs
Voc.	patrēs	ducēs	virginēs	uxōrēs
Acc.	patrēs	ducēs	virginēs	uxōrēs
Gen.	patrum	ducum	virginum	uxōrum
Dat.	patribus	ducibus	virginibus	uxōribus
Abl.	patribus	ducibus	virginibus	uxōribus

3rd declension neuter nouns

	body	name	head
Sing.			
Nom.	corpus	nōmen	caput
Voc.	corpus	nōmen	caput
Acc.	corpus	nōmen	caput
Gen.	corporis	nōminis	capitis
Dat.	corporī	nōminī	capitī
Abl.	corpore	nōmine	capite
Pl.			
Nom.	corpora	nōmina	capita
Voc.	corpora	nōmina	capita
Acc.	corpora	nōmina	capita
Gen.	corporum	nōminum	capitum
Dat.	corporibus	nōminibus	capitibus
Abl.	corporibus	nōminibus	capitibus

4th and 5th declension nouns

	4th decl.	5th decl.
Sing.	spirit	thing, matter
Nom.	spīritus (m.)	rēs (f.)
Voc.	spīritus	rēs
Acc.	spīritum	rem
Gen.	spīritūs	reī
Dat.	spīrituī	reī
Abl.	spīritū	rē
Pl.		
Nom.	spīritūs	rēs
Voc.	spīritūs	rēs
Acc.	spīritūs	rēs
Gen.	spīrituum	rērum
Dat.	spīritibus	rēbus
Abl.	spīritibus	rēbus

Adjectives and past participles: -us, -a, -um

bonus,-a,-um *good*			
Sing.	Masculine	Feminine	Neuter
Nom.	bonus	bona	bonum
Voc.	bone	bona	bonum
Acc.	bonum	bonam	bonum
Gen.	bonī	bonae	bonī
Dat.	bonō	bonae	bonō
Abl.	bonō	bonā	bonō
Pl.			
Nom.	bonī	bonae	bona
Voc.	bonī	bonae	bona
Acc.	bonōs	bonās	bona
Gen.	bonōrum	bonārum	bonōrum
Dat.	bonīs	bonīs	bonīs
Abl.	bonīs	bonīs	bonīs

3rd declension adjectives

omnis,-e *all, every*			
Sing.	Masculine	Feminine	Neuter
Nom.	omnis	omnis	omne
Voc.	omnis	omnis	omne
Acc.	omnem	omnem	omne
Gen.	omnis	omnis	omnis
Dat.	omnī	omnī	omnī
Abl.	omnī	omnī	omnī
Pl.			
Nom.	omnēs	omnēs	omnia
Voc.	omnēs	omnēs	omnia
Acc.	omnēs	omnēs	omnia
Gen.	omnium	omnium	omnium
Dat.	omnibus	omnibus	omnibus
Abl.	omnibus	omnibus	omnibus

ingēns *huge, vast* (and all present participles)			
Sing.	Masculine	Feminine	Neuter
Nom.	ingēns	ingēns	ingēns
Voc.	ingēns	ingēns	ingēns
Acc.	ingentem	ingentem	ingēns
Gen.	ingentis	ingentis	ingentis
Dat.	ingentī	ingentī	ingentī
Abl.	ingentī	ingentī	ingentī
Pl.			
Nom.	ingentēs	ingentēs	ingentia
Voc.	ingentēs	ingentēs	ingentia
Acc.	ingentēs	ingentēs	ingentia
Gen.	ingentium	ingentium	ingentium
Dat.	ingentibus	ingentibus	ingentibus
Abl.	ingentibus	ingentibus	ingentibus

fēlix: *happy, fortunate*			
Sing.	Masculine	Feminine	Neuter
Nom.	fēlīx	fēlīx	fēlīx
Voc.	fēlīx	fēlīx	fēlīx
Acc.	fēlīcem	fēlīcem	fēlīx
Gen.	fēlīcis	fēlīcis	fēlīcis
Dat.	fēlīcī	fēlīcī	fēlīcī
Abl.	fēlīcī	fēlīcī	fēlīcī
Pl.			
Nom.	fēlīcēs	fēlīcēs	fēlīcia
Voc.	fēlīcēs	fēlīcēs	fēlīcia
Acc.	fēlīcēs	fēlīcēs	fēlīcia
Gen.	fēlīcium	fēlīcium	fēlīcium
Dat.	fēlīcibus	fēlīcibus	fēlīcibus
Abl.	fēlīcibus	fēlīcibus	fēlīcibus

Numbers

1	ūnus,-a,-um[1]	7	septem
2	duo[1]	8	octō
3	trēs, tria[1]	9	novem
4	quattuor	10	decem
5	quīnque	100	centum
6	sex	1000	mīlle

[1] variable endings as below

ūnus,-a,-um *one*			
	Masculine	Feminine	Neuter
Nom.	ūnus	ūna	ūnum
Acc.	ūnum	ūnam	ūnum
Gen.	ūnīus	ūnīus	ūnīus
Dat.	ūnī	ūnī	ūnī
Abl.	ūnō	ūnā	ūnō

The singular of these adjectives is like **ūnus**: **sōlus** (*alone, sole*); **tōtus** (*whole, entire*); **nūllus** (*none, no*); **ūllus** (*any*). They have plurals like **bonī,- ae,-a.**

duo, duae, duo *two*			
Nom.	duo	duae	duo
Acc.	duōs	duās	duo
Gen.	duōrum	duārum	duōrum
Dat.	duōbus	duābus	duōbus
Abl.	duōbus	duābus	duōbus

trēs, tria *three*			
Nom.	trēs	trēs	tria
Acc.	trēs	trēs	tria
Gen.	trium	trium	trium
Dat.	tribus	tribus	tribus
Abl.	tribus	tribus	tribus

1st and 2nd person pronouns

	I, me	you (sing.)	we, us	you (pl.)
Nom.	ego	tū	nōs	vōs
Acc.	mē	tē	nōs	vōs
Gen.	meī	tuī	nostrī/-trum	vestrī/-trum
Dat.	mihi	tibi	nōbīs	vōbīs
Abl.	mē	tē	nōbīs	vōbīs

3rd person pronouns

hic, haec, hoc *this, this man, woman, he, she, it*			
Sing.	Masculine	Feminine	Neuter
Nom.	hic	haec	hoc
Acc.	hunc	hanc	hoc
Gen.	huius	huius	huius
Dat.	huic	huic	huic
Abl.	hōc	hāc	hōc
Pl.			
Nom.	hī	hae	haec
Acc.	hōs	hās	haec
Gen.	hōrum	hārum	hōrum
Dat.	hīs	hīs	hīs
Abl.	hīs	hīs	hīs

ille, illa, illud *that, that man, woman, he, she, it*			
Sing.	Masculine	Feminine	Neuter
Nom.	ille	illa	illud
Acc.	illum	illam	illud
Gen.	illius	illius	illius
Dat.	illī	illī	illī
Abl.	illō	illā	illō
Pl.			
Nom.	illī	illae	illa
Acc.	illōs	illās	illa
Gen.	illōrum	illārum	illōrum
Dat.	illīs	illīs	illīs
Abl.	illīs	illīs	illīs

is, ea id *this, that, he, she, it*			
Sing.	Masculine	Feminine	Neuter
Nom.	is	ea	id
Acc.	eum	eam	id
Gen.	eius	eius	eius
Dat.	eī	eī	eī
Abl.	eō	eā	eō
Pl.			
Nom.	eī (iī)	eae	ea
Acc.	eōs	eās	ea
Gen.	eōrum	eārum	eōrum
Dat.	eīs (iīs)	eīs (iīs)	eīs (iīs)
Abl.	eīs (iīs)	eīs (iīs)	eīs (iīs)

ipse, ipsa, ipsum: *himself, herself, itself, themselves* (emphatic)			
Sing.	Masculine	Feminine	Neuter
Nom.	ipse	ipsa	ipsum
Acc.	ipsum	ipsam	ipsum
Gen.	ipsius	ipsius	ipsius
Dat.	ipsī	ipsī	ipsī
Abl.	ipsō	ipsā	ipsō
Pl.			
Nom.	ipsī	ipsae	ipsa
Acc.	ipsōs	ipsās	ipsa
Gen.	ipsōrum	ipsārum	ipsōrum
Dat.	ipsīs	ipsīs	ipsīs
Abl.	ipsīs	ipsīs	ipsīs

sē: *himself, herself, itself, themselves* (reflexive)	
all genders, singular and plural	
Nom.	–
Acc.	sē
Gen.	suī
Dat.	sibi
Abl.	sē

Answer key

Unit 1

The answers include macrons. It is not wrong to leave them out, as macrons are not shown in the majority of texts, but you may wish to include them all the same. Macrons are not displayed in anglicized Latin (e.g. bona fide below).

Introduction

1 (b) **2** (a) **3** (b)

Practice 1a

1 (i) noun (ii) verb (iii) verb (iv) verb **2** The/a mule watches/is watching the wood.

Practice 1b

1 as subject: he, they; as object: me, her, us **2** (i) subject noun – mule; object noun – wood; neither – silence; (ii) subject noun – huntsman; object noun – animal; neither – wood; (iii) subject noun – woman; object noun – supper; neither – friends

Practice 1c

1 a sack **2** Paulus, mūlus, silva (subject nouns); (from) Paulum, sarcinam, silvam, mūlum (object nouns) **3** silvā, Paulō **4** silvam **5** as subject: silva, Paulus; as object: sarcinam, mūlum

Practice 1d

(i) mūlus; puellam; mūlum (ii) silva; silvā; Paulum; Paulō

Practice 1e

1 (i) cēnam – The mule longs for (his) dinner. Note that for many of these verbs it does not matter whether you use the English present simple tense (longs) or present continuous (is longing); (ii) silvā – Benedictus is not in the wood. (iii) mūlum – The girl loves the mule. (iv) Paulō – Benedictus is not walking with Paulus. (v) puella – Paulus is not a girl. **2** Paulus is carrying the sack.

Word discovery 1

1 spectat (watches); portat (carries) **2** favent, sentiō, vīnō **3** (i) subaqua, aqueduct, aquatic, etc (ii) mosquito (iii) equestrian, equitation, etc

Test yourself 1

1 Benedictum, Paulum, Catullum, Fabullum **2** sarcinā – Fabullus carries the dinner in the bag. (ii) puellam – Catullus loves the girl. (iii) mūlus – Now the mule carries water in the sack. (iv) musca – In the water (there) is a fly.

(v) cēnam – The fly watches the dinner. (vi) Fabullō – Catullus is walking with Fabullus. (vii) equum – Benedictus is watching the horse. (viii) Benedictum – The mule does not like Benedictus. (ix) Benedictus – Benedictus is not in the wood. (x) puella – The girl does not love/like Catullus but Fabullus. **3** (b)

Unit 2
Practice 2a
1 The students live in the monastery. **2** equōs. **3** Verbs which end **-nt** have a plural subject.
Practice 2b
(i) mūlōs – The flies like the mules. (ii) discipulīs – Stephanus is working in the school with the students. (iii) muscās – The mules do not like the flies. (iv) monachus – Catullus is not a monk. (v) puellīs – The student does not work with the girls.
Practice 2c
1 All are in the 1st person. **2** (i) venit – The mule comes into the wood. (ii) labōrat – Paulus works with the monks. (iii) amat – Fabullus loves the girl. (iv) iacet – The monk lies on the ground. (v) dēsīderat – The mule desires water. (vi) portat – Paulus carries the dinner in a bag. **3** (i) portat – The mule carries a sack. (ii) labōrant – The horses do not work with the mules. (iii) iacent – The girls are lying on the ground. (iv) dēsīderant – The horses desire water. (v) fugit – The student is fleeing. (vi) sunt – The flies are in the water /There are flies in the water/In the water (there) are flies. **4** At a burial site (here lies …).
Practice 2d
1 Benedictus likes wine. The mule does not like woods, shadows or sacks (or, previously, horses). **2** (i) umbrae – The mule does not like the wood because in the wood (there) are shadows. (ii) labōrant – The mule does not like the horses because the horses do not work with the mule. **3** (i) monachīs; (ii) sarcinae, sunt; (iii) discipulī, habitant; (iv) amīcōs **4** (i) umbrās – The mules watch the shadows. (ii) monachīs – The students work with the monks. (iii) muscae – In the sacks (there) are flies. (iv) mūlī, equīs – The mules do not live with the horses.
Word discovery 2
1 (i) silent (ii) lēgēs (iii) populum **2** Chester, Doncaster, Gloucester, Leicester, Manchester, etc; also Caer – in Welsh (Cardiff, etc) **3** habita(n)t, intellegit, labōra(n)t, tempora, vide(n)t.
Test yourself 2
1 silent **2** (i) puellae, sunt; (ii) puellās; (iii) muscae, amant, muscās
3 (i) mūlīs – The student often walks in the wood with the mules. (ii)

monachōs – The horses do not carry the monks. (iii) muscās – The mules like neither the flies nor the shadows. (iv) aquā – There are often flies in the water. **4** (c)

Unit 3
Practice 3a
(i) nominative; the eggs are in the bag/sack (ii) accusative; Benedictus desires cakes and wine (iii) nominative; there is gold in the meadow; (iv) accusative; the horse does not like leaves; (v) accusative; the monks do not long for war.

Practice 3b
(i) Benedictō – The maids come into the kitchen with Benedictus. (ii) monasteriō – Stephanus works in the monastery. (iii) discipulīs – The girls are not with the students in the library. (iv) silvā – The mule flees out of the wood. (v) silvam – Paulus walks through the wood to(wards) the monastery. (vi) monasterium – The monks flee into the monastery.

Practice 3c
1 (for example) per (viam – accusative); ad (Paulum mūlumque – accusative); in (equō or silvā – ablative); ē (viā – ablative); ex (equō – ablative); in (terram or silvam – accusative); sine (monachō – ablative)
2 equō, terram, viā – The hooded monk falls from the horse on to the ground and lies on the road/track. **3** (i) equum – Paulus hears a horse in the wood. (ii) oppidum – Benedictus sends Paulus into the town. (iii) prātō – The horses are lying in the meadow. (iv) ōva – The monk prepares the eggs in the kitchen. (v) per – Paulus is always walking through the wood with the mule. (vi) umbrās – The mule fears the shadows but does not flee out of the wood. (vii) unguenta, vīna, oleum – Benedictus is always seeking perfumes, wines and oil, but the mule always carries them. (viii) sarcinās – The mule groans because he is carrying the sacks.

Word discovery 3
1 (i) catēnās (ii) fugā (iii) fīliae (iv) rīpās (v) vēnerant **2** ambulat, habitat, labōrat, portat **3** ablative (by way of …)

Test yourself 3
1 (i) catēnīs – The monks do not work in chains! (II) terrā – The monk lies on the ground and the horse flees out of the wood. (iii) viam – The mule walks slowly along the track. (iv) bibliothēcā, culīnā – The students work in the library and the maids work in the kitchen. (v) fīliās – Ariovistus sees his daughters. (vi) ōva – Hey! The eggs are falling out of the bag on to the ground. (vii) equō – The girl sits on the horse. (viii) aquam – Suddenly the monk falls into the water. **2** (i) equus, labōrat (ii) discipulus, sedet (iii)

muscam (iv) ōvum, iacet (v) crustum (vi) sarcinā (vii) ancilla, parat (viii) catēnam **3** (b)

Unit 4
Practice 4a
1 (i) mūlī (ii) puellae (iii) vīnī (iv) puellārum (v) silvārum (vi) mūlōrum
2 Benedictī – The students desire the wine of Benedict (Benedict's wine).
Practice 4b
1 The horse is frightened of the shadows and of the branches with their leaves rustling in the wind. **2** fēminae – genitive (sing.); folia – accusative (pl.) **3** (i) oculōs – Paulus looks at the eyes of the woman. (ii) ōvum – An egg falls onto/ into the bag. (iii) foliōrum – The student carries a sack of leaves.
Practice 4c
(i) Who is lying on the ground? (ii) What is in the bag? (iii) Does the mule love the horses? (iv) Why do the students live in the monastery? (v) Where is the wine?
Practice 4d
1 (i) Why are you walking through the wood today? (ii) The monks are in the wood. (iii) What do you desire? (iv) The mule does not live in the wood. (v) Why are you shouting? (vi) Are the mules working in the meadow? (vii) We live in the monastery. (viii) What are the maids preparing? (ix) Are you a monk? (x) Does the mule always carry perfumes? **2** ambulāre, amāre, clāmāre, dēsīderāre, equitāre, habitāre, labōrāre, parāre, portāre, rogāre, spectāre
Practice 4e
(i) Can you walk? – Yes, for sure I can walk. (ii) Where is the horse? – It is absent. Now it is present in the monastery. (iii) Can the girl breathe? – Yes, thanks to God. (iv) Why cannot the maids work in the meadow? – Because they are always working in the kitchen. (v) Can the mule carry the perfumes and the eggs and the wine? – Yes, and the woman.
Word discovery 4
1 discordia, avāritia **2** (i) praesentiam (ii) commōtus (iii) ōrātiōnem
3 fēmina, figūra, spīrāre, scissus
Test yourself 4
1 (i) habitāmus; (ii) labōrant? (iii) clāmat (iv) monachōrum (v) equitāre (vi) sarcinās (vii) fēminae, adest **2** (i) Does the mule live in the wood? – No, he does not live in the wood but in the meadow. (ii) Where is the woman? Is she present in the wood? – Yes, today she is riding in the woods wearing a hood. (iii) Do the students desire Benedictus' wine? – Yes, for sure they desire (his) wine, but I always want water. (iv) Can the cook whisper? – Alas, he cannot. The fact is he always shouts. **3** (c)

Unit 5

Practice 5a

(i) magistrō (ii) librī puerī (iii) presbyterīs, agrīs

Practice 5b

1 (i) (a) anxius (b) Paulus (ii) (a) onerōsae (b) sarcinae; (iii) (a) scissus (b) cucullus; (iv) (a) multī (b) equī **2** (i) suntne epīscopī benignī? Are the bishops kind? (ii) mūlus meās sarcinās portat. The mule carries my sacks. (iii) cūr sunt fēminae cucullātae? Why are the women in hoods? (iv) librī magnī in bibliothēcā sunt. There are great books in the monastery.

Practice 5c

(i) Surely your mule desires water? (ii) Surely the dutiful/pious maids do not desire the wine of Benedictus?

Practice 5d

1 sānctus, benignus **2** sāncta, benigna **3** No, Paulus says nothing which describes the bishop's good or kindly qualities. **4** The adjectives should end **-us** if you are male and **-a** if female.

Practice 5e

sānctī

Practice 5f

Brūte

Word discovery 5

1 (i) dea (ii) domina (iii) filia **2** mūrus, schola, umbra, vīta **3** culinary, episcopal, filial, nocturnal, obscure **4** (i) church (ii) moon (iii) mother (iv) ship (v) sun

Test yourself 5

1 (i) gulōsa, saeva, vīnolenta – The woman is not bad, she is not greedy, not cruel, not drunk with wine. (ii) multa – Friends, why does Benedictus desire many perfumes? (iii) benigna – Is your mistress kind? (iv) saevus – Is the master harsh? (v) somnulentī – Do the sleepy students love your books? (vi) tuus, meā – O monk, your book is in my bag. (vii) multī – There are many (men/people) in the fields. **2** (i) The bad students are not working. – Surely they are not bad, but tired? (ii) The bishop orders/tells the student to lead the horse. – But the nervous horse is fleeing. **3** (b)

Unit 6

Practice 6a

1 monachus dominae unguentum dat. The monk gives perfume to the lady/mistress. **2** (i) coquō (ii) equīs (iii) dominae

Practice 6b

(i) dative (plural) (ii) ablative (plural)

Practice 6c

(i) mihi – The master gives a book to me. (ii) nōbīs – The monk shows us the monastery. (iii) mēne – Does the woman love me? (iv) tibi – I am always a slave to you. (v) vōs – Maids, surely you do not love the cook? (vi) tēcum – Paulus, who is walking with you in the wood?

Practice 6d

1 1st conjugation verbs have the 'a' in the ending, 2nd conjugation ones have 'e'. **2** (i) docet – Who is teaching you? (ii) iacent – Are the students lying on the ground? (iii) iubeō – I order you to carry the bags. (iv) ancillīs – Why do you always obey the maids? (v) sedēmus – We are sitting on the ground because we are tired. (vi) vidēre – Friend, you ought to see my book.

Word discovery 6

1 mister or master **2** don **3** (i) curriculum vitae (CV) (ii) et cetera (iii) ab initio (iv) ad infinitum **4** (for example) history, fable

Test yourself 6

1 (i) Who is lying on the track/road? (ii) Who is teaching the master's son? (iii) Why do you sing of your boss? (iv) Who obeys you? (v) Is the story of battles pleasing to you? (vi) The beasts are lying in the amphitheatre. (vii) Banquets for us are always lavish! (We always have …) (viii) Is the cook ever kind to the wretched maids? (ix) Sir, you have many votes! (x) The lady never tells me to sit! **2** (i) dative – The master often gives books to friends. (ii) dative – Surely there are enough stories of beasts for you? (Surely you have enough …) (iii) genitive – Is the cruelty of the games pleasing to Romans? **3** (a)

Revision: 1–6
Practice
1

	(i)	(ii)	(iii)
Sing.			
Nom.	servus	bēstia	bellum
Voc.	serve	bēstia	bellum
Acc.	servum	bēstiam	bellum
Gen.	servī	bēstiae	bellī
Dat.	servō	bēstiae	bellō
Abl.	servō	bēstiā	bellō
Pl.			
Nom.	servī	bēstiae	bella
Voc.	servī	bēstiae	bella
Acc.	servōs	bēstiās	bella
Gen.	servōrum	bēstiārum	bellōrum
Dat.	servīs	bēstiīs	bellīs
Abl.	servīs	bēstiīs	bellīs

2

	Masculine	Feminine	Neuter
Sing.			
Nom.	grātus	grāta	grātum
Voc.	grāte	grāta	grātum
Acc.	grātum	grātam	grātum
Gen.	grātī	grātae	grātī
Dat.	grātō	grātae	grātō
Abl.	grātō	grātā	grātō
Pl.			
Nom.	grātī	grātae	grāta
Voc.	grātī	grātae	grāta
Acc.	grātōs	grātās	grāta
Gen.	grātōrum	grātārum	grātōrum
Dat.	grātīs	grātīs	grātīs
Abl.	grātīs	grātīs	grātīs

3

I	narrō	doceō
you (sing.)	narrās	docēs
he/she/it	narrat	docet
we	narrāmus	docēmus
you (pl.)	narrātis	docētis
they	narrant	docent

Word revision

1

aura,-ae	air/breeze	aurum,-ī	gold
dea,-ae	goddess	deus,-ī	god
dīcit	he/she says	dūcit	he/she leads
domina,-ae	mistress	dominus,-ī	master
filia,-ae	daughter	fīlius,-ī	son
nōs	us	vōs	you
quid?	what?	quis?	who?
venit	he/she comes	videt	he/she sees
via,-ae	way/road	vīta,-ae	life
vir,-ī	husband/man	vīrus,-ī	poison/slime
parat	he/she prepares	pāret (+ dat.)	he/she obeys

2

cantō/cantāre	I sing/to sing
clāmō/clāmāre	I shout/to shout
dō/dare	I give/to give
narrō/narrāre	I tell, narrate/to tell, narrate
putō/putāre	I think/to think
recitō/recitāre	I read aloud/to read aloud
rogō/rogāre	I ask/to ask
spīrō/spīrāre	I breathe/to breathe
susurrō/susurrāre	I whisper/to whisper
verberō/verberāre	I beat/to beat

3

dēbeō/dēbēre	I ought, owe/to owe
doceō/docēre	I teach/to teach
iaceō/iacēre	I lie/to lie
iubeō/iubēre	I order/to order
maneō/manēre	I stay, remain/to stay, remain
respondeō/respondēre	I reply/to reply
rīdeō/rīdēre	I laugh/to laugh
sedeō/sedēre	I sit/to sit
timeō/timēre	I fear/to fear
videō/vidēre	I see/to see

4

ascendit	he/she climbs
cadit	he/she falls
carpit	he/she plucks
fugit	he/she flees
gemit	he/she groans
intellegit	he/she understands
petit	he/she seeks
vādit	he/she goes
vincit	he/she conquers

5

aqua,-ae	water
avāritia,-ae	greed
catēna,-ae	chain
causa,-ae	cause, case
cēna,-ae	dinner
fābula,-ae	story
īra,-ae	anger
lūna,-ae	moon
terra,-ae	earth, ground, land

6

amīcus,-ī	friend
caballus,-ī	horse
coquus, -ī	cook
lūdus,-ī	game
mūrus,-ī	wall
oculus,-ī	eye
populus,-ī	people
servus,-ī	slave
ventus,-ī	wind

7

bellum,-ī	war
convīvium,-ī	banquet
folium,-ī	leaf
oppidum,-ī	town
prātum,-ī	meadow
proelium,-ī	battle
silentium,-ī	silence
suffrāgium,-ī	vote

8

doctus,-a,-um	learned
grātus,-a,-um	pleasing, grateful
obscūrus,-a,-um	dark
opulentus,-a,-um	rich, lavish
paucus,-a,-um	little, few
pius,-a,-um	dutiful
prīmus,-a,-um	first
saevus,-a,-um	cruel
sānctus,-a,-um	blessed
vērus,-a,-um	true, real

9

deinde	then, next
ēheu	alas
enim	for, you see, the fact is
etiam	also, even
hodiē	today
igitur	therefore, accordingly
ita	so, thus, in this way
nunc	now
semper	always
vel	or (as you like)

10 (i) vel (ii) enim (iii) ita

Unit 7
Practice 7a
1

	(i)	(ii)
Sing.		
Nom.	pater	senātor
Voc.	pater	senātor
Acc.	patrem	senātōrem
Gen.	patris	senātōris
Dat.	patrī	senātōrī
Abl.	patre	senātōre
Pl.		
Nom.	patrēs	senātōrēs
Voc.	patrēs	senātōrēs
Acc.	patrēs	senātōrēs
Gen.	patrum	senātōrum
Dat.	patribus	senātōribus
Abl.	patribus	senātōribus

2 (i) ducēs semper clāmant. (ii) mīlitēs nōn in montibus sed in urbe habitant. (iii) quis uxōrem senātōris amat?

Practice 7b
(i) dat. sing. (ii) abl. sing. (iii) nom./voc./acc. sing. n. (iv) gen. sing. m./n.; nom./voc. pl. m. (v) dat./abl. sing. all genders (vi) nom./voc./acc. pl. n. (vii) nom./abl. sing. (viii) nom./voc./acc. sing. (ix) nom./voc./acc. pl. (x) gen. pl.

Practice 7c
1 (i) 3rd decl. (ii) 1st (iii) 3rd (iv) 2nd **2** (i) gen. sing. (ii) acc. sing. (iii) abl. sing. (iv) abl. pl. **3** (for example) discipulīs, hominibus, mortālibus **4** arborēs

Practice 7d

1

	(i)	(ii)	(iii)
Sing.			
Nom.	opus	flūmen	caput
Voc.	opus	flūmen	caput
Acc.	opus	flūmen	caput
Gen.	operis	flūminis	capitis
Dat.	operī	flūminī	capitī
Abl.	opere	flūmine	capite
Pl.			
Nom.	opera	flūmina	capita
Voc.	opera	flūmina	capita
Acc.	opera	flūmina	capita
Gen.	operum	flūminum	capitum
Dat.	operibus	flūminibus	capitibus
Abl.	operibus	flūminibus	capitibus

2 (i) cūr corpus in terrā iacet? (ii) ego carmina Catullī dēsīderō. (iii) omnia capita numerāre nōn possum. (iv) scelera Catilīnae vidēre possum!

Practice 7e

1 (i) manēre – The cook orders the boy to remain in the kitchen. (ii) portāre – The maids order the boy to carry the sacks into the kitchen. (iii) labōrāre – Everyone tells the boy to work in the kitchen. (iv) parāre – Does the boy have to prepare the dinner? (v) labōrāre – Are the maids willing to work in the kitchen? (vi) sedēre – Benedictus is certainly willing to sit in the garden! (vii) adesse – The boy ought to be present in the library with the students. (viii) labōrāre – Master, all us students are willing to work in the kitchen. **2** carmen, vīs – O lady/mistress, is nothing pleasing to you? Surely you want to hear my poem?

Word discovery 7

1 bus (omnibus – for all) **2** a creative person's major work **3** custōdia, hospitibus, latet, minimae, temptābam **4** mob

Test yourself 7

1

	(i)	(ii)	(iii)
Sing.			
Nom.	māter	arbor	lēx
Voc.	māter	arbor	lēx
Acc.	mātrem	arborem	lēgem
Gen.	mātris	arboris	lēgis
Dat.	mātrī	arborī	lēgī
Abl.	mātre	arbore	lēge

Pl.			
Nom.	mātrēs	arborēs	lēgēs
Voc.	mātrēs	arborēs	lēgēs
Acc.	mātrēs	arborēs	lēgēs
Gen.	mātrum	arborum	lēgum
Dat.	mātribus	arboribus	lēgibus
Abl.	mātribus	arboribus	lēgibus

	(iv)	(v)	(vi)
Sing.			
Nom.	regiō	nōmen	corpus
Voc.	regiō	nōmen	corpus
Acc.	regiōnem	nōmen	corpus
Gen.	regiōnis	nōminis	corporis
Dat.	regiōnī	nōminī	corporī
Abl.	regiōne	nōmine	corpore
Pl.			
Nom.	regiōnēs	nōmina	corpora
Voc.	regiōnēs	nōmina	corpora
Acc.	regiōnēs	nōmina	corpora
Gen.	regiōnum	nōminum	corporum
Dat.	regiōnibus	nōminibus	corporibus
Abl.	regiōnibus	nōminibus	corporibus

2 (i) Everyone is sitting under the trees. (ii) Accordingly the monk longs for peace, the soldier for war. (iii) The young woman's songs are pleasing to everyone. (iv) Who is the goddess of love? Is it Diana? (v) The maids have many tasks. (There are many tasks for the maids …)
3 (i) possumus – We are not able to work in the kitchen. (ii) corpus, vult – Who is willing to carry the body through the wood? (iii) flūmine – Why is the master's wife sitting in the river? (iv) omnibus – For sure I work with all the slaves/serfs. (v) iubet – The cook orders the maids to prepare the banquet. (vi) dēbent – Surely the gods ought to care for all mortals? **4** (a)

Unit 8
Practice 8a
1

cadō/cadere	I fall/to fall
cognōscō/cognōscere	I learn/to learn
crēdō/crēdere (+ dat.)	I believe, trust/to believe, trust
currō/currere	I run/to run
dīcō/dīcere	I say, tell/to say, tell
dūcō/dūcere	I lead, bring/to lead, bring
gemō/gemere	I groan/to groan

mittō/mittere	I send/to send
petō/petere	I seek/to seek
relinquō/relinquere	I leave/to leave
scrībō/scrībere	I write/to write
vincō/vincere	I conquer, win/to conquer, win

2 (i) gemimus – We are always groaning. (ii) dīcis – Master, what are you saying? (iii) dūcit – Who is leading the mule into the meadow? (iv) currere – I am unable to run out of the city. (v) scrībunt – All the students are writing in the library. (vi) crēdit – Does the lady/mistress trust you?

3

aperiō/aperīre	I open/to open
audiō/audīre	I hear/to hear
dormiō/dormīre	I sleep/to sleep
sciō/scīre	I know/to know
sentiō/sentīre	I feel/to feel
sepeliō/sepelīre	I bury/to bury
veniō/venīre	I come/to come

4

capiō/capere	I capture/to capture
cōnspiciō/cōnspicere	I catch sight of/to catch sight of
faciō/facere	I make, do/to make, do
fugiō/fugere	I flee/to flee

5 (i) veniunt – All the maids are coming into the garden. (ii) facimus – What are we doing? (iii) fugis – Friend, why are you fleeing? (iv) dormit – Is the student asleep in the wood? (v) audīre – Does Lucia want to hear Catullus' poem? (vi) capit – Does Diana capture many beasts by hunting?

Practice 8b

1 (i) 3rd (ii) 1st (iii) 4th (iv) 2nd (v) M. (vi) 3rd (vii) 2nd (viii) 1st (ix) 1st (x) 3rd
2 cognōscit/cognōscunt; cūrat/cūrant; custōdit/custōdiunt; favet/favent; incipit/incipiunt; legit/legunt; praebet/praebent; salūtat/salūtant; servat/servant; vādit/vādunt

Practice 8c

1 (for example) equitāre, exscrībere, vidēre, perficere, fīnīre, scrībere, vigilāre, pervigilāre, habēre, legere, cognōscere **2** (i) 3rd (ii) 3rd (iii) M. (iv) 4th (v) 3rd (vi) 3rd (vii) 4th (viii) 1st (ix) M. (x) 1st

Practice 8d

1 (i) irreparābile – Is time irretrievable? (ii) grave, dulce – It is serious to be awake all night, but charming to be awake with you. (iii) trīstēs – Why are the boys sad? (iv) fortibus – Fortune favours the brave. (faveō,-ēre

takes an object in the dative) (v) facilia – The tasks are easy! (vi) humilēs –
What do humble men seek? **2** trīstem, dulce – Today it is not pleasing to
Augustinus to write out the grim rule(s) but to read a sweet poem aloud.
Word discovery 8
dūcō,-ere; arbor,-is; dīligō-ere; fābula,-ae; pecūnia; rēgula,-ae; relinquō,-ere;
tōtus,-a,-um
Test yourself 8
1 (i) For he who is able to carry the huge sack is not a man but a horse. –
I am not a horse, but a humble mule. (ii) Fortunate is he who sits in the
garden with the maids. – We who work in the library are unfortunate. (iii)
For sure it pleases Fortuna to be awake all night. Why is she always cruel
to me? – But surely she also favours you? (iv) There are so many words! I
am groaning! – You write therefore you groan! (v) The boy is always willing
to obey the maids but never the cook. – The maids are charming, the
cook is cruel. **2** (i) magistrī, docent – The masters teach the boys. (ii) puerī,
crēditis – Boys, do you believe/trust me? (iii) ancillae, mittunt – The maids
send the boy to the town. (iv) mīlitēs turpēs, fugiunt – The disgraceful
soldiers flee beneath the trees. (v) nōs, exscrībimus – We always copy/
write out the book. (vi) uxorēs gemunt – Why are the wives groaning? **3** (a)

Unit 9
Practice 9a
(i) amāvit (ii) laudāvērunt (iii) parāvimus
Practice 9b
(i) rīsērunt (ii) docuistī (iii) vīdit
Practice 9c
(i) duxērunt (ii) dīxit (iii) mīsimus
Practice 9d
(i) fīnīvī/fīniī (or perfēcī) (ii) dormīvit/dormiit (iii) custōdīvērunt/
custōdiērunt
Practice 9e
(i) cēpimus (ii) fēcistis (iii) fūgērunt
Practice 9f
(i) relinquit (ii) īnflammat (iii) iubet
Practice 9g
1 labōrantēs – I saw the maids (who were/as they were) working in the
kitchen. **2** (i) cadentem (ii) iacentem **3** (i) fēminās, sedentēs – The poet
loves/likes the women (who are) sitting in the carriage. (ii) hominēs,
susurrantēs – Did you hear/have you heard the men (who were)
whispering in the wood? (iii) ōva, cadentia – I saw eggs falling from

the tree. (iv) mūlīs gementibus – The slave/servant/serf is working with groaning mules/with mules who are groaning.

Practice 9h

(i) it (ii) iit/īvit (iii) abiērunt/abīvērunt (iv) abīmus (v) adītis

Word discovery 9

1 (for example) moral, paginate, insomniac **2** dormiō,-īre; iūdicium,-ī; lascīvus,-a,-um; levis,-e; vīcīnus,-a,-um **3** vādō,-ere; ambulō,-āre; eō, īre

Test yourself 9

1

	(i)	(ii)	(iii)
I	parāvī	occīdī	incēpī
you (sing.)	parāvistī	occīdistī	incēpistī
he/she/it	parāvit	occīdit	incēpit
we	parāvimus	occīdimus	incēpimus
you (pl.)	parāvistis	occīdistis	incēpistis
they	parāvērunt	occīdērunt	incēpērunt

2 (i) Why has the monk already/now fled into the wood? (ii) Who (has) heard the monk (who is) groaning? (iii) The leader came/ has come, saw/ has seen, went away/has gone away. (iv) The laughing maids (have) taught me to prepare the dinner. (v) The monks (have) told the maids to go to the cook (who is) lying on the ground. **3** (i) laudāvit – The cook (has) never praised me. (ii) rīsit – Who (has) laughed in the carriage? (iii) scrīpsistī – Did you write/Have you written all the words? (iv) relīquit – At last the woman (has) left the carriage. (v) mīsimus – We (have) sent money to you. **4** (i) amāvit, abiit, relīquit. (ii) vīcistī, fūgistī, vēnī, vīdī, rīsī. (iii) dormientī **5** (c)

Unit 10

Practice 10a

was reading – imperfect; entered – perfect

Practice 10b

(i) mittēbat (ii) capiēbant (iii) habēbāmus (iv) audiēbat

Practice 10c

1 poterat – Was the monk able to/Could the monk hear the soldiers whispering in the wood? **2** (i) erās – Paulus, where were you? (ii) amabat – The master's daughter used to love[1] me. (iii) parābāmus – We always used to prepare/were preparing[1] the dinner. (iv) dormiēbant – The students were sleeping[1]. (v) poteram – I was able to/could see Theodorus. (vi) aderat – Who was present? **3** (i) iacēbat (ii) ducēbat (iii) scrībēbam (iv) aderās (v) fugiēbat (vi) sepeliēbant.

¹ Other renderings of the imperfect tense are possible: see the guide in the unit.

Practice 10d

(i) My boss/master should be praised. (ii) My money should be guarded. (iii) The work should be completed. (iv) The poems/songs should be heard.

Practice 10e

1 festīnāte **2** (i) ō Caesar, venī, vidē, vince! (ii) ō amīcī, bibite, rīdēte, dormīte!

Practice 10f

(for example) (i) līberā, cavē, ōrā (ii) cantandum, dormienda

Practice 10g

(i) versūs – Can you hear the verses of Augustinus? (ii) manūs – The cook was stretching his hands to(wards) the wine. (iii) exercitū – Are the Danes present/here with an army? (iv) metū – We were fleeing out/because of fear. (v) cāsū, lacū – By accident/chance I saw you in the lake. (vi) strepitum gemitūsque, poterās – Were you able to/Could you hear the noise and the groans in the wood?

Word discovery 10

1 (i) dīvidendus,-a,-um/dividend (ii) propāgandus,-a,-um/propaganda (iii) addendus,-a,-um/addendum (sing.) and addenda (pl.) (iv) agendus,-a,-um/ agenda (agendum (sing.), occasional and archaic) **2** Brenda (Amanda – f. to be loved; Miranda – f. to be admired) **3** Imperative (first word of a recipe – 'take …') **4** (i) cāsus,-ūs (ii) domus,-ūs (iii) manus,-ūs **5** (for example) frustrate, juxtaposition

Test yourself 10

1 (i) erat – Who was in the lake? (ii) vādēbant – By chance Lucia and Paulus were going into the wood. (iii) portābat – Stephanus was carrying from the church the body for burial (to-be-buried). (iv) poterant – The students could hear the groans of Stephanus in the whole monastery. (v) timēbāmus – For many years we all used to be afraid of the woods out of fear of the Danes. (vi) volēbat – Oh no, Benedictus was wanting to drink all the wine alone! **2** (i) ōrō (ii) ōrā **3** (i) I never drank/have never drunk any poison! (ii) The monk sits with a sad face under the tree. (iii) O goddess, give me things to be desired/that should be desired. (iv) Why should the Danes be feared? **4** (c)

Unit 11

Practice 11a

(i) Who has faith in the soldiers? (ii) Paulus looked at the face of the young woman lying on the ground. (iii) The soldier places hope and faith in weapons. (iv) Surely we all have faith in the monks?

Practice 11b

1

	(i)	(ii)	(iii)
I	parābō	vidēbō	amābam
you (sing.)	parābis	vidēbis	amābās
he/she/it	parābit	vidēbit	amābat
we	parābimus	vidēbimus	amābāmus
you (pl.)	parābitis	vidēbitis	amābātis
they	parābunt	vidēbunt	amābant

2 (i) laudābit. (ii) iubēbō. (iii) sedēbunt.

Practice 11c

1

	(i)	(ii)	(iii)
I	faciam	dīcam	veniam
you (sing.)	faciēs	dīcēs	veniēs
he/she/it	faciet	dīcet	veniet
we	faciēmus	dīcēmus	veniēmus
you (pl.)	faciētis	dīcētis	veniētis
they	facient	dīcent	venient

2 (i) audiam! (ii) custōdiet? (iii) vincent.

Practice 11d

(i) aderit (ii) volent (iii) ībit (iv) dūcet

Practice 11e

(i) acc. sing. – Who wanted to kill him? (ii) nom. sing. – Who is she (that woman)? (iii) acc. sing. – Do you want to see her? (iv) acc. pl. – I never saw/ have never seen them. (v) acc. sing. – Why do they bury/are they burying him so quickly? (vi) nom. sing.; acc. sing. – I shall greet her (that woman).

Practice 11f

(i) nom. m. sing. – That lazy boy walks with the devil. (ii) abl. f. sing. – Are (there) Danes in this wood? (iii) nom. f. sing. – That young woman comes into the church. (iv) nom. f. pl. – Those were voices of Danes. (v) nom. m. sing. – Who is that boy who is looking at you? (vi) abl. m. sing. – Why are you present in this place?

Practice 11g

1 (i) ipsa – The young woman herself swam in the pond. (ii) sē – The mule could see himself. **2** (i) nom. – Lucia herself was preparing the dinner. (ii) gen. – Lucia heard the voice of the abbot himself. (iii) abl. – Paulus led the mule with him into the wood. (iv) acc.; acc. – Egberta caught sight of Benedictus looking at her herself.

Practice 11h
(i) praedicābit (ii) volēs (iii) audiet (iv) redībit
Word discovery 11
1 (i) bombus,-a,-um (ii) crēdō,-ere (iii) quaerō,-ere (iv) centum (v) referō,
referre **2** i.e. (that is)
Test yourself 11
1 (i) vidēbis – Mule, you will see shadows in the woods. (ii) recitābō –
Mistress, shall I recite to you my hundred verses? (iii) veniet, vidēbit,
vincet – Caesar will come, will see, will conquer. (iv) relinquam – I'll never
leave you. (v) amābis – Will you alone always love me? **2** (i) abl. – I order
you to remain in this kitchen. (ii) acc. – I (have) never heard those poems/
songs. (iii) acc. – The mule caught sight of himself in the water. (iv) gen. –
Here lies Lucius Agrippa, leader of this city. (v) gen; acc.; – Clodia loves his
poems/songs but not the poet himself. **3** (i) The lady's (ii) Fabullus' **4** (b)

Unit 12
Practice 12a
(i) amō, amāre, amāvī, amātum *love*; parō, parāre, parāvī, parātum *prepare*;
spectō, spectāre, spectāvī, spectātum *watch* (ii) doceō, docēre, docuī,
doctum *teach*; habeō, habēre, habuī, habitum *have*; iubeō, iubēre, iussī,
iussum *order, tell*; teneō, tenēre, tenuī, tentum *hold* (iii) dīcō, dīcere, dīxī,
dictum *say, tell*; dūcō, dūcere, dūxī, ductum *lead*; mittō, mittere, mīsī,
missum *send*; relinquō, relinquere, relīquī, relictum *leave, abandon*; scrībō,
scrībere, scrīpsī, scrīptum *write*; vincō, vincere, vīcī, victum *conquer* (iv)
audiō, audīre, audiī (-īvī), audītum *hear*; custōdiō, custōdīre, custōdiī (-īvī),
custōdītum *guard*; veniō, venīre, vēnī, ventum *come* (v) capiō, capere, cēpī,
captum *take, capture*; faciō, facere, fēcī, factum *make, do*; fugiō, fugere, fūgī,
fugitum *flee*
Practice 12b
1 (i) cōnfirmātus – Was that rumour/has that rumour been confirmed?
(ii) ēlevātīs – The lady/mistress spoke to me with her hands raised. (iii)
territus – The terrified monk fled out of the wood. (iv) audītum – After they
had heard the poem/song, everyone praised it. (v) scissa – The woman's
tunic was/has been torn. **2** audīta
Practice 12c
1 (i) lēgerō – If I read your book, I shall sleep. (ii) vīderit – If Ricardus sees you
sleeping, he will beat you. (iii) cēperint – If those soldiers capture the master/
teacher, who will teach us? **2** (i) dormīverat/dormierat (ii) custōdīverāmus/
custōdierāmus (iii) cēperant (iv) vīderam (v) verberāverat (vi) lēgerās

Practice 12d

aestāte veniente; habēnīs … ligātīs; veste dēpositā

Word discovery 12

1 (i) exhauriō,-īre, exhausī, exhaustum (ii) frīgidus,-a,-um (iii) trādō,-ere, trādidī, trāditum **2** (i) audītum/audition (for some there are a number of derived words) (ii) dictum/diction (iii) invāsum/invasion (iv) narrātum/narration (v) parātum/preparation (vi) salūtātum/salutation (vii) scrīptum/description (viii) statum/station

Test yourself 12

1 (i) scrībentem – Did you see/Have you seen the student writing in the library? (ii) dēvorātum – The entire cake was/has been devoured by the cook. (iii) occīsum – Did you see/Have you seen the monk (who was) killed in the wood? (iv) perfecta – Many tasks were/have been completed by the students. (v) recitātum – Did you hear/Have you heard the poem recited by Catullus? (vi) parantēs – I (have) heard the maids preparing the dinner. **2** (i) hīs dictīs – With these things said (having said this) Stephanus went from the church. (ii) Paulō natante – The mule brayed as/while Paulus was swimming. (iii) magistrō audītō – The students hushed with the master having been heard (after the master had been heard/after hearing the master). (iv) crustīs dēvorātīs – After the cakes had been devoured (After he had devoured/After devouring the cakes) Benedictus desired wine. **3** (b)

Revision: 7–12

Final Practice

1 (i) abl. (ii) abl. (iii) acc. **2** (for example) nūllō respondente, sagittā (ē pharetrā) ēreptā **3** (for example) (i) veniēbat, adībat (ii) audiit, susurrāvit, dēscendit, dūxit, agnōvit (iii) fuerat, cōnstituerat **4** (i) dēscēnsus,-a,-um (ii) doctus,-a,-um (iii) ductus,-a,-um (iv) inceptus,-a,-um (v) iussus,-a,-um (vi) missus,-a,-um (vii) occīsus,-a,-um (viii) scissus,-a,-um (ix) tacitus,-a,-um (x) vīsus,-a,-um **5** (i) adhaereō,-ēre, adhaesī, adhaesum *stick* (ii) immergō,-ere, immersī, immersum *dip, immerse* (iii) intendō,-ere, intendī, intentum *aim* (iv) percutiō,-ere, percussī, percussum *strike, hit* **6** (i) dūcō,-ere *lead* (ii) eō, īre *go* (iii) sum, esse *be* (iv) pōnō,-ere *put, place* (v) cēdō,-ere *withdraw* (vi) vādō,-ere *go* (vii) capiō,-ere *take, capture* (viii) eō, īre *go* (ix) vādō,-ere *go* (x) veniō,-īre *come* (xi) faciō,-ere *make, do* (xii) vigilō,-āre *be awake* (xiii) veniō,-īre *come* (xiv) rīdeō,-ēre *laugh* (xv) pōnō,-ere *put, place* (xvi) eō, īre *go* **7** (c)

Latin–English vocabulary

ā, ab (+ abl.) *by, from*
abbas,-ātis (m.) *abbot*
abbātissa,-ae (f.) *abbess*
abeō,-īre,-iī (-īvī),-itum *go away*
absum, abesse, āfuī *be away, absent*
ad (+ acc.) *to, towards, at*
addō,-ere, addidī, additum *add*
addūcō,-ere, addūxī, adductum *lead to, bring to*
adeō,-īre,-iī,-itum *go to, approach*
adhaereō,-ēre,-haesī,-haesum *stick*
adhūc *still, as yet*
adiuvō,-āre, adiūvī *help, assist*
adsum, adesse, affuī *be at hand, be present*
aequor,-oris (n.) *surface, sea*
aestās,-ātis (f.) *summer*
aestuōsus,-a,-um *hot*
ager, agrī (m.) *field*
agnōscō,-ere, agnōvī, agnitum *recognize*
agō,-ere, ēgī, āctum *do, perform*
albus,-a,-um *white*
aliēnus,-ī (m.) *stranger*
alius, alia, aliud *other, another*
allegoria,-ae (f.) *allegory*
alter,-era,-erum *one/other of two, another, the next*
amābilis,-e *lovely, attractive*
ambō *both*
ambulō,-āre,-āvī,-ātum *walk*
amīca,-ae (f.) *friend, girlfriend*
amīcus,-ī (m.) *friend*
amō,-āre,-āvī,-ātum *love, like*
amor,-ōris (m.) *love, passion*
amphitheātrum,-ī (n.) *amphitheatre*

amphora,-ae (f.) *jar, pitcher*
anas,-atis (f.) *duck*
ancilla,-ae (f.) *maidservant*
angelus,-ī (m.) *angel*
anima,-ae (f.) *soul*
annus,-ī (m.) *year*
ānser,-eris (m./f.) *goose*
ante (+ acc.) *before, in front of*
anxius,-a,-um *anxious, uneasy*
aperiō, -īre, aperuī, apertum *open*
aptus,-a,-um *suitable, proper*
apud (+ acc.) *at the house of*
aqua,-ae (f.) *water*
āra,-ae (f.) *altar*
arbor,-oris (f.) *tree*
arcus,-ūs (m.) *bow*
arma,-ōrum (n.) *arms, weapons*
ars, artis (f.) *art, skill, practice*
ascendō,-ere, ascendī, ascēnsum *climb on to, go up*
āter, ātra, ātrum *black, gloomy*
atque *and*
audiō,-īre, audīvī (-iī), audītum *hear*
audītor,-ōris (m.) *hearer, pupil*
aura,-ae (f.) *air, breeze*
aurum,-ī (n.) *gold*
aut *or*
autem *indeed, but, yet*
avāritia,-ae (f.) *greed*

balbus,-a,-um *stammering*
bāsium,-ī (n.) *kiss*
Bellōna,-ae (f.) *Bellona (spirit of war)*
bellum,-ī (n.) *war*
bene *fine, well*
Benedictus,-ī (m.) *Benedictus*

benignus,-a,-um *kind*
bēstia,-ae (f.) *beast*
bibliothēca,-ae (f.) *library*
bibō,-ere, bibī *drink*
bombus,-a,-um *droning*
bonus,-a,-um *good*
bōs, bovis (m./f.) *ox*
brevis,-e *brief, short*

caballus,-ī (m.) *horse*
cadō,-ere, cecidī, cāsum *fall, fall down*
caelum,-ī (n.) *heaven, sky*
calamus,-ī (m.) *reed*
calidus,-a,-um *warm, hot*
campana,-ae (f.) *bell*
candēla,-ae (f.) *candle*
candidus,-a,-um *bright, radiant*
canis,-is (m./f.) *dog*
cantō,-āre,-āvī,-ātum *sing*
capiō,-ere, cēpī, captum *take, capture*
captō,-āre,-āvī,-ātum *chase*
caput, capitis (n.) *head*
carmen,-inis (n.) *poem, song* **carpō,-ere, carpsī, carptum** *pluck*
cārus,-a,-um *dear*
castellum,-ī (n.) *castle*
castitās,-tātis (f.) *chastity*
cāsus,-ūs (m.) *accident, chance*
catēna,-ae (f.) *chain*
Catullus,-ī (m.) *Catullus*
causa,-ae (f.) *case, cause*
caveō,-ēre, cāvī, cautum *be careful, wary*
cēdō,-ere, cessī, cessum *give way, go, submit*
celebrō,-āre,-āvī,-ātum *celebrate*
celeriter *quickly*
cella,-ae (f.) *cell, room*
cēlō,-āre,-āvī,-ātum *hide*
cēna,-ae (f.) *dinner*
cēnō,-āre,-āvī,-ātum *dine*
centum *hundred*
certē *certainly, for sure*
cēterus,-a,-um *the other, remaining*

chorus,-ī (m.) *choir*
Christiānus,-a,-um *Christian*
Christus,-ī (m.) *Christ*
circum (+ acc.) *about, around*
circumspiciō,-ere,-spexī,-spectum *look around*
cīvīlis,-e *civil*
clāmō,-āre,-āvī,-ātum *shout, cry*
clāmor,-ōris (m.) *shout, cry*
claudō,-ere, clausī, clausum *shut, close*
cōgitō,-āre,-āvī,-ātum *think, ponder, reflect*
cognōscō,-ere, cognōvī, cognitum *learn, become familiar with*
comes,-itis (m./f.) *companion* (class.); *count* (med.)
comitissa,-ae (f.) *countess*
computō,-āre,-āvī,-ātum *reckon, sum up*
cōnfirmō,-āre,-āvī,-ātum *confirm, establish*
coniūnx, coniugis (m./f.) *husband, wife, spouse*
cōnspiciō,-ere,-spexī,-spectum *catch sight of, perceive*
cōnstituō,-ere, cōnstituī, cōnstitūtum *decide*
cōnsul,-is (m.) *consul*
contemplō,-āre,-āvī,-ātum *consider, gaze at*
contentiō,-ōnis (f.) *dispute, controversy*
contrā (+ acc.) *against*
convalēscō,-ere *recover, regain health*
convīvium,-ī (n.) *banquet*
coquus,-ī (m.) *cook*
cor, cordis (n.) *heart*
Corinthiī,-ōrum (m.) *Corinthians*
corpus,-oris (n.) *body*
crās *tomorrow*
creātor,-ōris (m.) *creator*
crēdō,-ere, crēdidī, crēditum (+ dat.) *believe, trust*
crēdulus (+ dat.) *trusting*

crepitō,-āre *rustle, creak*
crēscō,-ere, crēvī, crētum *grow*
crūdēlis,-e *cruel, unfeeling*
crustum,-ī (n.) *cake, pastry*
cucullātus,-a,-um *hooded*
cucullus,-ī (m.) *hood*
culīna,-ae (f.) *kitchen*
cum (+ abl.) *with, together with*
Cupīdō,-inis (m.) *Cupid*
cupiō,-ere, cupīvī (-iī), cupītum
desire, want
cūr? *why?*
cūra,-ae (f.) *care, anxiety*
cūrō,-āre,-āvī,-ātum *care for*
curriculum,-ī (n.) *(race)course, career*
currō,-ere, cucurrī, cursum *run*
custōdia,-ae (f.) *protection, guard*
custōdiō,-īre,-īvī (-iī),-ītum *guard*
custōs,-ōdis (m./f.) *guard*

Dānus,-ī (m.) *Dane, Scandinavian*
dē (+ abl.) *concerning, about, down*
(from)
dea,-ae (f.) *goddess*
dēbeō,-ēre,-uī, dēbitum *ought, owe*
decem *ten*
dēclīnō,-āre,-āvī,-ātum *bend from,*
swerve
dēiciō,-ere, dēiēcī, dēiectum *lower,*
cast down
deinde *then, next*
dēmittō,-ere, dēmīsī, dēmissum *lower,*
let down
dēmōnstrō,-āre,-āvī,-ātum *point out*
dēpōnō,-ere, dēposuī, dēpositum *put*
down
dēscendō,-ere, dēscendī, dēscēnsum
get down, go down
dēsīderō,-āre,-āvī,-ātum *desire, long for*
dēsinō,-ere, dēsiī *stop*
deus,-ī (m.) *god*
dēvorō,-āre,-āvī,-ātum *consume,*
devour

diabolus,-ī (m.) *devil*
dīcō,-ere, dīxī, dictum *say, tell*
diēs, diēī (m./f.) *day*
difficilis,-e *difficult*
dīligenter *attentively*
dīligō,-ere, dīlēxī, dīlēctum *esteem,*
value, love
discēdō,-ere, discessī, discessum
depart
discipulus,-ī (m.) *student*
discordia,-ae (f.) *discord*
diū *for a long time*
dīvidō,-ere, dīvīsī, dīvīsum *distribute,*
divide, part
dō, dare, dedī, datum *give*
doceō,-ēre,-uī, doctum *teach*
doctus,-a,-um *learned, educated*
dolus,-ī (m.) *deceit, trick*
domina,-ae (f.) *lady, mistress*
dominus,-ī (m.) *boss, lord, master*
domus,-ūs (f.) *house, home*
dormiō,-īre, dormīvī (-iī), dormītum
sleep
dubitō,-āre,-āvī,-ātum *hesitate, doubt*
dūcō,-ere, dūxī, ductum *lead, bring*
dulcis,-e *sweet, charming*
dux, ducis (m.) *leader*

ē, ex (+ abl.) *from, out of*
ēbrius,-a,-um *drunk, sated*
ecce *see here, behold*
ecclēsia,-ae (f.) *church*
ecquis? *who?*
ego *I*
ēheu *oh no!, oh dear!, alas!*
eho *eh, indeed*
ēlevātus,-a-um *raised*
enim *for, indeed, you see, the fact is*
eō, īre, iī (īvī), itum *go*
epīscopus,-ī (m.) *bishop*
epistula,-ae (f.) *letter*
equitō,-āre,-āvī,-ātum
ride

equus,-ī (m.) *horse*
ergō *so, accordingly, therefore*
ēripiō,-ere, ēripuī, ēreptum *take out, snatch*
et *and*
et ... et *both ... and*
etiam *also, even*
ēvādō,-ere, ēvāsī, ēvāsum *go out, come out, escape*
ēvānēscō,-ere, ēvānuī *vanish, disappear*
ex (+ abl.) *from, out of*
excitō,-āre,-āvī,-ātum *arouse, wake,*
exemplum,-ī (n.) *example, model*
exerceō,-ēre,-uī, exercitum *keep busy, practise*
exercitus,-ūs (m.) *army*
exhālō,-āre,-āvī,-ātum *exhale*
exhauriō,-īre,-hausī,-haustum *drain, empty*
exhilarō,-āre,-āvī,-ātum *cheer, gladden*
exiguus,-a,-um *slender, small*
exscrībō,-ere,-scrīpsī,-scrīptum *write out, copy*
exsequiae,-ārum (f.) *funeral*
exspectō,-āre,-āvī,-ātum *wait for*

fābula,-ae (f.) *story, play*
Fabullus,-ī (m.) *Fabullus*
faciēs, faciēī (f.) *face, shape, appearance*
facilis,-e *easy*
faciō,-ere, fēcī, factum *do, make*
fāma,-ae (f.) *rumour, common talk, reputation*
famulus,-ī (m.) *attendant, servant*
faveō,-ēre, fāvī, fautum (+ dat.) *favour, support*
fēlīx *happy, fortunate, successful*
fēmina,-ae (f.) *woman*
fenestra,-ae (f.) *window*
fessus,-a,-um *tired*
festīnō,-āre,-āvī,-ātum *hurry, hasten*
fībula,-ae (f.) *brooch, clasp, pin*
fictilia,-ium (n.) *earthenware*

fidēs, fideī (f.) *faith, trust, confidence*
figūra,-ae (f.) *shape, sketch*
fīlia,-ae (f.) *daughter*
fīlius,-ī (m.) *son*
fīniō,-īre, fīnīvī (-iī), fīnītum *finish, end*
flōs,-ōris (m.) *flower*
flūmen,-inis (n.) *river*
folium,-ī (n.) *leaf*
forās *out of doors*
fortasse *perhaps, possibly, probably*
fortis,-e *brave, strong*
fortuītus,-a,-um *accidental*
fortūna,-ae (f.) *fortune*
frīgidus,-a,-um *cool*
frīgus,-oris (n.) *cold, chill*
frūstrā *in vain, to no purpose*
fugāx *fleeing*
fugiō,-ere, fūgī, fugitum *flee, escape*
fundō,-ere, fūdī, fūsum *pour*
fūrtim *stealthily*
furtum,-ī (n.) *theft*

gelidus,-a,-um *cold*
gemitus,-ūs (m.) *groan*
gemō,-ere, gemuī, gemitum *groan, sigh*
gena,-ae (f.) *cheek*
gradātim *little by little, gradually*
gradus,-ūs (m.) *step*
grātiās (agō) (+ dat.) *(I give) thanks*
grātus,-a,-um *pleasing, grateful*
gravis,-e *heavy, serious*
gulōsus,-a,-um *greedy*

habēna,-ae (f.) *rein*
habeō,-ēre,-uī, habitum *have, hold, consider*
habitō,-āre,-āvī,-ātum *live*
heu *oh!, oh no! oh dear*
heus! *hey!*
hīc *here*
hic, haec, hoc *he, she, this*
hiems, hiemis (f.) *winter*

historia,-ae (f.) *story, history*
hodiē *today*
homō, hominis (m.) *man, person*
honōrō,-āre,-āvī,-ātum *honour, adorn*
horrendus,-a,-um *dreadful*
hortus,-ī (m.) *garden*
hospes,-itis (m.) *host, guest*
humilis,-e *humble, insignificant*

iaceō,-ēre,-uī, iacitum *lie*
iam *now, already*
iānua,-ae (f.) *door, entrance*
Iēsus (m.; voc.: **Iēsū**; acc.: **Iēsum**) *Jesus*
igitur *therefore*
īgnāvus,-a,-um *lazy*
īgnōscō,-ere, īgnōvī, īgnōtum (+ dat.) *forgive, excuse*
īgnōtus,-a,-um *unfamiliar, strange*
ille, illa, illud *he, she, that*
immergō,-ere,-ersī,-ersum *dip, immerse*
immortālis,-e *immortal*
immōtus,-a,-um *unmoved, motionless, still*
in (+ abl.) *in, on*
in (+ acc.) *into, on to, against*
incendium,-ī (n.) *fire*
incēnsum,-ī (n.) *incense*
incertus,-a,-um *uncertain*
incipiō,-ere,-cēpī,-ceptum *begin*
incrēdibilis,-e *incredible*
inde *then, from then on, from that place*
indūcō,-ere,-dūxī,-ductum *lead in, into*
ineō,-īre,-iī (-īvī),-itum *go in*
ineptus,-a,-um *foolish*
īnfēlīx *unfortunate*
īnfīnītus,-a,-um *unbounded, endless*
īnfirmus,-a,-um *sick*
īnflammō,-āre,-āvī,-ātum *inflame*
ingenium,-ī (n.) *nature, disposition*
ingēns *huge*
inimīcus,-a,-um *hostile*
inimīcus,-ī (m.) *enemy*

initium,-ī (n.) *beginning*
iniūria,-ae (f.) *harm*
innō,-āre,-āvī,-ātum *swim, float*
inquit *(he/she) says, said*
īnsolentissimus,-a,-um *very/most insolent*
īnsolitus,-a,-um *unusual, unfamiliar*
intellegō,-ere,-lēxī,-lēctum *understand*
intendō,-ere, intendī, intentum *aim*
inter (+ acc.) *among, between*
intereā *meanwhile*
intrā (+ acc.) *within*
invādō,-ere,-vāsi,-vāsum *enter*
inveniō,-īre,-vēnī,-ventum *come upon, find*
invidia,-ae (f.) *grudge, jealousy*
iō! *hurrah!, yes!, oh!*
iocōsus,-a,-um *having a laugh, full of jokes*
Iōsēphus,-ī (m.) *Joseph*
ipse, ipsa, ipsum *(my/your/him/her/it) self*
īra,-ae (f.) *anger*
irreparābilis,-e *irretrievable*
is, ea, id *he, she, it, this, that*
ita *thus, so, in this way, in such a way*
itaque *and so, therefore*
iterum *again*
iubeō,-ēre, iussī, iussum *order, tell*
iūcundus,-a,-um *delightful, enjoyable*
iūdicium,-ī (n.) *judgment*
iūs, iūris (n.) *right, justice*
iuxtā (+ acc.) *next to*

Karolus,-ī (m.) *Charles*
Katharīna,-ae (f.) *Katharine*

labor, labōris (m.) *toil, work*
labōrō,-āre,-āvī,-ātum *work*
lacrima,-ae (f.) *tear*
lacus,-ūs (m.) *lake*
lascīvē *wantonly*

lascīvus,-a,-um *playful, wanton, lewd*
laudō,-āre,-āvī,-ātum *praise*
Lazarus,-ī (m.) *Lazarus*
legiō,-iōnis (f.) *legion*
legō,-ere, lēgī, lēctum *read*
lentē *slowly*
lentus,-a,-um *slow*
levis,-e *light, unimportant*
lēx, lēgis (f.) *law*
liber, librī (m.) *book*
Līber,-erī (m.) *Bacchus*
līber,-era,-erum *free*
līberō,-āre,-āvī,-ātum *free, deliver*
lībertās,-tātis (f.) *freedom*
lībertus,-ī (m.) *freedman*
libīdō,-inis (f.) *desire, lust*
ligō,-āre,-āvī,-ātum *tie*
linteum,-ī (n.) *linen cloth*
locus,-ī (m.) *place*
longē *far, distant*
lūdus,-ī (m.) *game*
(pl. *public games, shows*)
lūna,-ae (f.) *moon*
lūx, lūcis (f.) *light, daylight*

magister,-trī (m.) *master, teacher*
magnus,-a,-um *great, large*
maledīcō,-ere,-dīxī,-dictum (+ dat.)
abuse, slander
malus,-a,-um *bad*
maneō,-ēre, mānsī, mānsum *remain, stay*
manus,-ūs (f.) *hand*
mare,-is (n.) *sea*
Marīa,-ae (f.) *Mary*
Martiālis,-is (m.) *Martial*
māter,-tris (f.) *mother*
medius,-a,-um *mid-, middle of*
meherclē *by Hercules! heavens!*
mēns, mentis (f.) *mind*
mēnsa,-ae (f.) *table*
mēnsis,-is (m.) *month*
merīdiēs,-ēī (m.) *midday*

metuō,-ere, metuī *fear*
metus,-ūs (m.) *fear*
meus,-a,-um *my*
mīles, mīlitis (m.) *soldier*
mīlle *thousand*
mīrābilis,-e *wonderful, extraordinary*
miser,-era,-erum *wretched*
miseria,-ae (f.) *distress, suffering*
misericordia,-ae (f.) *pity, mercy*
missa,-ae (f.) *mass*
mittō,-ere, mīsī, missum *send*
modicus,-a,-um *modest, small*
modo … modo *one minute … the next*
molestus,-a,-um *troublesome*
mollis,-e *soft*
monachus,-ī (m.) *monk*
monasterium,-ī (n.) *monastery*
mōns, montis (m.) *mountain*
mors, mortis (f.) *death*
mortālis,-e *mortal*
mortuus,-a,-um *dead*
mōs, mōris (m.) *habit, custom, manner*
mox *soon, presently*
multus,-a,-um *much, many*
mūlus,-ī (m.) *mule*
mūnīmentum,-ī (n.) *protection*
mūrus,-ī (m.) *wall*
musca,-ae (f.) *fly*

nam *for, in fact*
narrō,-āre,-āvī,-ātum *tell, narrate*
nātālis,-e *natal, of birth*
natō,-āre,-āvī,-ātum *swim*
nausea,-ae (f.) *sickness*
neque (nec) *and … not, but … not*
neque (nec) … neque (nec) *neither … nor*
nesciō,-īre,-īvī (-iī), nescītum *not to know, be ignorant*
nihil, nīl *nothing*
nisi *unless, except*
nōbilis,-e *noble*
nōmen,-inis (n.) *name*

nōn *not*
nōndum *not yet*
nōnne *surely*
nōs *we/us*
noster, nostra, nostrum *our*
novus,-a,-um *new*
nox, noctis (f.) *night*
nūdus,-a,-um *naked*
nūgae,-ārum (f.) *trifles, nonsense*
nūllus,-a,-um *no, not any*
num *surely ... not*
numerō,- āre,-āvī,-ātum *count*
numquam *never*
nunc *now*

obdormiō,-īre,-īvī (-iī), obdormītum *fall asleep*
obscūrus,-a,-um *dark*
observō,-āre,-āvī,-ātum *observe, honour*
occīdō,-ere, occīdī, occīsum *kill*
ōcius *more quickly*
oculus,-ī (m.) *eye*
odōrō,-āre,-āvī,-ātum *give a fragrance to*
oleum,-ī (n.) *oil*
ōlim *once (upon a time)*
omnis,-e *all, every*
onerōsus,-a,-um *heavy, burdensome*
operiō,-īre, operuī, opertum *cover, close, hide*
oppidum,-ī (n.) *town*
optō,-āre,-āvī,-ātum *choose, desire*
opulentus,-a,-um *rich, lavish*
opus, operis (n.) *work, task*
ōrātiō,-ōnis (f.) *speech, language*
ōrātor,-ōris (m.) *speaker*
ōrō,-āre,-āvī,-ātum *plead, beg* (class.), *pray* (med.)
ostentō,-āre,-āvī,-ātum *show (off)*
ōtiōsus,-a,-um *idle*
ovis, ovis (f.) *sheep*
ōvum,-ī (n.) *egg*

pāgānus,-ī (m.) *countryman* (class.), *pagan* (med.)
pānis, pānis (m.) *bread*
pāreō,-ēre, pāruī, pāritum (+ dat.) *obey*
parō,-āre,-āvī,-ātum *prepare*
pater, patris (m.) *father*
paucus,-a,-um *little, few*
Paulus,-ī (m.) *Paul*
pāgina,-ae (f.) *leaf, page*
pāx, pācis (f.) *peace*
peccātor,-ōris (m.) *sinner, wrongdoer*
peccō,-āre,-āvī,-ātum *do wrong*
pecūnia,-ae (f.) *money*
per (+ acc.) *through, across, along, by means of*
percutiō,-ere, percussī, percussum *strike, hit*
pereō,-īre, periī (-īvī), peritum *pass away, perish*
perficiō,-ere, perfēcī, perfectum *complete, finish*
perpetuus,-a,-um *unending*
pervigilō,-āre *be awake throughout*
pēs, pedis (m.) *foot*
petō,-ere, petīvī (-iī), petītum *seek, ask, attack*
Petrus,-ī (m.) *Peter*
pharetra,-ae (f.) *quiver*
philosophus,-ī (m.) *philosopher*
piscis,-is (m.) *fish*
pius,-a,-um *pious, dutiful*
placet (+ dat.) *it pleases*
pluvia,-ae (f.) *rain*
poena,-ae (f.) *punishment, penalty*
poēta,-ae (m.) *poet*
pompa,-ae (f.) *procession*
pōmum,-ī (n.) *fruit*
pōnō,-ere, posuī, positum *put, place*
populus,-ī (m.) *people*
pōpulus,-ī (f.) *poplar-tree*
porta,-ae (f.) *gate*
portō,-āre,-āvī,-ātum *carry*
possum, posse, potuī *be able*

post (+ acc.) *after, behind*
post (adv.) *afterwards*

posteā *afterwards*
potius ... quam *rather than*
praebeō,-ēre,-uī, praebitum *offer, supply*
praeceptor,-ōris (m.) *teacher*
praeda,-ae (f.) *gain, plunder, profit*
praedicō,-āre,-āvī,-ātum *proclaim, preach*
praepōnō,-ere,-posuī,-positum *put before*
praeter (+ acc.) *besides, except*
prātum,-ī (n.) *meadow*
presbyter,-erī (m.) *elder, priest*
prīdem *long since, long ago*
prīmus,-a,-um *first*
prīnceps, prīncipis (m.) *leading person*
prō (+ abl.) *in return for, in place of, on behalf of*
probus,-a,-um *good, virtuous*
proelium,-ī (n.) *battle, combat*
profectō *truly, indeed*
prohibeō,-ēre, prohibuī, prohibitum *hold back, prevent*
prope (+ acc.) *near*
prope (adv.) *almost, nearby*
propter (+ acc.) *because of*
prōtegō,-ere,-tēxī,-tēctum *cover, protect*
pūblicus,-a,-um *public*
puella,-ae (f.) *girl*
puer,-erī (m.) *boy*
purpureus,-a,-um *purple*
putō,-āre,-āvī,-ātum *think, suppose, deem*

quaerō,-ere, quaesīvī (-iī) quaesītum *ask, seek*
quam (acc.f.) *whom, which; as, than, how*
quārē *for what reason, why, how*
-que *and*
quī *who*

quia *because, that*
quid? *what?, why?*
quidem *indeed*
quis? *who?*
quō *to where*
quod *because, which, that which*
quoniam *for the reason that*
quoque *also, too*

raeda,-ae (f.) *carriage*
rāmus,-ī (m.) *branch*
rapiō,-ere, rapuī, raptum *seize*
recipiō,-ere, recēpī, receptum *take, regain*
recitō,-āre,-āvī,-ātum *recite, read aloud*
recuperō,-āre,-āvī,-ātum *recover*
redeō,-īre, rediī, reditum *come back, return*
referō, referre, rettulī, relātum *bring back, report*
regiō, regiōnis (f.) *region*
rēgula,-ae (f.) *rule*
reiciō,-ere, reiēcī, reiectum *reject, refuse*
relinquō,-ere,-līquī,-lictum *leave, abandon*
requiēscō,-ere,-quiēvī,-quiētum *rest, relax*
rēs, reī (f.) *thing, matter*
rēs pūblica *republic*
resonō,-āre,-āvī,-ātum *resound*
respondeō,-ēre, respondī, respōnsum *reply*
reveniō,-īre,-vēnī,-ventum *come back*
rīdeō,-ēre, rīsī, rīsum *laugh (at)*
rīpa,-ae (f.) *bank*
rīvus,-ī (m.) *stream, channel*
rogō,-āre,-āvī,-ātum *ask (for)*
Rōmānus,-ī (m.) *Roman*
rudō,-ere, rudīvī, rudītum *bray*
rūmor,-ōris (m.) *rumour, gossip*

saepe *often*
saevitia,-ae (f.) *cruelty*
saevus,-a,-um *cruel, harsh*
sagitta,-ae (f.) *arrow*
sagittāria,-ae (f.) *archeress*
sāl, salis (m.) *salt* (also *sea*), *wit*
saltem *at least*
salūtem dīcō,-ere *say hello*
salūtō ,-āre,-āvī,-ātum *greet*
salvātiō,-ōnis (f.) *salvation*
sānctus,-a,-um *holy, sacred*
sānus,-a,-um *healthy*
sapiēns *wise*
sarcina,-ae (f.) *bag, sack*
satis *enough*
saucius,-a,-um *wounded, smitten*
scelus,-eris (n.) *crime, wicked deed*
schola,-ae (f.) *school*
scientia,-ae (f.) *knowledge*
scīlicet *to be sure, obviously*
scindō,-ere, scīdī, scissum *tear, cut up*
sciō,-īre, scīvī (-iī) , scītum *know*
scrībō,-ere, scrīpsī, scrīptum *write*
sē *himself, herself, itself, themselves*
sēcūritās,-tātis (f.) *security, safety*
sēcūrus,-a,-um *free from çare*
sed *but*
sedeō,-ēre, sēdī, sessum *sit*
semper *always*
senātor,-ōris (m.) *senator*
senātus,-ūs (m.) *senate*
sentiō,-īre, sēnsī, sēnsum *feel, perceive*
sepeliō,-īre,-īvī (-iī), sepultum *bury*
servō ,-āre,-āvī,-ātum *keep*
servus,-ī (m.) *slave*
sevērus,-a,-um *severe, hard*
sī *if*
sīc *thus, so, as you see*
sīcut *just as, as if*
silentium,-ī (n.) *silence*
sileō,-ēre, siluī *be silent, inactive*
silva,-ae (f.) *wood*

simulācrum,-ī (n.) *likeness, image*
sine (+ abl.) *without*
sitiēns *thirsty*
sīve ... sīve *whether ... or*
sōl, sōlis (m.) *sun*
sollicitus,-a,-um *alarmed, disturbed*
sōlus,-a,-um *alone, only, single*
sōlum (adv.) *only*
somnulentus,-a,-um *sleepy*
somnus,-ī (m.) *sleep*
sonitus,-ūs (m.) *sound, noise*
spatium,-ī (n.) *space, extent*
spectō ,-āre,-āvī,-ātum *watch, look at*
spērō,-āre,-āvī,-ātum *hope (for)*
spēs,-ēī (f.) *hope*
spīritus,-ūs (m.) *spirit*
spīrō ,-āre,-āvī,-ātum *breathe*
splendeō,-ēre *be bright, shine*
sponte *willingly, of one's own accord*
sst! *ssh!*
stabulum,-ī (n.) *stable*
stāgnum,-ī (n.) *pond*
statim *immediately*
stella,-ae (f.) *star*
Stephanus,-ī (m.) *Stephen*
stertō,-ere *snore*
stō,-āre, stetī, statum *stand*
strēnuus,-a,-um *energetic*
strepitus,-ūs (m.) *noise, din*
strīdeō,-ēre, strīdī *hiss, whistle*
studiōsus,-a,-um *hard-working*
studium,-ī (n.) *study*
sub (+ acc./abl.) *beneath, under*
subitō *suddenly*
subsellium,-ī (n.) *bench, pew*
suffrāgium,-ī (n.) *vote*
sum, esse, fuī *be*
superbus,-a,-um *proud, arrogant*
surrīdeō,-ēre, surrīsī *smile*
sūrsum *upwards*
suspīrō,-āre,-āvī,-ātum *sigh*
susurrō,-āre,-āvī *whisper, murmur*
suus,-a,-um *his, her, their own*

taberna,-ae (f.) *inn, shop*
taceō,-ēre, tacuī, tacitum *hush, be quiet*
tam *so*
tamen *yet, however*
tandem *at last*
tēctum,-ī (n.) *ceiling*
temptō,-āre,-āvī,-ātum *try, test*
tempus,-oris (n.) *time*
tendō,-ere, tetendī, tentum *stretch*
teneō,-ēre, tenuī, tentum *hold, keep*
tentātiō,-ōnis (f.) *temptation*
terra,-ae (f.) *land, earth, ground*
terreō,-ēre,-uī, territum *scare, terrify*
terribilis,-e *terrible*
tertius,-a,-um *third*
testāmentum,-ī (n.) *testament, will*
theologus,-ī (m.) *theologian*
thēsaurus,-ī (m.) *store*
timeō,-ēre, timuī *fear*
tollō,-ere, sustulī, sublātum *raise*
tot *so many*
tōtus,-a,-um *entire, whole*
trādō,-ere, trādidī, trāditum *hand over*
trāns (+ acc.) *across, over*
trānseō,-īre,-iī (-īvī), trānsitum *go by, pass*
tremō,-ere, tremuī *tremble*
trepidus,-a,-um *nervous*
trīstis,-e *sad, gloomy, grim*
trucīdō,-āre,-āvī,-ātum *slaughter, butcher*
tū *you* (sing.)
tum *then, at that time*
tunica,-ae (f.) *tunic, dress*
turbulentus,-a,-um *stormy*
turpis,-e *disgraceful*
turpitūdō,-dinis (f.) *disgraceful behaviour*
tūtus,-a,-um *safe*
tuus,-a,-um *your* (sing.)

ubi *when, where*
ūllus,-a,-um *any*
ululō,-āre,-āvī,-ātum *howl*
umbra,-ae (f.) *shadow, shade*

umbrōsus,-a,-um *shady, full of shadows*
umquam *ever*
unde *from where*
unguentum,-ī (n.) *perfume*
ūnus,-a,-um *one*
urbs, urbis (f.) *city*
usque *without interruption*
ut (+ indic.) *as, when;* (+ subj.) *that, so that*
ūtilis,-e *useful, suitable*
uxor,-ōris (f.) *wife*

vādō,-ere, vāsī *go, walk*
valeō,-ēre, valuī, valitum *be well*
vel *or, or rather, for example, or as you like*
vēnātiō,-ōnis (f.) *hunting*
vēnātrīx, -īcis (f.) *huntress*
venēnum,-ī (n.) *poison*
veniō,-īre, vēnī, ventum *come*
ventus,-ī (m.) *wind*
vēr,-is (n.) *spring*
verber,-is (n.) *blow* (pl. *beating*)
verberō,-āre,-āvī,-ātum *beat*
verbum,-ī (n.) *word*
vērē *really, in fact*
vērō *indeed, really, yes*
versus,-ūs (m.) *verse*
vērus,-a,-um *true, real*
vester, vestra, vestrum *your* (pl.)
vestiō,-īre,-īvī (-iī), vestītum *clothe, dress*
vestis,-is (f.) *clothing*
via,-ae (f.) *road, track, way*
viātor,-ōris (m.) *traveller*
videō,-ēre, vīdī, vīsum *see*
vigilō,-āre *be awake*
vīlla,-ae (f.) *villa, country-house*
vincō,-ere, vīcī, victum *conquer, win*
vinculum,-ī (n.) *chain, rope*
vīnolentus,-a,-um *full of wine, drunk with wine*
vīnum,-ī (n.) *wine*
vir,-ī (m.) *man, husband*
vīrēs, vīrium (f.) *strength, resources*

virgō,-ginis (f.) *maiden, young woman*
virtūs,-tūtis (f.) *virtue, courage*
vīrus,-ī (n.) *poison, slime*
visitō,-āre,-āvī,-ātum *visit, go to see*
vīta,-ae (f.) *life*
vitium,-ī (n.) *vice*
vīvō,-ere, vīxī, vīctum *live*

vix *scarcely, hardly, barely*
volō, velle, voluī *want, wish*
vōs *you* (pl.)
vōx, vōcis (f.) *voice, cry, sound*
vultus,-ūs (m.) *face, look*

English–Latin vocabulary

The English to Latin vocabulary is limited to words needed for the exercises.

able, be **possum, posse, potuī**
absent, be **absum, abesse, āfuī**
accident **casus,-ūs** (m.)
all **omnis,-e**
and **et, -que**
approach **adeō,-īre, adiī, aditum**
army **exercitus,-ūs** (m.)

bag **sarcina,-ae** (f.)
be **sum, esse, fuī**
beat **verberō,-āre,-āvī,-ātum**
Benedictus **Benedictus,-ī** (m.)
body **corpus,-oris** (n.)
book **liber, librī** (m.)
boy **puer,-erī** (m.)
brave **fortis,-e**
bury **sepeliō,-īre,-īvī (-iī), sepultum**
but **sed**
by **ā, ab** (+ abl.)

capture **capiō,-ere, cēpī, captum**
carry **portō,-āre,-āvī,-ātum**
Catullus **Catullus,-ī** (m.)
chain **catēna,-ae** (f.); **vinculum,-ī** (n.)
charming **dulcis,-e; suāvis,-e**
city **urbs, urbis** (f.)
come **veniō,-īre, vēnī, ventum**
conquer **vincō,-ere, vīcī, victum**
cook **coquus,-ī** (m.)
crime **scelus,-eris** (n.)
cruel **crūdēlis,-e; saevus,-a,-um**

daughter **fīlia,-ae** (f.)
desire **cupiō,-ere, cupīvī (-iī), cupītum; dēsīderō,-āre,-āvī,-ātum; optō,-āre,- āvī,-ātum**
dinner **cēna,-ae** (f.)
do **faciō,-ere, fēcī, factum**
drunk with wine **vīnolentus,-a,-um**

easy **facilis,-e**
egg **ōvum,-ī** (n.)
eye **oculus,-ī** (m.)

Fabullus **Fabullus,-ī** (m.)
fall **cadō,-ere, cecidī, cāsum**
fear **timeō,-ēre, timuī**
field **ager, agrī** (m.)
finish **fīniō,-īre, fīnīvī (-iī), fīnītum; perficiō,-ere,-fēcī,-fectum**
flee **fugiō,-ere, fūgī, fugitum**
fly **musca,-ae** (f.)
from **ā, ab; dē; ē, ex** (all + abl.)

girl **puella,-ae** (f.)
go **eō, īre, iī (īvī), itum**
go away **abeō,-īre,-iī (-īvī),-itum**
greedy **gulōsus,-a,-um; avārus,-a,-um**
grim **trīstis,-e**
groan **gemitus,-ūs** (m.)
groan **gemō,-ere, gemuī, gemitum**
ground **terra,-ae** (f.)
guard **custōdiō,-īre,-īvī (-iī),-ītum**

harsh **saevus,-a,-um**
have **habeō,-ēre,-uī, habitum**
head **caput, capitis** (n.)
hear **audiō,-īre, audīvī (-iī), audītum**
horse **equus,-ī** (m.); **caballus,-ī** (m.)
humble **humilis,-e**

I/me **ego/mē**
in **in** (+ abl.)
into **in** (+ acc.)
irretrievable **irreparābilis,-e**

kind **benignus,-a,-um**
kitchen **culīna,-ae** (f.)

lady **domina,-ae** (f.)
lake **lacus,-ūs** (m.)
laugh **rīdeō,-ēre, rīsī, rīsum**
lead **dūcō,-ere, dūxī, ductum**
leader **dux, ducis** (m.)
leaf **folium,-ī** (n.)
leave **relinquō,-ere,-līquī,-lictum**
library **bibliothēca,-ae** (f.)
lie **iaceō,-ēre,-uī, iacitum**
long for **dēsīderō,-āre,-āvī,-ātum**
love **amō,-āre,-āvī,-ātum**

maid **ancilla,-ae** (f.)
make **faciō,-ere, fēcī, factum**
many **multus,-a,-um**
master **dominus,-ī** (m.); **magister,-trī** (m.)
meadow **prātum,-ī** (n.)
mistress **domina,-ae** (f.); **amīca,-ae** (f.)
monk **monachus,-ī** (m.)
mortal **mortālis,-e**
mountain **mōns, montis** (m.)
mule **mūlus,-ī** (m.)
my **meus,-a,-um**

noise **strepitus,-ūs** (m.)

oil **oleum,-ī** (n.)
on **in** (+ abl.)

onto **in** (+ acc.)
order **iubeō,-ēre, iussī, iussum**
ought **dēbeō,-ēre,-uī, dēbitum**
out of **ē, ex** (+ abl.)

Paulus **Paulus,-ī** (m.)
perfume **unguentum,-ī** (n.)
poem **carmen,-inis** (n.)
praise **laudō,-āre,-āvī,-ātum**
pray **ōrō,-āre,-āvī,-ātum**
present, be **adsum, adesse, affuī**
priest **presbyter,-erī** (m.)

read **legō,-ere, lēgī, lēctum**
recite **recitō,-āre,-āvī,-ātum**
river **flūmen,-inis** (n.)
road **via,-ae** (f.)
run **currō,-ere, cucurrī, cursum**

sack **sarcina,-ae** (f.)
sad **trīstis,-e**
say **dīcō,-ere, dīxī, dictum**
see **videō,-ēre, vīdī, vīsum**
senator **senātor,-ōris** (m.)
send **mittō,-ere, mīsī, missum**
serious **gravis,-e**
shadow **umbra,-ae** (f.)
shout **clāmō,-āre,-āvī,-ātum**
sit **sedeō,-ēre, sēdī, sessum**
sleep **dormiō,-īre, dormīvī (-iī), dormītum**
sleepy **somnulentus,-a,-um**
song **carmen,-inis** (n.)
student **discipulus,-ī** (m.)
sweet **dulcis,-e**

teach **doceō,-ēre,-uī, doctum**
through **per** (+ acc.)
to, towards **ad** (+ acc.)
town **oppidum,-ī** (n.)
track **via,-ae** (f.)
trust **crēdō,-ere, crēdidī, crēditum** (+ dat.)

verse **versus,-ūs** (m.)
want **volō, velle, voluī**
we/us **nōs**
whisper **susurrō,-āre,-āvī**
wife **uxor,-ōris** (f.)
willing, be **volō, velle, voluī**
wine **vīnum,-ī** (n.)
with **cum** (+ abl.)
without **sine** (+ abl.)
woman **fēmina,-ae** (f.)

wood **silva,-ae** (f.)
work **labōrō,-āre,-āvī,-ātum**
write **scrībō,-ere, scrīpsī, scrīptum**

you (pl.) **vōs**
you (sing.) **tū**
your (pl.) **vester, vestra, vestrum**
your (sing.) **tuus,-a,-um**

Abbreviations

abl.	ablative
acc.	accusative
AD	after Christ
adj.	adjective
adv.	adverb
BC	before Christ
class.	classical
dat.	dative
e.g.	for example
f.	feminine
gen.	genitive
i.e.	that is
indic.	indicative
l.	line
lit.	literally
M.	mixed conjugation
m.	masculine
med.	medieval
n.	neuter
nom.	nominative
occas.	occasionally
perf.	perfect
p.	page
pl.	plural
prep.	preposition
pres.	present
sing.	singular
subj.	subjunctive
voc.	vocative